WR THE

GR EL

DANIEL COONEY
PETER Palmiotti

WRITING AND ILLUSTRATING THE GRAPHIC NOVEL

DANIEL COONEY

A QUARTO BOOK

Published in 2011 by
A&C Black Publishers
36 Soho Square
London W1D 3QY
www.acblack.com

A CIP record for this book is available from the British Library.

ISBN-13: 978-1-408-13944-8

QUAR. IGN2

Conceived, designed, and produced by
Quarto Publishing plc
The Old Brewery
6 Blundell Street
London N7 9BH

Project editor: Chloe Todd Fordham
Art director: Caroline Guest
Designer: Jon Wainwright
Creative director: Moira Clinch
Publisher: Paul Carslake

Colour separation by PICA Digital Pte Ltd, Singapore

Printed in Singapore by Star Standard Pte Ltd

9 8 7 6 5 4 3 2 1

Contents

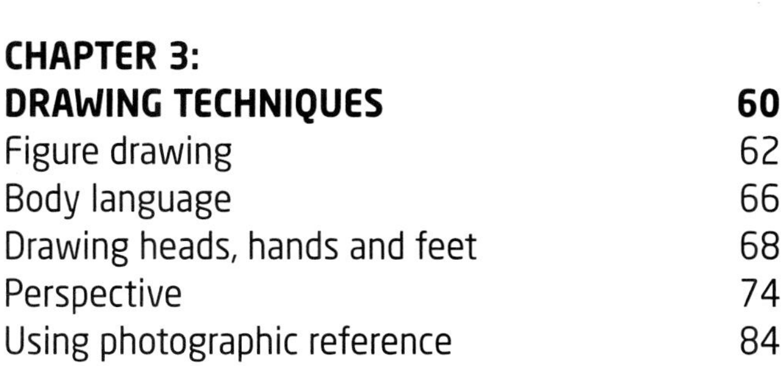

FOREWORD

The purpose of this book is for aspiring writers and artists to learn how to create their own comics and graphic novels. Every artist has to start somewhere and that somewhere begins with your idea and vision. The content in these 160 pages will give you information, professional tips, tools and techniques for creating your own comic book, but you have to work hard to develop them. Writing and drawing comics has its own vocabulary and language as a medium that requires a learned set of skills unlike any other medium of storytelling, and takes an intense level of commitment.

Learning how to be a good storyteller is a lifelong experience. The principles presented in this book are tried-and-tested methods that have worked for me in my two-decade career as a comic artist and instructor. Some of the techniques I learnt in school, and others I have developed through my own experiences along with observing others in the process. You may discover that some of the drawing mechanics in this book will also suit you in other fields (illustration, storyboarding, animation, etc.), or realise you're doing it just for fun. It is important to have fun while you work and develop your skills.

Above all else, I encourage you to be fearless with your ideas for stories and take chances with your drawing styles when it comes to comics. As an artist, you need to develop your own unique visual language and style once you've learnt the language of comics. Perfection is an elusive mistress, and experimenting and learning from your mistakes will set you on a path for success in the world of comics and graphic novels.

ABOUT THE AUTHOR

Daniel Cooney is an accomplished comics writer, educator and illustrator of such books as ***Valentine, The Tommy Gun Dolls*** and ***The Atomic Yeti***. Cooney has established himself as an illustrator for various book publishers, and licensed properties of comics, television and film. Cooney resides on Martha's Vineyard, Massachusetts, U.S., with his wife and their son, Dashiell. He teaches writing and drawing comics for The Academy of Art University and works as a freelance illustrator.

WHAT IS A GRAPHIC NOVEL?

So what exactly is a graphic novel? Even more difficult, what is understood by the term? What do people think of when you mention 'graphic novel'? An overpriced comic book, or a kid's comic with delusions of grandeur?

THE CLASSICS

Many classic novels have made it into graphic format, along with characters from myth and legend, and figures of popular culture, such as Superman.

To start with definitions, a novel is usually described as something like 'a lengthy fictional prose narrative, normally dealing with human relationships, the plot unfolding through the actions, speech and thoughts of the characters.' 'Graphic' means pictures. A 'graphic novel' is therefore a long work of fiction in pictures, which makes a comic book the equivalent of a short story, or an episode in a longer story, right?

These, unfortunately, are false analogies. Novels deal with people – lots of characters, all interacting in some way and driving the story forward, so that by the end there will have been major changes in the main characters, as well as the status quo. The short story, meanwhile, is usually about an idea – the effect on a small group of characters, or sometimes just a mood piece. Many monthly comic books, to use an analogy that will occur frequently in this book, are more like episodes of a television series, back in the days when each episode closed with order restored. No matter how crazy it became during an episode, by the end it was as if nothing had occurred. (This was simply so that a television series could be shown in any order when it went to syndication). A graphic novel, however, is a full, feature-length film.

WHERE DID IT ALL START?

Most people in the field consider the birth of graphic novels to have occurred in 1978 with Will Eisner's ***A Contract with God***. Eisner actually coined the phrase 'graphic novel' while the book itself dealt with 'real' people – not weirdos in funny costumes. It was concerned with the heartbreak and hope of real life, and loudly proclaimed that the comic book format could deal with any subject – and do it in a sensitive, adult manner. The book was also printed on quality paper and bound with heavy card covers. Everything from the quality of the writing and artwork to the production values said this was something special.

Since then, Eisner's regular output has certainly fit this definition: long, complex, character-led stories (often with strong autobiographical elements) that are beyond the normal comic book. His most recent book, ***Fagin the Jew***, is a prequel, of sorts, to Dickens' ***Oliver Twist***.

Not all critics, however, agree that graphic novels are a mere 25 years old. Back in the 1930s, Lynd Ward produced novels told entirely as woodcut images (***God's Man, Madman's Drum***), with no narrative or dialogue text. In 1967, artist Gil Kane (***Green Lantern, The Atom***) experimented with a violent, noir-like black-and-white book, ***His Name Is Savage***. It received a mixed response: the critics were horrified, but the readers loved it – probably because they were the same ones who had grown used to such underground comics as ***The Fabulous Furry Freak Brothers***, ***Fritz the Cat*** and ***Mr. Natural***. The old Classics Illustrated series of comic books of the 1950s and 1960s were literally books in comic format. Dickens, Jules Verne, H. G. Wells and many more were adapted – and often grossly oversimplified – for the books. Because each title was rarely much longer than the average comic book, often badly drawn and cheaply produced, they can probably be relegated to the 'close, but no cigar' tray.

Meanwhile in Europe

In Britain, during the post-World War II era, the Scottish newspaper and magazine company, D. C. Thomson, used to publish several titles of 'picture digests' – small, pulp-sized comics with 70-odd pages of black-and-white artwork, which, although almost all have since disappeared, were probably the last examples of a uniquely British phenomena. In mainland Europe, the tradition for large-format comic books is well established and dates back decades. Hergé's ***Tintin*** is probably one of the most familiar comic characters on the planet. His books sell in all corners of the world and in countless translations. The same is true of ***Asterix the Gaul***, created by Goscinny and Uderzo. Somehow, the anarchic humour manages to rise above translation. The French artist Phillipe Druillet was also creating his own unique brand of decadent science fiction and fantasy books. The coffee table-sized books ***Lone Sloane/ Delirius*** and ***Yragael/Urm*** were originally published from 1972–75 (English translations published by Paper Tiger).

The Manga story

Japan has long had a near-obsessive love affair with comics. The word 'Manga' is now as familiar in the West as the East, with the form's unique stylisation instantly recognisable. In Japan, Manga covers a bewildering range of subjects and genres, but in the West the science fiction dystopias typified in Katsuhiro Otomo's ***Akira*** and Yukito ***Kishiro's Battle Angel Alita*** are the most familiar. This said, there are more graphic novels sold in Japan than anywhere in the world.

DREAMWALKER

Created by Diane Pascual, this is the story of Isis, a troubled 16-year-old, who often finds herself mingling in the astral plane – a spirit world where Isis can manifest anything she wills into form.

EUROPEAN GENIUS

Created by Hergé (real name George Rémi), Tintin is recognised worldwide. One of the most popular characters from graphic novels, he's probably the most long-running.

Adaptations

Early on, it was clear that graphic novels would be an ideal vehicle for adaptations of existing conventional novels and stories. Byron Preiss published books in a variety of formats and genres, ranging from ***The Illustrated Harlan Ellison*** and ***The Illustrated Roger Zelazny*** to the Howard Chaykin-illustrated adaptation of Alfred Bester's ***The Stars My Destination***. But it wasn't just adaptations. Established authors were also drawn to the new medium. Science fiction author Samuel R. Delany wrote, with Howard Chaykin drawing, ***Empire for Byron Preiss*** (1978), a stunning space opera that eschewed normal speech bubbles and text panels and instead concentrated on the artwork, arranging text and speech outside the panels. The following year ***The Swords of Heaven, the Flowers of Hell*** was produced, a new adventure of Michael Moorcock's Eternal Champion character, plotted by Moorcock and realised by Chaykin.

Turning point

You'll notice that superhero titles have yet to be mentioned. At first, there seemed to be a deliberate attempt to keep graphic novels away from character clichés. Following Eisner's lead, writers and artists wanted to go somewhere different with graphic novels, even if it was just creating a novel told in pictures.

It would be impossible to overview graphic novels without mentioning two titles: ***The Dark Knight Returns*** and ***Watchmen***, both from DC Comics. They met an unprepared world in 1986 with impeccable timing. Frank Miller's reinvention of a darker, more vengeful Batman and Alan Moore and Dave Gibbons' post-modern evaluation of a world where superheroes really exist hit a nerve with the reading public. The impact of both titles can be felt to this day throughout comic book publishing. But more significantly, neither title was originally published as a graphic novel. Both were published as mini-series, only collected into graphic novel form after the initial series run had completed. In fact, they work perfectly as graphic novels, each episode flowing flawlessly with the others, acting like chapters of a larger work. This method has precedents in the field of conventional novels – Dickens' books were all originally published as magazine serials, and no one seriously argues that the finished articles are anything but novels. That ***The Dark Night Returns*** and ***Watchmen*** had the same artists throughout also created a sense of cohesion. As a result, the majority of graphic novels published by the larger companies (DC, Marvel, etc.) tend to be repackaged mini-series, or issues from a continuing title. Not exclusively, of course. DC's ***Elseworlds*** series – where familiar characters are set in different, sometimes experimental, roles – is a perfect vehicle for a one-shot. Other examples would be Alan Davis's ***The Nail and Gotham*** by Gaslight. In fact, Batman seems to be a favourite for both ***Elseworlds*** stories and one-shot graphic novels that are set in the DC universe, but outside the regular monthly titles.

PRIZE-WINNING

The Escapist and Luna Moth are meta-fictional characters, featured in the Pulitzer Prize-winning novel The Amazing Adventures of Kavalier and Clay, *by Michael Chabon.*

The future of the graphic novel

Whether the graphic novel was born in the 1930s or 1970s, in the U.S. or Europe, we've come to understand what most people expect when reading one. It is a lengthy work of fiction, told in pictures, that will stand on its own, needing no prequels or sequels to explain it. Generally, it will also be aimed at a more mature audience, and will have superior production values to regular monthly titles. By its very nature it can be experimental – taking the familiar and subverting it. It can be anything between 30 to over 100 pages long. The subject matter will be as wide-ranging as that found in conventional novels – the only limits are the writer's and artist's imaginations and the publisher's nerve. It can be written specifically as a whole, collected from a multi-part mini-series or even an ongoing title. Taking the emotional world of conventional novels, the familiar visual techniques of comics and a few ideas from the movies, graphic novels are a new voice for the 21st century.

TOOLS OF THE TRADE

The requirements for drawing comics are pretty basic, but there are a few essentials that you really need in order to do it properly.

Prices can be misleading on art supplies, so rather than assuming the most expensive is the best, you will need to experiment with materials to find what produces the best results for you. Here is the lowdown on what you'll need for pencilling, inking, lettering and colouring your comics. For more on specialist lettering tools, see pages 132–133.

DRAWING TOOLS

Pencils

The chart below gives an idea of the varieties of pencil lead available to you. Softer, darker leads, such as B and 2B, are generally considered best for sketching. For finished comic book art on art boards, use harder and lighter leads, such as 2H, H and F, to avoid smearing and smudging the lead on the paper. You want to have clean line art before you ink your work, and it's a good habit to get into when drawing comics.

A clutch pencil (or lead holder) tends to use thicker leads of 2–4 mm (1⁄16–1⁄8 inch). Most hold only one piece of lead at a time. A clutch pencil is a pencil that contains one large piece of lead, exceeding the entire pencil's length. For this, use a 2H or F for drawing comic pages.

Mechanical pencils come in three widths: 0.7 mm (thick line), 0.5 mm (the most commonly used) and 0.3 mm (fine line).

Sharpeners

Use an ordinary electric sharpener for sketching and drawing pencils, and a regular lead pointer for a clutch pencil.

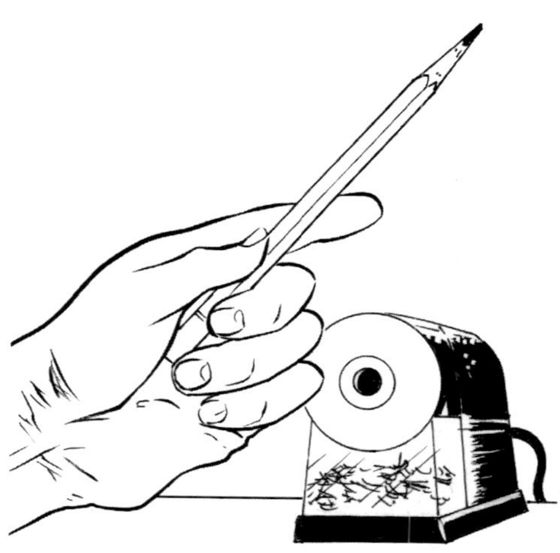

Electric sharpener

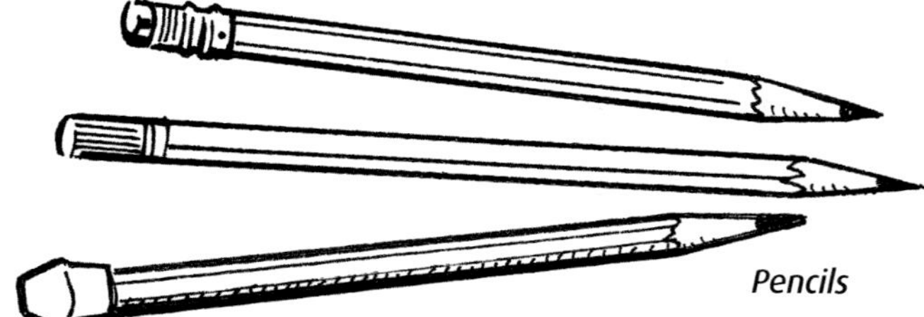

Pencils

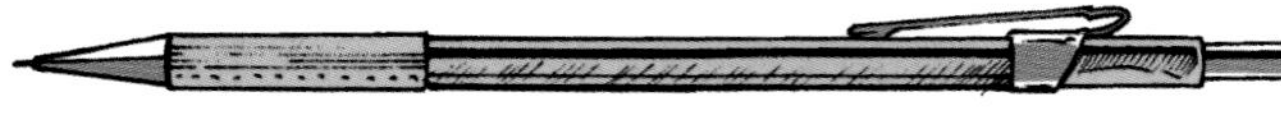

Clutch pencil

PENCIL LEAD

Extremely hard - 9H to 7H	Very hard - 6H to 5H	Hard - 4H to 3H
Medium hard - 2H to H	Medium - F to HB	Medium soft - B to 2B
Soft - 3B to 4B	Very soft - 5B to 6B	Extremely soft - 7B to 9B

Lead pointer

Erasers

A putty eraser that you can shape into form is good for cleaning up pencil smudges and unwanted construction lines. For smaller areas use a Pentel Clic or Sanford Tuff Stuff eraser. To remove pencil lines from larger areas after you've inked a page, use a white plastic eraser.

Light box

A light box is a useful drawing tool that should be a part of your art equipment. A light box provides a brilliant underlighting illumination on your piece of paper, making it easier to see a drawing on top of your comic art board. This enables you to trace pencil work when inking, allowing for a looser finish.

Inking tools

Inks

Pelikan, Higgins, Speedball, FW acrylic and Holbein inks are all suitable and available at most craft or art supply stores.

Correction fluid

There are several types of pen and bottle correction fluids that work well. Pelikan Graphic White, Pro White and FW acrylic all work for covering up ink while being opaque enough to ink over when dry. The Pentel Presto! correction pen is great for special effects after you've inked over your pencils. It doesn't work so well for actual corrections, it's difficult to ink over, and gives a rougher surface than standard correction ink. White gouache works just as well for making corrections.

Pens

Hunt crowquill, Gillot and Speedball pens with holders work best for inking comic book artwork. There are a variety of pen nibs ranging from fine point to coarse. Some nibs are more flexible than others. You may want to try a few different types to see what results work best for you. (See page 110 for more about pens.)

Technical pens

Rotring pens are very similar to rapidograph pens but don't clog as easily. The advantage of using a Rotring pen is a replaceable cartridge with a new pen tip, as opposed to the maintenance-heavy rapidograph pens you have to take completely apart to clean thoroughly. Both these pens come in several pen tip sizes, from thick to thin lines.

After filling your pen and starting it, continue using it, even if it is for multiple days, until your project is completed. Do not leave ink in your pen for an extended period of time. Here is a fail-safe way to maintain your pen and always have it in good working condition.

1 Disassemble the pen parts.
2 Use the nib wrench that came with your pen and remove the pen point from the body.
3 Rinse the pen parts under tap water until no ink is evident.

After taking the pen apart, store the pen tip and the pen body in a small container (a film canister works wonderfully) filled with household ammonia – any brand or type will suffice. Submerge the two parts in ammonia and store them in it until the next time you have a project to work on. When ready to start a new project, take the tip and body out of the ammonia. Wipe and tap onto a paper towel to remove ammonia. No need to rinse; just add ink to the cylinder, assemble, write across paper, and within a few seconds the ink cancels out any ammonia that would be up in the steel tip, and you have ink flow!

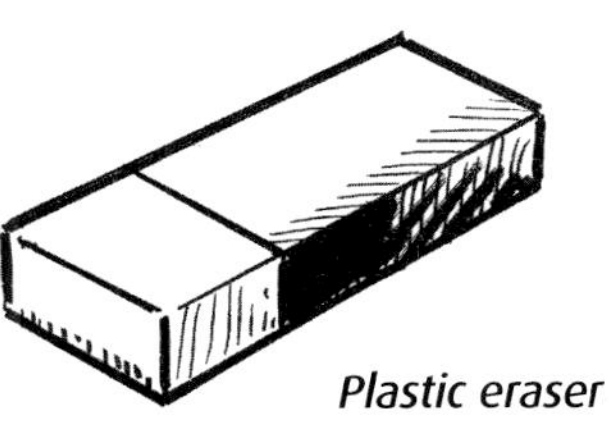

Plastic eraser

Putty eraser

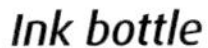

Ink bottle

Correction fluid

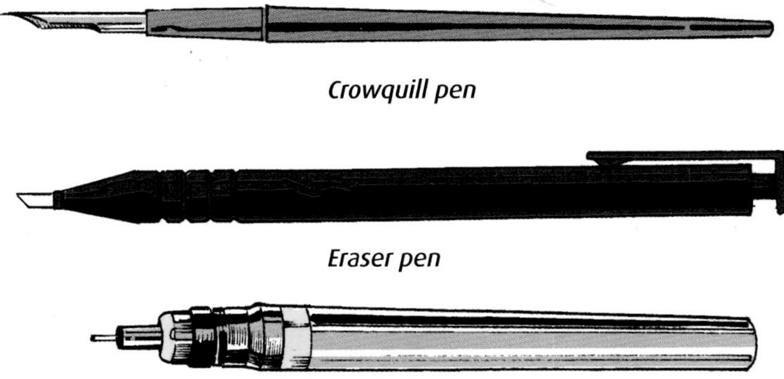

Crowquill pen

Eraser pen

Technical pen

Pigment liners

These pens are basically felt-tip pens with permanent ink that won't bleed when mixed with India ink. There is a variety of brands to choose from, from Sakura's Micron pens to Copic's Multiliner steel-tip pens. These are ideal for inorganic objects such as buildings, automobiles and other structures that require precision lines and detail using a template, triangle or ruler.

Brushes

The brushes that are considered the industry standard are Kolinsky red sable round, Raphael 8404 size 4 and Winsor & Newton Series 7 sable brush size 2 or 3. See page 108 for more on brush types and brushwork tips.

Technical tools

French curves

A set of French curves is handy for drawing clean, curved lines in pencil or pen. They are useful for figure work, automobiles, spaceships, architecture, special effects and more.

Templates

Circle and elliptical templates are great for word balloons, vehicle tyres and more. It's useful to get into a good habit of drawing clean, precise shapes throughout your comic book when it's called for.

Drawing compass

A compass with a pencil and ink attachment is great for drawing large circles that adjust into different sizes.

Straightedge tools

A 30- or 40-cm (12- or 15-inch) ruler, 45- or 60-cm (18- or 24-inch) T-square and a set of triangles (45/90-degree and 30/60-degree) can be used for pencilling and inking straight lines as well as panel borders and special effects.

Ames lettering guide

A useful device for drawing lettering guidelines, the Ames guide is still the standard tool for lettering professional comic books by hand. See page 132 for more on specialist lettering tools.

Proportion wheel

Before computers made it possible to scale things up or down by dragging a corner or typing in a number, the proportional scale was an indispensable studio tool, which made it easy to calculate relative measurements when you needed to make enlargements or reductions.

The proportion wheel looks like a circular slide rule. The smaller inside wheel represents the size of the original, while a larger outside wheel measures the size of the reproduction. Each wheel is marked in a gradually increasing scale from 2.5 to 254 cm (1 to 100 inches). The two wheels rotate independently, held concentrically by a grommet.

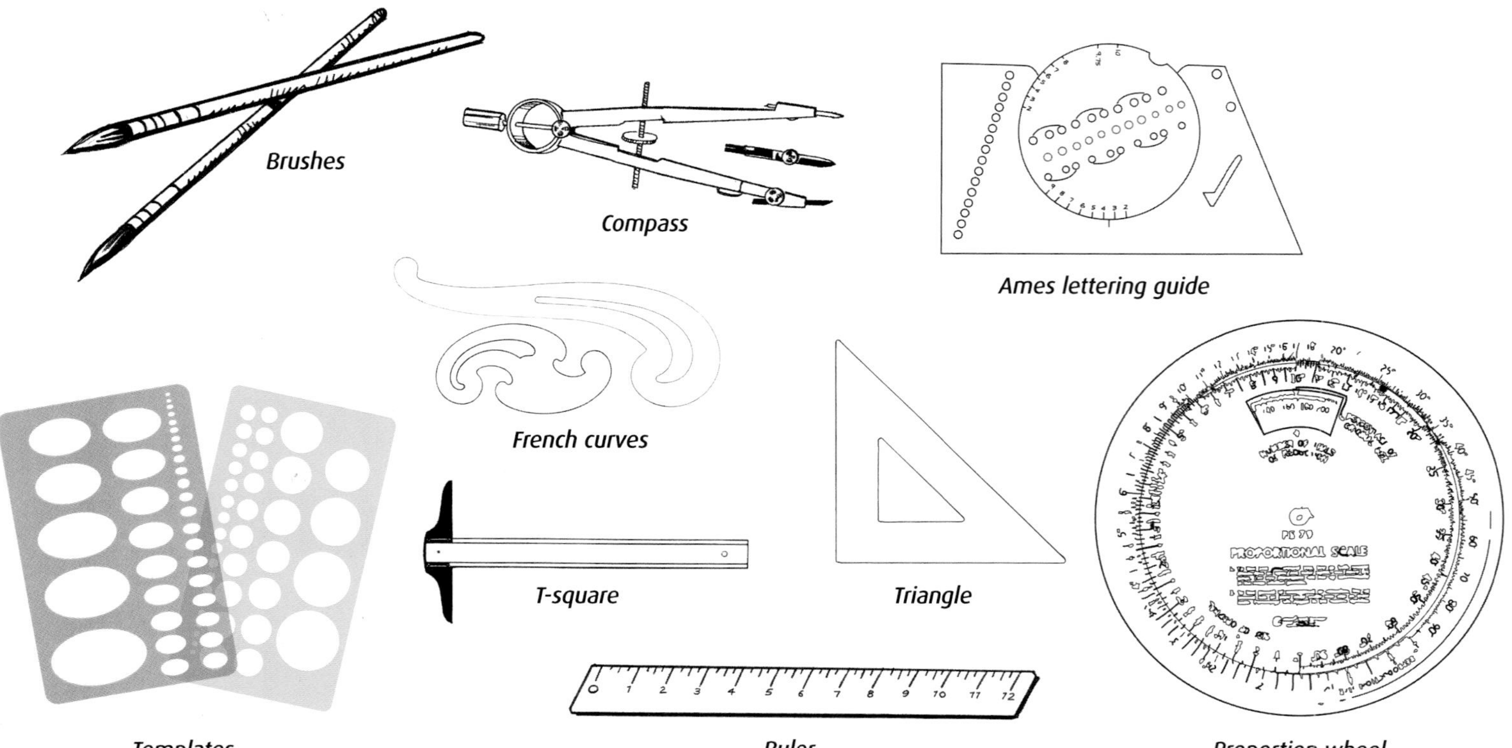

Brushes

Compass

Ames lettering guide

French curves

T-square

Triangle

Templates

Ruler

Proportion wheel

Additional materials

Dusting brush

A 25-cm (10-inch) dusting brush with a wooden comfort-fitting handle can be used to sweep away eraser particles. Other useful extras include drafting tape, a glue stick, an X-acto knife and an eraser shield.

Paper and tracing paper

There are several types of paper made specifically for drawing comic books. Canson produces a series of comic book papers suitable for pencilling and inking, as well as Strathmore 500 series paper. Common paper types used are 2-ply semismooth or vellum surface. The semismooth surface is slightly textured, making it well suited for pen and ink tools, pencil, speciality pens and markers, while the vellum surface is slightly rougher, ideal for pencil rendering and dry-brush effects. A suggestion would be to try different types of paper to see what you like best.

It's always good to have some tracing paper on hand for sketching and refining drawings that can take a beating from erasing and redrawing. Tracing paper is great for transferring your loose sketches onto a light box with your comic art board over it, in order to draw through for clean, revised line art.

Computer and software requirements

First determine which platform is best for you to use: Apple or PC? Ideally, use a computer that has sufficient speed for working Adobe Photoshop and Illustrator. These two software programs are the industry standard for image editing, lettering and colouring. Files are compatible with either one to get the job done. There are certainly other graphics programs out there, and it is recommended that you work with the one you are most comfortable with.

The software programs you are likely to use are:

- Microsoft Word or similar for script writing.
- Adobe Acrobat Pro or similar for making PDFs.
- Adobe Photoshop for scanning, image correction and colouring.
- Adobe Illustrator for lettering, sound effects and logo design.

A Wacom graphics pen tablet (30 x 40 cm/ 12 x 15 inches) is optional, while a Mustek 30 x 42-cm (11.7 x 17-inch) scanner is one of the more affordable large, flatbed scanners useful for scanning line art.

Practising good posture

When drawing or inking, artists should maintain good posture by keeping their backs straight. You should never draw flat for long periods of time, since your neck, shoulders and lower back will become strained by looking down at your work, thus creating bad posture over time from not sitting at your drawing table properly.

Instead, while seated at the drawing table, position your knees lower to simulate a higher seat and work surface. This is the most suitable position for long periods of sitting, with the muscles relaxed and the body in perfect posture. A front seat tilt and higher work surfaces are valuable alternatives that can eliminate lower back strain and ultimately prevent chronic back pain.

The recommended chair height is one-third of the artist's height, and the desk height one-half. Most people with back pain will find this very comfortable, but for the first weeks you will only be able to sit like this for 5 to 10 minutes, because your back muscles need training. You may also reduce the tension of painful tendons and back muscles by moving to the front of the seat of a traditional chair, or by using a forward-sloping cushion. Most desks are far too low, and this may be improved by placing wooden blocks under the legs.

It's a good idea to take breaks for 5 to 10 minutes to stretch, and even go for a short walk if working long hours at the drawing table.

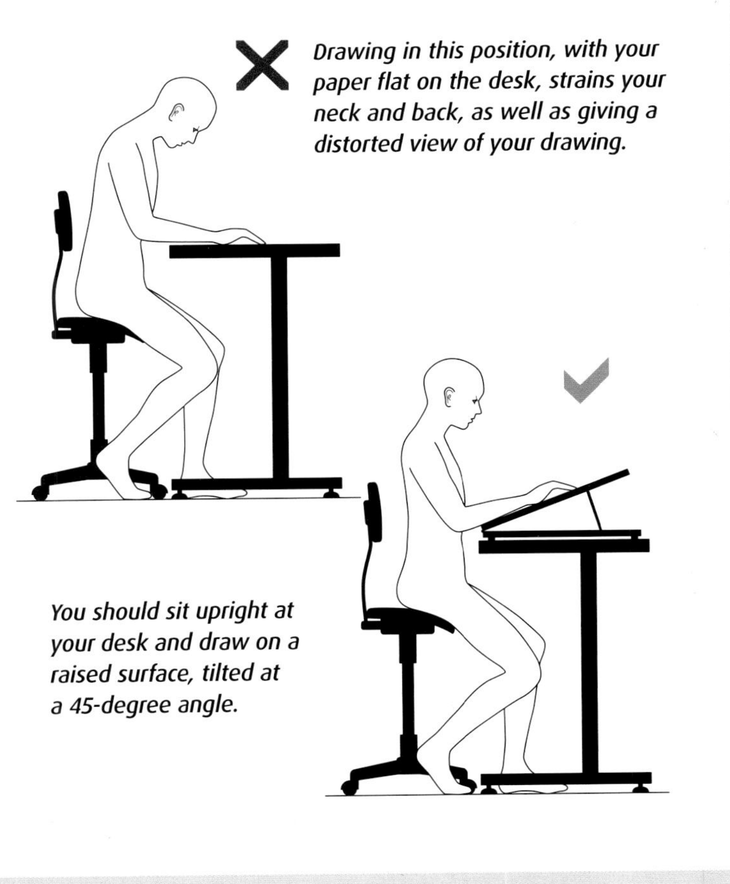

Drawing in this position, with your paper flat on the desk, strains your neck and back, as well as giving a distorted view of your drawing.

You should sit upright at your desk and draw on a raised surface, tilted at a 45-degree angle.

Recommended Reads

Watchmen by Alan Moore and Dave Gibbons

Watchmen is a graphic novel published by DC Comics in 12 instalments in 1986-87. It has sometimes been described as a postmodern or deconstructionist take on the comic book superhero.

Kingdom Come by Mark Waid and Alex Ross

Set just after the dawn of the 21st century, in a world spinning inexorably out of control, comes this grim tale of youth versus experience, tradition versus change, while asking the timeless question: what defines a hero? ***Kingdom Come*** is a riveting story, pitting the old-guard Superman, Batman, Wonder Woman and their peers against a new, uncompromising generation of heroes in the final war against each other, to determine nothing less than the future of the planet.

Wanted by Mark Millar and J. G. Jones

What if everything in your life was out of your hands and those around you propelled your fate? Your girlfriend left you for your best friend; your boss gave your job to someone better. What if then, after all this, someone gave you back total control? What if he revealed you were the next in line to join a secret society of supervillains that controlled the entire planet? Mark Millar and J. G. Jones provide a look at one man who goes from being the world's biggest loser to the deadliest assassin alive.

Rip Kirby Volume 1 by Alex Raymond

Raymond's follow-up to ***Flash Gordon*** featuring scientist-turned-private-detective Rip Kirby, an ex-marine, a former athlete and a genuine intellectual, a bookish-looking urbanite who smoked a pipe and even wore glasses. ***Rip Kirby*** was a fresh approach to the genre, a departure from the prevailing hard-boiled style of detective fiction.

ESTABLISHING CHARACTER

'First, find out what your hero wants, then just follow him!'

Ray Bradbury

GETTING INSPIRED

The keys to good characterisation are all around you. By observing the traits of everyday people you can deepen and enrich the characters of your story.

As a writer, carry an idea journal with you wherever you go, and as an artist, a visual journal for ideas on characters and settings.

Some of the best character designs you write for an artist may involve someone that caught your eye in the context of character development. Grab a pen and paper, your laptop or voice recorder, and step outside. Go to a coffee shop, a railway station, airport, bus stop, library or book shop, and make notes on what people are doing and what they are wearing. Observe their mannerisms when they interact with other people. Listen to what they're saying and how they say it. Make notes on their physical appearance, the clothes they wear and the objects they have with them. Some of these characters may work well visually in the background of your story.

WRITE WHAT YOU KNOW

There may be character traits in people you know – yourself, your family, friends, co-workers and more – that could work for your protagonist or antagonist. Writers write what is familiar to them and use it as a starting point to develop characters, even ones who might only have one scene in a story.

DON'T BE AFRAID TO USE THE NEGATIVE

Think about an experience you may have had, or of someone you know who had a negative impact on you, and use them for character material and story. Newspapers and the evening news are full of negative reports that you can use for any character in your story. Don't be afraid to tap into the darker stuff to give your character and story emotional weight.

TURN RIGHT, INSTEAD OF LEFT

When writing about a character to build a story around, you may go down the familiar road when considering their background. Try writing the road less travelled for your character, if your instinct is to turn right because that's what you know, how about asking yourself 'what if?' and turning left? You may find the answer surprising and more exciting to write about than your original idea. Writing is rewriting, and the journey of creating a character can be just as exciting as writing the story itself.

DRAW WHAT YOU SEE

A serious artist is never without a sketchbook – you never know what interesting characters you might bump into on your expeditions.

OBSERVATIONAL DRAWING

Observe a number of different people in a public place and write a fictionalised background for each of them. For example: an elderly man walking through the park; a couple having an intense conversation; an artist drawing from life. Start out by drawing a physical description, then fictionalise the person based on your observation – as shown in the strip, right.

A DAY IN THE CAFETERIA...

The germ of the idea for this sequence began in a roadside diner. The lesson here is to keep your eyes open and your pen and paper ready wherever you go. You never know when an idea might strike.

ON THE BUS

On a rickety old bus a young girl sits in a vacant seat, eyes fixed on a small notebook, with pen in hand on a cold Saturday morning: a gorgeous-looking person of Asian heritage and small stature, with dark black hair, shoulder length. Her hypnotic eyes don't break concentration and she remains in a state of constant focus, and she can't hide that behind her vintage glasses. What could she be writing that is so important? Seems too essential to be something simple like a grocery list. Perhaps she's doodling?
Or could it be something a little more devious? A hit list perhaps? Is it possible that such an innocent and charming female could be capable of carrying out an insidious plot? What's that in the bag next to her? Could it be a weapon cloaked in disguise?
The possibilities are of course endless. Is she ever going to stop writing so aggressively...?

IN THE STREET

It's 5 a.m. A man staggers the desolate sidewalks of San Francisco. He looks broken. His clothes are dirty, shoes torn, and he has the look of an individual who has seen the end of the world, and is traumatised by the vision. He staggers along. An evident handicap in the context of a limp on this man's left leg has no way of concealing itself. He staggers along. Withered face and all, the man forges ahead with a fixed gaze. Is he on some sort of mission? It seems so. What could it be though? What makes this person different from any of the other residents in San Francisco? He staggers along.

OBSERVATIONAL STORYTELLING

Character notes are really important, regardless of whether you are an artist or a writer. It's easy to see how these notes might be developed into fully-fledged comic book characters. It all starts here, with the note-taking.

CONCEPTUALISING YOUR CHARACTER

CHARACTERISATION IS ONE OF THE MOST IMPORTANT ASPECTS OF ANY STORY. YOU NEED TO KNOW WHO YOUR PEOPLE ARE AND WHAT MOTIVATES THEM, AND DECIDE WHAT YOUR CHARACTERS' OBJECTIVES WILL BE.

To create good characters for your story you need to invent and understand their complexities and the world they inhabit.

MAIN CHARACTERS

Your main character, or protagonist, is the focus of the story and determines its plot; he or she must be the most complex. This character usually has a desire to do or gain something (how they achieve their aim is what drives your story), but they may think twice about their actions, and this internal conflict gives them depth.

SUPPORTING CHARACTERS

Supporting characters reflect the qualities of the main character. A supporting character can be symbolic of the conscience of the main character, and be there to remind him of the consequences

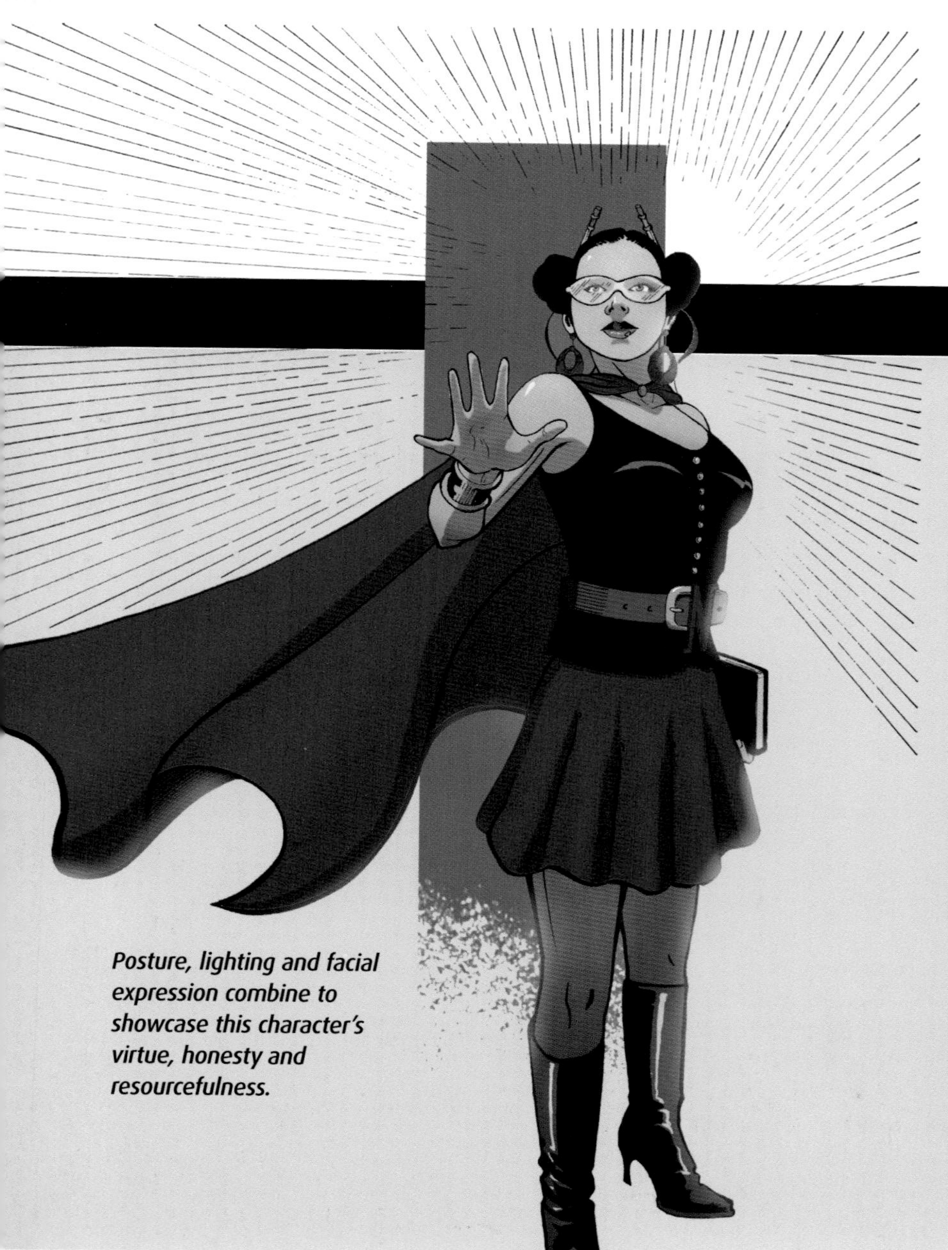

Posture, lighting and facial expression combine to showcase this character's virtue, honesty and resourcefulness.

HEROES AND VILLAINS

Heroes don't buckle under pressure, and neither do villains worthy of their opponents. There's no story if the villain gives up after losing the first battle to his arch-nemesis, the hero.

HEROIC ATTRIBUTES

» **Honest**
Honest within their own frame of reference. You can vary the amount of truth your character exhibits to those close to them or strangers in your story.

» **Self-sacrificing**
This is what raises your hero above the common herd – willingness to sacrifice himself for an ideal.

» **Resourceful**
Your hero will be able to dig herself out of a hole. Whether it's with specialist knowledge, a special talent or plain stubbornness, she will prevail. It's how she faces adversity that counts.

» **Knows what's right and wrong**
This doesn't mean that the hero always does good. Your hero committing bad acts for a good cause, especially if it causes some self-doubt, is interesting – just don't overdo the moral ambiguity.

» **Morally conflicted**
The hero sometimes doubts the morality of his cause, because your good guy has a conscience.

of his actions. This character may also be used to reveal to the reader information about the main character's motives, history and flaws without the main character addressing them in a direct way, which can be boring to readers.

Incidental characters

Incidental characters exist only to move the story along and have the least amount of development. For example, an incidental character could be an innocent bystander telling your main character, the policeman, which way the bank robbers escaped.

Levels of characterisation

For a main character there are different levels of characterisation. Take, for example, Superman and Batman. In his heroic, colourful costume, Superman is the ultimate boy scout, who fights for truth and justice. What you see is what you get. Batman, on the other hand, is a brooding crime fighter with a darker costume. He is more human than Superman can ever be. Both have origins of tragedy, but unlike Superman, Batman is a man with deep emotional scars and complex motives. Batman struggles to do the right thing and doesn't always get the credit he deserves, where Superman does. To understand this character, you need to look deeper into the man, not just at the surface. Batman may be intended for older audiences looking for a character with deeper motives than some, whereas Superman is often intended for younger readers. Who are you writing for?

Purpose and conflict: the antagonist

There can be no story without conflict, and this is where the antagonist comes in. An antagonist does not have to be a villain; it could be your character's best friend who wants the same thing in your story. The way each character goes about realising their purpose is what determines why readers will care about them. Your antagonist should think and act differently from your protagonist.

Villainous Attributes

» **Arrogant**
The graphic novel or comic book villain has very little doubt about his or her own abilities or causes. Most are megalomaniacs. They may not actually be classifiably insane, but they're certain to have a few tics. Psychopaths and sociopaths are usually loners, which makes them much harder to detect.

» **Resourceful**
In the course of your story their plans will be upset several times by the hero, but the villains will adapt and improvise.

» **Self-serving**
Villains regard their troops as cannon fodder, so if there's a problem, the villain will think of ways for his followers to solve it.

» **Absolute ideals**
Your villain knows the difference between right and wrong: he is right and everyone else is wrong. He may not see himself as evil - real bad guys never do - but as simply carrying out necessary work.

The knife and skull-tipped staff suggest this character will stop at nothing. Her stance also typifies her bravado - her absolute certainty that she is in the right.

GIVING YOUR CHARACTER DEPTH

Graphic novels are a visual medium, so a character's appearance is very important. There must be something in the portrayal of a character that gives instant clues to his or her nature.

William Shakespeare was known for creating several archetypal characters, such as Romeo and Juliet, the ill-fated lovers; Richard II, the hero who dies with honor; and Falstaff, the bawdy, rotund comic knight who appeared in three of his plays. Contemporary heroic archetypes include J. K. Rowling's Harry Potter, George Lucas's ***Star Wars*** character Darth Vader, DC Comics' Superman and Marvel Comics' Spider-Man. These examples are famous because they bring to mind the archetypal hero or villain, while challenging conventional perceptions of these archetypes. Drawing on stereotypes can be very powerful, but it's not enough to create characters that are based on stereotype alone. You must flesh out your characters; you can do this with words, but also visually.

SUBVERTING STEREOTYPE WITH VISUAL CLUES

Visual clues are a signpost to your reader of a character's nature. A fully rounded superhero cannot remain in costume at all times, so the

FIVE QUESTIONS FOR YOUR CHARACTER

The following questions will help you to shape a believable character for your story. Remember, characters in your story are people with feelings, attitude, goals, personality, secrets, family and friends. When creating characters for the first time, you want to know some basic things about them. The more you learn about your character, the clearer your story is going to be. Answering these five questions could help you to get started. Obviously, this is just a springboard to further develop your character's details that may or may not be relevant to your story. The character profile on the right is good, but there is so much more to Frank – as the five questions below reveal.

CHARACTER PROFILE

The character's name is Frank, short for Franklin (Sullivan). He is fifty-two years old. He is a fair-skinned Irishman with hazel eyes, short, greying hair combed back, and is 1.80 m (5 feet 10 inches) tall.

Frank is quiet and reserved, intellectually quick and assertive when he needs to be. He feels a strong sense of responsibility and duty to his job and others who employ his services. Frank's likes include cigarette smoking and good scotch, walking alone in the rain and seafood.

1 What does your character do?
Frank is a detective, a former policeman tired of the corrupt system and bureaucracy who decided to open his own private-eye service.

2 What interests does your character have?
Reading pulp novels, solving mysteries, spending time with his son and working on his automobile.

3 Where does your character live?
Just outside the Barbary Coast on Bush Street in San Francisco.

4 What is your character's secret?
Frank lost the woman he loved to an illness and married her sister and became stepdad to her only child, as a promise to his fiancée to take care of them. His heart died with his fiancée.

5 What does your character want?
Frank wants to have enough money to take care of his stepson and retire to enjoy his remaining days in the tropics. He believes he's meant to solve one big case that will earn him enough to do both. Which is where the story hook comes into play.

artist will draw consistently on other features – such as hairstyle and the way a person stands – that should not change when the hero returns to his everyday persona. You should note that costumed superheroes are often several inches taller than the ordinary guy, so they'll stand out even when they're not in spandex.

The villain shouldn't look villainous; instead he or she should give themselves away by subtler means. There should be a sense of menace around them, even when they are at their most genial. Their true nature will be revealed only in private; but luckily, our omnipresent readers will be able to listen in on such moments like a fly on the wall, and not be fooled at all.

Adding depth through body language

You can disguise or reveal your characters' true motives by considering their body language, the unconscious physical signals we make to each other without realising. When anyone lies, for example, there are certain signs to look for. They often can't meet your eyes directly (although this isn't always the case, if they are a particularly good liar), the pupils dilate a little, and breathing changes, as does pulse rate. They sweat a little, too, which is what the polygraphs rely on: the increased conductivity of the skin. The question presented to you is how do you visualise all of that in your graphic novel?

Well, of course, you can't. Not all of it certainly. It'll be up to you, the writer, to think of ways in which you can convey to the reader that your character is being conservative with the truth. And, most importantly, these character traits have to be visualised by the artist for clarity. You must write these nuances about your character for your artist to effectively draw them convincingly. Subtle positioning of the body, failure to meet someone's eyes, looking away, hunching the shoulders or keeping to the shadows are all aspects of body language that you could draw upon.

For the purpose of your book, gestures of body language will have to be exaggerated to make them obvious visually, to ensure that readers see what you want them to see with clarity.

Quiet demeanour, neat but unflashy clothes and a deadly weapon. Classic hit man.

The combination of wild hair, tight black clothing and a sultry expression gives the impression of a femme fatale.

A loud dresser, complete with pompadour, cigarette, and a sneer; your basic low-level street thug.

The tension in the body language and the hidden object behind the back give this man the demeanour of someone waiting to pounce.

Strong, aggressive posture gives this guy the impression of being a leader, or at least a force to be reckoned with.

Glasses, a button-up shirt and a pocket protector give an air of intellectualism; someone to go to for information.

Is she here to love you or kill you?

WRITING A CHARACTER BRIEF

Writing a character brief is essential for bringing your vision to the page. Writing for an artist or yourself, this is an opportunity to develop the visual clues that define your characters.

As a writer of graphic novels you will need to give notes to the collaborating artist that describe each character, for example, their clothing, hair, any obvious physical features and emotions that could be conveyed through the artwork. A good character description will allow the artist to easily visualise what the author imagines, while leaving enough room for the artist's own interpretation.

If you are both writing and drawing your graphic novel, it is worth considering what comes first; the artwork or the words. Words and pictures must work together for visual clarity and structure. Will your characters evolve as you draw them, or are they already carved in stone?

DON'T FORGET THE LITTLE GUYS

There's a reason they give Oscars for Best Supporting Actor. Give even your most incidental characters unique traits; make them interesting. It doesn't take much, and it makes the world your reader is visiting that much more vibrant.

WRITE A WINNING CHARACTER BRIEF

Your character description for the artist needs to be clear and have a strong visual element. It should describe appearance and personality, explain something of the character's origins and give an indication of any significant events in the story. Here, two writers describe the same character, Dana Valentine. Notice how much fuller the first (the 'good' character description) is.

'GOOD' CHARACTER DESCRIPTION

Title: Valentine: Assassin For Hire
Character: Dana Valentine
Description: Female, age 22. The story takes place in the United States and some settings abroad in 2010. Dana's physique is like that of a track and field athlete, wearing a black tank top tucked in black jeans with knee-high street boots over her jeans. Dana will wear a beat-up old black leather jacket with duct tape covering up bullet holes and tears. She has straight, raven black hair that she wears in a ponytail from time to time. Her hair hangs over part of her face, concealing one eye in most of the visuals in the graphic novel. Dana rarely smiles and carries a stoic expression most of the time. Her personality can be described as tough, cynical, dry sarcasm, but incredibly loyal to those she's allowed to get close to her. Behind her ice-cold glare lies a vulnerable side as well.

Her stance is a defensive one most of the time, one hand clenched and the other close to her concealed gun or knife. She's never relaxed and always on guard, even when she's not on assignment.
Physical Appearance: Athletic, raven black hair, green eyes, noticeable scars on her shoulders and back.
Meaning of Name: 'Arbiter. Someone with the power to settle matters at will.'
Ethnicity: Irish, Spanish, French.

'BAD' CHARACTER DESCRIPTION

Title: Valentine: Assassin For Hire
Character: CIA Agent Kevin Harper
Description: A field agent for the CIA who follows the book and is loyal to the agency, but breaks protocol when it comes to helping Valentine, an assassin working above the law. Agent Harper hides his feelings for the attractive yet deadly assassin, while his actions to protect her say otherwise.

WHAT MAKES THIS A GOOD DESCRIPTION?

- Visual clues are provided for the artist, as are details that will make sense later in the story.
- Indicating the time the story takes place is very useful, and the artist can use this information to research settings, automobiles, technology, fashion and more.
- Body language is detailed. This will give the reader a hint to the nature of the character before reading the first line of dialogue.
- Although clearly defining the character, this description allows plenty of room for the artist's input.

WHAT MAKES THIS A BAD DESCRIPTION?

- This minimal description tells the artist nothing of the character's appearance.
- Something of the character's motives are revealed, but not enough. Will the character's reasons for aiding a known criminal be enough to explore?
- There is no visual description, only vague character traits that the artist cannot draw. Your character description serves to develop the character's background for the story, but should also detail the visuals for your artists to draw clearly.

SHOT BY SHOT

The brief, brought to life. The artist has incorporated all aspects of Dana Valentine's body language and attire, making her a solid character.

VISUALISING A CHARACTER

Once you know who your characters are, it's time to give them life on the page. That's where your artist comes in, or, if you are writing and illustrating your novel, it's time to pick up your drawing pencil.

Once you've fleshed out your characters, it's time to start collaborating with the artist (even if the artist is you). This is a process of creative tennis, so be patient and keep your wits about you. You and your artist should spend time building each character's appearance from the ground up. Remember, the visual representation of a character is their calling card. If their looks aren't consistent, the best writing still won't save you.

Start with rough sketches, trying out different expressions, hairstyles, accessories, etc. Gradually develop the character, tightening the edges and working out a solid and consistent look. Do they have any defining physical attributes? A costume? A favourite hat? Is their personality coming through in the body language? Are there any visual problems that have to be worked out, such as the character being an android or a mutant? Work with your artist to get the character just right, but do remember to let your artist be an artist. They may see visual problems or cues that you don't. Listen to them and treat them as an equal partner in the creation of your characters, and the result will be that much stronger.

This sequence shows the developmental sketches produced as a result of the 'good' character brief on page 22.

1 INITIAL ROUGHS

The artist quickly sketches out ideas as they occur. This is the time to try out anything and everything, and not get too precious about it. This is visual brainstorming; it's supposed to get messy.

Note the differing hairstyles; experimenting is the only way to get the right look.

2 DEVELOPING THE CHARACTER

A trial run of the whole figure, with attempts to capture the defensive stance. The artist is getting comfortable with Valentine's face and is moving on to understanding and communicating her whole body language.

Sketches are used to capture Valentine's stoic demeanour.

Think about your character's posture in light of her props.

3 ALMOST THERE

The roughs have evolved into something more complete. Notice how much more consistent the demeanour, hair and whole look are. This now feels like several sketches of one distinct character.

Facial close-ups clearly depict Valentine's stoic expression.

4 THE FINAL DRAFT

The figure captures Valentine perfectly - her tough demeanour, as well as the sense that at any time she could lift her gun and fire off a few rounds if threatened. Her clothes, hair and general distinguishing marks have solidified and she is very clearly herself.

Both guns drawn show Valentine is ready to take care of trouble.

Her head is half turned in awareness of her surroundings, and the eyes show she knows exactly where the threat is coming from.

Recommended Reads

***The Dark Knight Returns* by Frank Miller**
This masterpiece of modern comics storytelling brings to vivid life a dark world and an even darker man. Together with inker Klaus Janson and colourist Lynn Varley, writer/artist Frank Miller reinvents the legend of Batman in his saga of a near-future Gotham City gone to rot, ten years after the Dark Knight's retirement.

***Black Orchid* by Neil Gaiman**
After being viciously murdered, Susan is reborn fully grown as the Black Orchid, a hybrid of plant and human, in order to avenge her own death. Now as this demigoddess attempts to reconcile her human memories and botanical origins, she must also untangle the webs of deception and secrets that led to her murder. Beginning in the cold streets of a heartless metropolis and ending in the lavish heartland of the thriving Amazon, this book takes the reader through a journey of secrets, suffering, and self-rediscovery.

***Asterios Polyp* by David Mazzucchelli**
An engrossing, epic story of one man's search for love, meaning, sanity and perfect architectural proportions.

***Bone* by Jeff Smith**
After being run out of Boneville, the three Bone cousins - Fone Bone, Phoney Bone and Smiley Bone - are separated and lost in a vast, uncharted desert. One by one, they find their way into a deep-forested valley filled with wonderful and terrifying creatures. It will be the longest - but funniest - year of their lives.

***Blacksad* by Juan Diaz Canales and Juanjo Guarnido**
Private investigator John Blacksad is up to his feline ears in mystery, digging into the backstories behind murders, child abductions and nuclear secrets. Guarnido's sumptuously painted pages and rich cinematic style bring the world of 1950s America to vibrant life, with Canales weaving in fascinating tales of conspiracy, racial tension and Communist witch hunts.

STORYTELLING

'Every sensible invention must have a purpose, every planned sprint a destination.'

Outlining and researching your plot

outlining your plot may seem counterintuitive, but only by defining your story's boundaries will you be free to run around within it and go mad.

Organising your ideas and looking into the broader world you seek to create will not only add credibility to your story, but also make your life a lot easier. The construction of a cogent outline enables you to develop your tale before you even write the script. Conducting research beforehand – as well as throughout the project – invites details and authenticity that might otherwise be lacking in the final product.

Creating an outline of the plot through the use of note cards, a word processing program or even pen and paper assures you the flexibility of rearranging scenes, plotting points, and beats, or even eschewing them altogether. Your completed outline acts as a blueprint, a defined structure that allows you to exercise your creativity within.

Research methods

Through various types of research, you can add the facts, details and colour that make your story come to life. Your method of research can take many forms – the internet, book shops, libraries, classes, personal interviews or public records. If you find yourself working on an established character or property, researching its history will be key. Try not to rely too heavily on outside sources, or else you run the risk of giving too much over to the 'facts' at the expense of creatively telling your story.

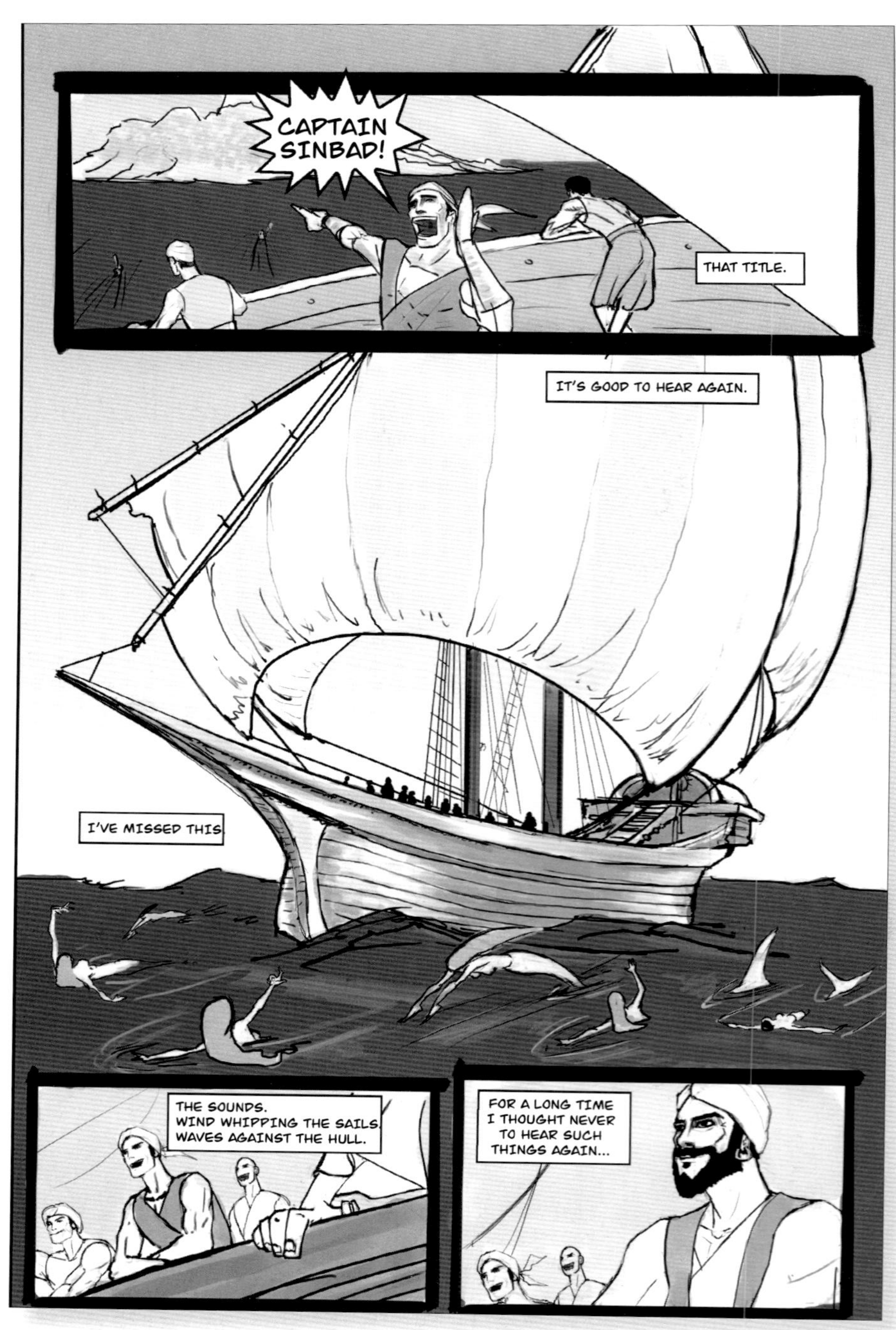

WHAT THE EXPERTS SAY

Brian Schirmer is a writer, filmmaker and educator living in San Francisco. He is the author of the comic anthology ***Worlds Apart***. His graphic novel ***Wavelength*** will be published by Committed Comics in 2011.

THE VALUE AND THE FUN OF RESEARCH BY BRIAN SCHIRMER

Once upon a time, I couldn't be bothered with researching anything more than a page or two on a topic. If that. I'd either wing it, or I'd find some way to get around whatever the topic, covering my tracks, hoping no one would notice.

But I noticed.

For the Sinbad script (shown on these pages) I knew that I wanted to craft a tale rooted in not only Arabic mythology, but also the history of the land. Who were the common people? Who was the ruling power? What could I learn about the day-to-day business of the different classes? Where did so-and-so sleep? And with whom? The only way to answer these questions was to tackle the big R – research.

I read up on the history of seamanship and on Islamic dynasties in the eighth and ninth centuries and on obscure demons and their kin. You know what? It was suddenly no longer a chore. Research became a fun exploit in itself.

A question I get asked a lot is 'When are you done researching?' Well, probably only when you're done with the script. You'll look things up throughout the process. It's unavoidable. That said, if I've done the proper amount of research, I find I have to fight myself off, wanting so desperately to include as many titbits and details as I've gleaned. I find I'm done when I've taken in so much information that I'm rushing to the keyboard, wanting to pour everything I've absorbed into my script.

ALTERNATE HISTORIES

For **The Final Voyage of Sinbad,** *historical figures, locations and events intermingle with legendary characters and mythological creatures, creating a sense of an alternate history of the Arab world, circa 800 A.D.*

Writing the Premise

Your premise is the backbone around which you will build the rest of your story. It is the foundation used to build your characters, your theme and the plot. A great premise is best expressed in a short paragraph, rather than condensed into a single sentence.

The premise is used to lay out the primary goals of your main character, and to lay out the path that the protagonist will use to achieve the story's goals. Read on to learn about the theory and practice of writing premises.

Where the story is going, and why

When you undertake the development of your story's premise, there are a few things that you must take into account. First, you must quickly introduce your main character. Then you must make a decision about this character's objectives: what is it that they are trying to accomplish in the story? This will explain to the reader what it is that your character desires. An explanation of your main character's driving desire can go a long way to explaining most of the character's actions throughout the story, especially when those actions are not directly beneficial to the character's personal well-being. The premise must also include a sense of where the story is going and what the outcome will be.

Premise as writing tool

Writing a premise can be intimidating but also liberating for your story. The more you refine your premise, the better your story is going to be. Character is story and without a good character, you have no story.

Your premise is not meant to be artistic, or even pretty. You are not looking to create originality or a unique idea when you build your premise. Instead, you are looking to set out the foundation to help support your developing story. A premise on its own is nothing. In order for it to matter, you must take the time to build it up until it becomes an exciting representation of the story that you intend to tell. Use your premise as a tool to help you create the best novel that you can.

Stories are metaphors for life

Fiction has the power to give meaning to the meaninglessness of life. Life is chaotic and hard to understand for many of us. Fiction can bring order and sense to it all. You, the writer, have the powers of a god when you craft a story. You decide what happens, when, and how. You must construct events in a logical, but unpredictable pattern that points inevitably to the conclusion raised by your premise.

The choices your character makes in the course of the story should further enhance the statement of your premise. This way, the audience lives through the hero's experiences and witnesses the validation of the premise.

Remember the following points as you build on your premise.

- Stories are about life; life means change.
- Your audience needs to see change.
- Anything static is boring.
- Stories that don't affect the characters or don't make a difference are dull stories.
- Changes in the story need to validate the argument of the premise; this is done by employing the power of choice.

Put in the groundwork

A good premise lays out the building blocks of your story and serves as a support to launch you into your writing. Character, conflict and motivation are all introduced here. Using your premise as your road map will prevent you from taking detours that will dilute your narrative. Is the dramatic issue clear? What is the protagonist's key motivation? How are the characters working to resolve the conflict and what will begin to unfold before them? Stumped? Ask yourself 'what if' and start writing, the same way an artist hones ideas in a sketchbook. Experiment, refine and persevere and your premise will emerge.

Alicia is a shy high school girl who discovers that her dreams have the ability to alter waking reality. Overcome with grief after accidentally erasing her home town, she attempts to stay awake so as to do no more harm, but her dreams only become more dire. She soon finds herself miraculously pregnant, stealing stimulants to stay awake and on the run from a pharmaceutical police state. Allied with an unstable band of outlaws and armed with uppers, she tries to evade the agents of her anxiety long enough to have her baby.

WHAT MAKES THIS
A GOOD PREMISE?

- » You understand the main character's motivation.
- » The setup and conflict is clear.
- » The action is inspired by the conflict.
- » The conflict escalates.
- » Structured enough to help you stay on course.
- » Loose enough to let your characters evolve and drive elements of the plot.

Alicia was your typical suburban teenager until her dreams started altering reality. She discovers, to her horror, the destructive power of her subconscious and attempts to stop sleeping but this only makes it worse. After dreaming the world into a living nightmare, she'll do anything to stay awake, with disastrous effect.

WHAT MAKES THIS
A BAD PREMISE?

- » The main character has no clear motivation or attributes.
- » The action is inert.
- » It's unclear what's at stake.
- » Too vague to aid you in the writing process.

HOW TO WRITE A PREMISE

It is important that your premise is planned out well and is easily recognizable to your readers. If you fail to properly present the premise of the story to the audience, you may end up losing their interest. The premise will contain the introduction of your main character, the event that starts the action and some sense of the direction in which the story will go.

First step

Quickly write down one sentence that explains your entire story. Include who your story is about, what is going to happen to your main character or characters and where the story is going to go.

> ***'A man travels to Prague in 1994 to avenge a friend's death and retrieve a secret document.'***

This sentence introduces the character and his objectives, while establishing a sense of the direction the story may take, and explains why the character must undertake this journey.

Moving on

Now you need to add to this basic premise. Keep in mind that your premise need not be artistic or creative; it needs to be functional. Start adding strong verbs and nouns to help enhance your premise.

> ***'Upon hearing about the bloody murder of a close friend, a retired detective undertakes an expedition to Prague to find his friend's killer. Once he arrives, his investigations and inquiries begin to unearth evidence of a government cover-up, and incriminating evidence - last seen in the hands of a mysterious woman - that has disappeared.'***

THREE-ACT STORY STRUCTURE

In its simplest form, the classic three-act structure is a common formula found in a majority of narrative comics and films. The structure is divided into a beginning, middle and end.

THREE-ACT BREAKDOWN

When you're working up a new story, refer to this simple structure that comics' writer and editor Denny O'Neil stands by for writing comics and graphic novels.

To begin, introduce the status quo of your character and set up the situation through an inciting incident, 'the hook', using a major visual action. The beginning of your graphic novel must show the readers the establishment of the central characters, setting and problem or conflict.

In the middle, develop and complicate the situation by using setbacks, reversals, suspense and 'rising action' that leads to a dramatic conclusion. For each rising action you expound to your readers, give them a chance to breathe by using 'falling action', to allow them to absorb the ramifications of the complications in the story.

The action/complication in the story increases as the story nears its climax. Each complication you build into your story should be more important with greater consequences than the one before it, as you race to the finish line.

The events you write leading to the dénouement after reaching the climax of your story are similar to using falling action, in which your readers are presented with a brief scene that gives them some closure and possibly something to think about when easing out of the story's world. For those of you writing a series of graphic novels with the same central character, give the readers some sense of completion, while leaving them with a taste of what's to come by posing a question they feel compelled to know the answer to, which can be found in a future instalment.

THREE-ACT BREAKDOWN

ACT I: BEGINNING

SETUP

Introduction of characters, environment and genre of your story. Everything the reader needs to know to understand and follow the rest of the book gets laid out here. Your inciting incident should happen within the first pages; the sooner the better.

ACT II: MIDDLE

CONFRONTATION

Your protagonist encounters setbacks and rising conflict. Complications build and they are at the furthest from their goal. There should be major visual action here – make it worth drawing and worth looking at.

ACT III: END

RESOLUTION

The protagonist takes clear and final action to resolve their central conflict. A dénouement adds crucial closure to the story, but leaves doors open for future tales.

WHAT THE EXPERTS SAY

Michael Davidson has been writing about comic books and graphic novels for the past ten years. Since graduating from the University of Oregon with a degree in Magazine Journalism, he has been working steadily as a freelance writer and journalist, most notably for Suite101.com. In his free time, he spends entirely too much energy daydreaming about Spider-Man.

'DRAMATIC STRUCTURE IN INFINITE NARRATIVE' BY MICHAEL DAVIDSON

Traditional comic books are serials, which means that they are intended as a constant narrative rather than a fully complete work, like a novel. For example, ***Spider-Man*** comic books are consumed in a different way than ***Moby-Dick***, because Spider-Man stories form a larger, years-long narrative, while Ahab and his great white whale exist as a single volume.

SERIES, STORY ARCS AND SINGLE ISSUES

An issue of ***Spider-Man*** is usually a part of a designated story arc, which tells a smaller story within the framework of his character narrative. A story arc will usually feature the titular hero in pursuit of a single goal, with obstacles and challenges spaced over a number of issues.

Any issue of a story arc comprises a complete story, intended to be read as a stand-alone narrative. Knowledge of the character's complex back-story is beneficial to the reader, but the story does end with some closure. In a decades-long serial, closure is rarely final. Closure comes in bursts, with the fulfilment of smaller goals that aid consumption and understanding.

Single issues are interesting in that even though they are intended as twice-removed steps in a larger whole (first as part of a story arc, then a series), they still conform to a three-act structure. Every issue still requires setup, then rising action, then a climax. Many issues have a climax that is a cliffhanger, or a moment that resolves the mini-story contained within the issue, but leads into the next.

Finally, each issue and arc becomes a piece of the series, or continued adventures of the protagonist. ***Spider-Man*** has existed as a continuing story since August 1962. Although some writers have sought to change certain aspects of the character, all changes come from within the text. The continuing Spider-Man story is fairly basic. Nebbish teenager Peter Parker gains the proportional abilities of a spider after he is bitten by a radioactive insect. This is the facet character that never changes, and the story that never ends. Each smaller piece builds upon that simple premise, creating a story that fulfils its dramatic structure in segments rather than a single conclusion.

CLOSURE

To achieve the lofty goal of a story that never truly ends, especially one crafted by thousands of individuals, knowledge of the three-act structure is essential. Infinite narratives are all about the process of building, and for something to never truly end, a reader must still be able to feel a sense of closure.

Without closure, a story isn't a story. It would be a mess incapable of providing any true understanding, merely events strung together. A conclusion, even if it is really the illusion of an ending, is integral to a story's meaning. The journey is important, but only insomuch that it leads to a certain kind of truth.

STORMS AT SEA

As dire as things may look for the star of the ongoing serial, don't worry, this too shall pass. All good stories come to an end, after all.

Creating conflict

Good stories involve conflict, and this is what keeps the story moving. The drama you create for your story is conflict, every single bit of it. No conflict, no connection to your audience.

Conflict can be emotional, mental, physical, spiritual, sociological or elemental. It can be two friends at odds over the same girl, two armies on opposing sides about to wage battle or a man with a gambling addiction struggling to keep his family together while being tempted by a high-stakes winner-takes-all card game. You cannot have a good story without having a well-developed character that goes through some type of metamorphosis internally, or deals with an external problem.

Types of conflict

A character's conflict can be external (a struggle with a force outside of themselves) or internal (a struggle within one's self – perhaps if he or she must make a difficult decision, overcome pain, quieten their temper or resist an urge). Creating a believable conflict through the development of your characters' needs – whether it's your protagonist's desire for life, love or inner peace, or your antagonist's desire for power, control or destruction – could have the biggest impact on whether or not your story is effective.

The most typical types of conflict are man-versus-man, man-versus-circumstance, man-versus-society and man-versus-himself, but it's important to note that a character typically has multiple conflicts to resolve. Goals change during the course of the novel. New information or insight can alter motivations and goals, and lead to new conflicts and new potential solutions.

You need to be cognizant of your character's choices because there is a cause and effect to them not related to one scene or incident, but throughout your entire story. As you complicate the characters' situations and equip them with new knowledge and strength to resolve their conflict, their change becomes a story.

Conflict and action

Be careful not to confuse conflict with action. Action is a circumstantial event or crisis, like an automobile accident, a robbery or getting fired from a job. Conflict is the choices or struggles the character has to make, sometimes because of that crisis. Conflict usually precedes action, building up to the action scene, not the other way around. Your story could be filled with all kinds of action scenes, but will be rendered useless without any conflict or tension to keep the reader engaged.

WITH COLD DELIBERATION MING FORCES FLASH TOWARD A SMOULDERING PIT...
HE'S AMAZING! I CAN'T GET THROUGH HIS GUARD.

MAN VS MAN

In man-versus-man conflict, the leading character struggles with his physical strength against other men (right), forces of nature or animals (above).

ESTABLISHING CONFLICT

For an action scene to be effective between two characters, the conflict must be established prior to their confrontation. Above, a woman has taken a prized dog from an abusive owner, who knows she's lying. She refuses to hand the dog over to the owner. The action is compounded by their conflict.

CONFLICT OF CHOICE

In this sequence, an assassin encounters a setback when she has a flat tyre. She has no spare tyre and no mobile phone signal. The tension building from this scene begs the question of whether or not she'll take a passerby's truck by force.

Suspense and surprise

You can use suspense throughout your entire story, but the element of surprise has to be used sparingly for it to effectively impact your audience. If you want to use suspense effectively in your story, be sure to include the audience, so the reader knows at least – and preferably more than – what the main character knows. Giving the readers this insight enables their thoughts and feelings to be involved with the character and the story.

The director and producer Alfred Hitchcock described the difference between suspense and surprise like this:

'Four men are sitting at a table playing poker. The scene is rather boring. Suddenly, after fifteen minutes, we hear a big bang – it turns out there was a bomb under the table. This is called "surprise", as it isn't what we expected would happen.

'If we watch the same scene again with the important difference that we have seen the bomb being placed under the table and the timer set to 11 a.m., and we can see a watch in the background, the same scene becomes very intense and almost unbearable – we are sitting there hoping the timer will fail, the game is interrupted or the hero leaves the table in time, before the blast. This is called "suspense".'

Finding the MacGuffin

A MacGuffin (sometimes McGuffin or Maguffin) is a plot device that motivates the characters and advances the story, but has little other relevance to the story. Hitchcock popularised both the term 'MacGuffin' and the technique. Hitchcock explained the term in a 1939 lecture at Columbia University: 'We have a name in the studio, and we call it the "MacGuffin". It is the mechanical element that usually crops up in any story. In crook stories it is always the necklace and in spy stories it is always the papers.'

What distinguishes a MacGuffin from other types of plot devices is that it is not important what object the MacGuffin specifically is. Anything that serves as a motivation will do. A true MacGuffin is essentially interchangeable. Its importance will generally be accepted completely by the story's characters, with minimal explanation. From the audience's perspective, it is not the point of the story.

The technique is commonly used in movies, especially thrillers. Often the MacGuffin is the central focus of the film in the first act, then declines in significance as the struggles and motivations of the characters take centre stage. Try incorporating a MacGuffin into your novel.

BEST OF BOTH

Mark Schultz effectively combines suspense and surprise in one page! The first panel establishes the situation, while the subsequent panels build the suspense, using a close-up shot of the woman for impact. As our hero defeats the man with the gun, he is surprised to see the woman pointing one at him in the last panel.

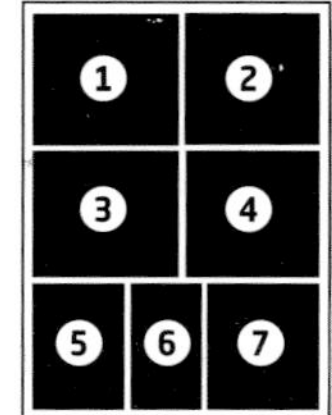

COMMENTARY

1: The composition reflects the predicament our hero finds himself in. The man in the hat has the advantage.

2: Tension is increased by the gunman's body language as he leans in towards our hero with his gun.

3: A struggle ensues with the gun falling to the ground. The slight tilt of the composition impacts the action.

4: To convey suspense effectively, include your audience by giving them close-ups of the characters reacting to the conflict.

5: Our hero throws the knockout punch.

6: The suspense appears to be over as our hero stands over his attacker.

7: A surprise twist occurs when the woman pulls a gun on our hero as he's reaching for his attacker's gun. Suspense can be built from a few panels or more, while surprise can be shown in one.

FAMOUS MACGUFFINS

The statuette in **The Maltese Falcon** *(1941) is a prime example of a MacGuffin. A private detective takes on a case that involves him with three eccentric criminals, a gorgeous liar and their quest for a priceless statuette.*

Because a MacGuffin is, by definition, ultimately unimportant to the story, its use can test the suspension of disbelief of audiences. Works that are done well will compensate for this with a good story, interesting characters, talented acting/writing and so on. Inferior novels or films, which fail in those areas, often only highlight a MacGuffin, sometimes to the point of absurdity. MacGuffins may be acceptable to the general audience, but fail to be believable for experts in the subject matter (such as a particular technology or historical detail).

MacGuffins in the graphic novel

» In the perennial classic ***Watchmen*** the MacGuffin that reunites the retired super heroes is the threat of a giant squid attacking Manhattan. It lent so little to the book's purpose that it was excised entirely for the film adaption.

» In the ***Martian Confederacy***, a trio of outlaws band together to retrieve a stolen scientific sample that could free the people of Mars from corporate tyranny. The theft of the sample sets the story in motion but its importance fades as the characters' motivations play out.

» In ***The Sandman's Preludes and Nocturnes***, Dream sets out to reclaim a stolen helm, a pouch of sand and a ruby, which provide his driving motivation for the whole book but by the end are either destroyed or inconsequential.

» In the Cerebus graphic novel ***Jaka's Story***, Oscar attracts a new customer to the bar by painting a statue called a Guffin. Eventually, the MacGuffin is also what attracts the attention of the Cirinists, which sets the stage for the story's ending.

MacGuffins in the movies

» One famous MacGuffin is Rosebud, the sleigh seen at the end of the film ***Citizen Kane*** (1941), meant to symbolise the lost innocence of the millionaire protagonist, Charles Foster Kane (Orson Welles).

» In ***Notorious*** (1946), the uranium hidden in wine bottles is a MacGuffin. It is the reason the story takes place, but could just as easily have been diamonds, gold or rare wine. In fact, during production, there was discussion of changing it to diamonds to be more believable.

» In ***North by Northwest*** (1959), the MacGuffin is the unspecified secret information known by a man for whom Roger Thornhill (Cary Grant) is mistaken. Throughout the movie, Thornhill tries to find the man, without realizing that he does not exist.

» In Sergio Leone's famous Western ***The Good, The Bad, and The Ugly***, the gold that the main characters are searching for is a MacGuffin.

Orson Welles in **Citizen Kane.**

WHAT THE EXPERTS SAY

A Xeric Award winner, **Jason McNamara's** comic titles include ***Less Than Hero***, ***First Moon***, ***Continuity***, ***The Gastometrist***, ***Short Hand***, ***Sucker***, ***The Martian Confederacy*** and its sequel, ***From Mars with Love***. He recently co-created the PIE Theory Alternate Reality Game and co-adapted the animated graphic novel ***Project Ajax***. He's a redhead, a Pisces and looks great in a Spider-Man suit. Look out!

MONKEY IN A MAN-SUIT

I was asked to be in a monkey-themed anthology. After accepting, I quickly realised that I didn't have a monkey story to tell. As the deadline loomed, all I could think of was 'escaping' my obligations and, through that anxiety, discovered the premise of my story.

It's a daily struggle, for your story and yourself.

When building a story, my first inclination is to make my protagonist, and the supporting cast, the best of friends. They agree on everything, respect each other's feelings and compliment each other's outfits. 'Can you believe it? I got it on sale!' Isn't that what we'd all like in our lives? But writing graphic novels isn't the real world, kids. Next time someone asks you, 'Why can't we all just get along?' you have my permission to smash a bottle over their head and scream 'Because it's dull'.

In fiction, your characters need to have differences; they need to chafe under pressure, screw each other over and basically do what they said they wouldn't do. And, especially for comics, they need to look different. The more physical, emotional, social and ideological differences you can put between your characters, the better. There's a goldmine of conflict in odd-couple pairings. Look at Abbott and Costello, Harold and Maude, Chris Farley and David Spade, Christopher Walken and, well, anybody else.

But characters aren't created entirely on the page. Sometimes they need to cook a little longer in the toaster oven of your mind. Lock your cast up in a virtual room and listen to them. You can do this on the bus, at the gym or while your boss is talking. What's the worst thing that

Page one

Page two

can happen to each of your characters? Who falls in love? Who cracks? Motivation is key; even characters working towards a common goal will have different reasons for doing so. The more attention you give your characters, the more likely the story conflict will deepen and grow.

My favourite stories are ones that connect personal and environmental conflicts. The 1953 film ***The Wages of Sin*** is a great example of this. Four expatriates hiding in South America are offered a fortune to drive two trucks, filled with unstable nitroglycerin, over a hazardous mountain terrain. The guys don't get along, they could blow up at any minute and they're running out of time.

Now if you took that same plot and made them best friends, from high school, and had it take place on Long Island, and had the trucks filled with golf balls, the 'will they or won't they' becomes 'who cares?' even though it's still four guys on a road trip. Where your story takes place, and how your characters interact with that environment, is an unmissable opportunity for conflict.

Writing a graphic novel, or anything, can be a Herculean task, no matter where you are in your career. That is our conflict, as creators. Take every raw emotion this process ignites in you and throw it back at the page. You are the protagonist of your own journey.

Page three

Page one *Page two* *Page three*

COMMENTARY

Page One

1: An exterior establishing shot establishes when and where your story takes place and invites the reader in to the world you've created.
2: This close-up effect introduces Simon, acknowledges a conflict and creates suspense because you don't know who he's talking to.
3: Valerie's introduction is made stronger by moving her to the foreground. Simon's body language suggests he's being pulled between two worlds.
4: Notice the way Simon walks, it reinforces his character while foreshadowing his 'secret'. Altering the camera angles in a quiet scene keeps it visually interesting.
5: The inciting action (the kiss) is more powerful because of the differences between the characters. The first act closes with Simon's decision to go to the party.

Page Two

1: Another location change, another establishing shot putting the characters in context with their environment. Second act begins.
2,3,4: Escalating emotional conflict. Character low point.
5: Simon makes a decision and the conflict becomes physical. Third act begins.
6: The line between Simon's two worlds is crumbling. Borderless panels are a great way to showcase action while being conservative with space.

Page Three

1: Objects breaking out of panel make the action seem more dynamic.
3: Off-panel reveal builds suspense and enables you to share an emotion with your character.
4: The story's climax attempts to resolve all previous plot points.
5: A brief epilogue resolves the emotional conflict.

Scripting your story

when it comes to scripting your story, there are two approaches that are considered the industry standard for scripting comic books and graphic novels.

There are two basic methods of writer/artist collaboration in comics: 'plot first' (or 'marvel style') and full script. Read on to find out about their advantages and disadvantages, and see how they differ in the sample scripts, right.

Plot first (or 'marvel style')

The Marvel Method is a form of comic book writer–artist collaboration in which the artist works from a story synopsis, rather than a full script, creating page-by-page plot details on his or her own. The technique takes its name from its widespread use at Marvel Comics, beginning in the 1960s, primarily under writer–editor Stan Lee and artists Jack Kirby and Steve Ditko.

Advantages

- Writer knows exactly what the art looks like, and how much room there is for text.

Disadvantages

- Writer gives up some control over pacing and composition, and may get undesired results.
- You can't use this method unless you have an existing relationship with the artist and editor.

Full script

This is generally the more accepted writing style for comic book scripting. A writer breaks the story down in sequence, page by page and panel by panel, describing the action, characters and sometimes backgrounds and 'camera angles', as well as all captions and dialogue balloons. For decades this was the preferred format for books published by DC Comics.

Advantages

- Writer has full control of the story and pacing.
- Writer can improve on their original idea.
- Writer is not relying on anyone else to get the job done – the full script.

Disadvantages

- You may need to trim or otherwise revise your dialogue and captions after seeing the art.
- Full scripts take longer to write than plot-first breakdowns.

Plot first (or 'marvel style')

Panel One: Establishing shot of a large yacht anchored off the island of Malta in the southeastern part of the Mediterranean. This sequence takes place late in the afternoon. The water is calm and glasslike, reflecting the nearby island and the yacht itself.

Colourist Notes: Use warm colours reflecting the sunset setting behind the yacht.

Panel Two: A group of wealthy middle-aged men are on the deck of the yacht preparing to grill fish as the captain, also a known crime lord, gives a speech while opening a bottle of champagne. The art of sabering plays a key part in both the beginning and end of the story. Several women are seen 'partying' it up, scantily clad in bikinis and sarongs, and flirting with the crime lord's bodyguards.

Panel Three: A close-up shot of the saber sword slicing off the bottleneck of the champagne bottle.

Panel Four: Zoom in to a medium shot to get a closer look at the people on board. We see a blonde woman on the left, wearing a two-piece bikini and wrapped in a sarong from the waist down. She has a large sunhat and glasses, and is holding a champagne glass. The man walking over is the captain of the ship, considerably older and wearing only Speedos and a captain's hat. He is lean but with a paunch stomach, and is holding the saber sword and the broken champagne bottle. In the background, other folks on the deck of the boat frame the background of the sea. A small speedboat can be seen in the distance.

Panel Five: Zoom in on the speedboat approaching fast towards the reader at a slight three-quarter low angle. The driver of the boat is a mid-thirtysomething woman with dark hair, wearing slick sunglasses and a two-piece bikini covered in a sarong.

Panel Six: Close-up of woman's face with a sly smile as she holds up a Glock with a silencer.

Checklist for scripting

When you're writing a full script, you're telling the artist everything that's going to be on the page. If the comic book is like a film, you are the director. Each panel is an individual shot. You're telling your artist (your director of photography) what you want.

» Is the storytelling clear from the first panel to the last on the page?
» Are the panels clearly numbered?
» Is there a focal point in each panel?
» Is your character conducting one action per panel? A red flag is multiple actions by one character in the same panel, when a series of panels is actually required to complete the action sequence.

FULL SCRIPT

Panel One: Establishing shot of a large yacht anchored off the island of Malta in the southeastern part of the Mediterranean.

Caption: Near the island of Malta.

CAPTAIN: Today, my friends, we celebrate the acquittal of all charges brought against me.

CAPTAIN: I stand before you an innocent man, whose only crime is successfully building an enterprise of commerce between our beloved Greece and the Americas.

CAPTAIN: Thank you all for coming to what's sure to be an unforgettable day!

Panel Two: A blonde woman reclines, holding up her glass of champagne in the foreground. The Captain's bodyguard is sandwiched between two women in the background as their Captain (a Greek/American crime lord) gives a speech while opening a bottle of champagne.

CAPTAIN: Eis igian!

BLONDE: To your health!

BODYGUARD: To your health!

Panel Three: A close-up shot of the saber sword slicing off the bottleneck of the champagne bottle.

Panel Four: Zoom in to a medium shot to get a closer look at the people on board. We see a blonde woman on the left, wearing a two-piece bikini and wrapped in a sarong from the waist down. She has a large sunhat and glasses, and is holding a champagne glass. The man walking over is the captain of the ship, considerably older and wearing only Speedos and a captain's hat. His hair is slicked back, he is lean but with a paunch stomach, and he is holding the saber sword and the broken champagne bottle. In the background, other folks on the deck of the boat frame the background of the sea. A small speedboat can be seen in the distance.

CAPTAIN: Welcome my lovely, allow me. And you are…?

BLONDE: Cassandra, Captain. Thank you.

Panel Five: Zoom in on the speedboat approaching fast towards the reader at a slight three-quarter low angle. The driver of the boat is a mid-thirtysomething woman with dark hair, wearing slick sunglasses and a two-piece bikini covered in a sarong.

Panel Six: Close-up of woman's face with a sly smile as she holds up a Glock with a silencer.

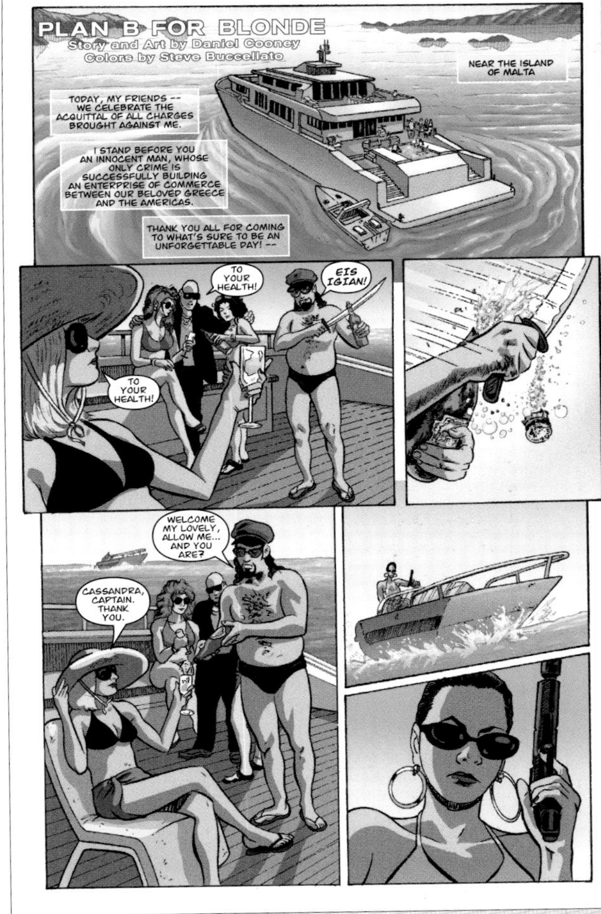

SETTING THE SCENE

This opening page establishes the setting for where the story takes place in the first panel. The characters involved and what they are doing are clearly illustrated in the panels that follow, with a threat introduced in the last panel. Character, place and situation are the components for clear storytelling in comic book scripting.

- » What are your characters doing with their hands?
- » Are the facial expressions clearly showing an emotion?
- » Did you describe the body language necessary for your character's actions?
- » Is the background clearly defined?
- » Is there a sense of depth in your composition from foreground to background?
- » Does each scene start with a description of the setting?
- » Are scene changes clearly indicated?
- » Did you start with an interesting hook? (Try a 'people' angle. Take what is compelling about your story and put it up front in your story.)
- » Are your sentences short, concise and clear? Do you make sense?
- » Are your subjects and verbs close together?
- » Are your verbs all in present or future tense (if possible)?
- » Are your verbs active rather than passive? ('The forward scored a goal' instead of 'A goal was scored by the forward'.)
- » Is your script conversational?
- » Is your information correct?

WHAT THE EXPERTS SAY

Brian Schirmer is a writer, filmmaker and educator living in San Francisco. He is the author of the comic anthology ***Worlds Apart***. His graphic novel ***Wavelength*** will be published by Committed Comics in 2011.

'WRITING A MODEL SCRIPT' BY BRIAN SCHIRMER

When writing a comic script, you are aiming to create a document - a blueprint - that clearly conveys your ideas to the artist. How much detail goes into a script is a matter of preference and taste. Some writers exert control over even the most minor detail, while others offer only the barest outline to their artist. Most illustrators thrive when given simple boundaries - basic restrictions that give them a target and space to be creative. ***Friends of a Friend*** cried out for the even rhythm of the nine-panel grid and a sparseness of setting details. The artist was free to exercise his own vision.

PAGE TWO

Panel One: An over-the-shoulder shot of Celine, now seated at a small table in the back of the bar. She has her beer in hand. Behind her: a dartboard, a restroom labelled 'Women', and a neon sign for Pabst Blue Ribbon.
CELINE: We start rehearsals next week, which is just crazy. I've been working so much I haven't even looked at the script.
RICKY (OFF-PANEL): What is it you do again?

Panel Two: Now, an over-the-shoulder shot of Ricky, with the bar and patrons behind him. His beer rests on the table before him.
CELINE (OP): I'm a marketing consultant. Local wineries mostly, which definitely has some perks.
RICKY: Nice.

Panel Three: Two-shot of them sitting across from each other. They share an uncomfortable silence.

Panel Four: Same framing as panel 3, but now Celine has a wry smile.
CELINE: So, Ricky, what did Paul say to you?
RICKY: He just told me he had a friend – he didn't say who – and that this friend had just gotten out of a relationship and she was looking for something with no strings.

Panel Five: Wide shot of the bar. They share a laugh – the kind reserved for two people engaged in an awkward situation who also realise its absurdity.
CELINE: 'No strings'? Is that what he said?
RICKY: Actually, I think he used the term 'booty call'.

Panel Six: Another two-shot of them across from each other. Ricky leans forward, elbows on the table, apprehensive.
RICKY: So, Celine, how do we actually . . . plan this?
CELINE: Are you kidding? I thought you'd done this before.
RICKY: Nope.

Panel Seven: Over-the-shoulder shot of Celine. She's very matter-of-fact, like she's ordering from a menu.
CELINE: Okay. Well, let's just say we'll do it the one time.
RICKY (OP): And let's have a sense of humour about it.

Page two

PANEL COUNT

The quantity of panels on a page plays as vital a role in conveying the story as the images and the text. Assuming your goal is to make your story easy-to-read, one of the most effective page layouts is the grid system. The page is divided horizontally and vertically into panels of equal size, creating a comfortable rhythm for the reader. Six and nine panel grid layouts have been in use since the early days of the medium and still thrive today.

Panel Eight: Another two-shot of them sitting across from each other. Ricky's lifting his beer.

CELINE: My place or yours?

RICKY: Whatever's more comfortable for you.

CELINE: Let's do mine then.

Panel Nine: Over-the-shoulder shot of Ricky, about to drink.

CELINE (OP): How about Tuesday night?

RICKY: Tuesday works.

PAGE THREE

Panel One: A coffee table. Two bottles of wine – one empty, the other halfway there.

CELINE (OP): Thirteen years.

RICKY (OP): Wow.

Panel Two: The couch – big, puffy, leathery. Celine and Ricky sit on either end, having a good time but still keeping that extra seat cushion between them. Celine's cat lies in a curled ball near Ricky's feet. Nice art on the walls, not reproductions of Starry Night or anything. Real paintings by talented artists no one's ever heard of.

CELINE: My husband and I bought it right after we were married. I'm glad I'm the one who got to keep it. I love this house.

Panel Three: Medium shot of Ricky, wine glass in hand.

RICKY: It's really nice...

THIRTEEN YEARS.
WOW.
WE BOUGHT IT RIGHT AFTER WE WERE MARRIED. I'M GLAD I'M THE ONE WHO GOT TO KEEP IT. I LOVE THIS HOUSE.
IT'S REALLY NICE. I DOUBT I COULD EVER AFFORD A PLACE IN THIS TOWN.
I KNOW. I MEAN, IF I DIDN'T ALREADY HAVE THIS PLACE, I'D BE BACK TO RENTING FOR SURE.
HERE'S WHAT I THINK WE SHOULD DO.
WE SHOULD JUST GO IN THE BEDROOM AND GET NAKED.
BUT FIRST, I NEED TO GO TO THE BATHROOM.

Page three

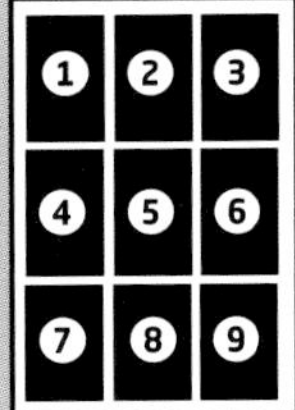

Page two

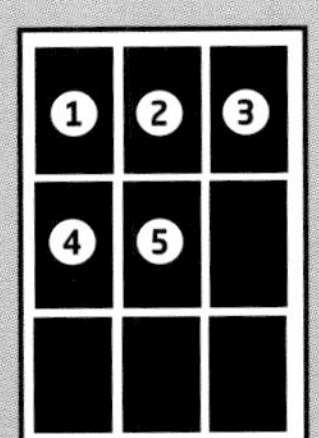

Page three

COMMENTARY

Page Two

1: Dialogue balloons can trump panel details. Celine has so much to say that it obscures background items called for in the script.

2: Note the eye-line match between Ricky here and Celine in the previous panel. They're clearly together, though separated by the gutter.

3: Though the script called for a two-shot, artist Mark Simmons pulled back to accentuate their awkwardness. I regularly encourage such digressions, deferring to the artist's skill and experience.

4: As per the script, Mark keeps the same framing as Panel 3, but adds body language to both characters that brings the scene to life.

5: This panel works – no thanks to my script. The dialogue is solid, but the description is too vague and subjective.

6: Mark does this great thing here that wasn't in the script, dropping out the background to accentuate Ricky's apprehension in the moment.

7: The detail with Celine's fingers and downcast gaze was not explicit in the script. This showcases the artist's interpretation of her behaving 'matter-of-fact'.

8: As Celine and Ricky finalise the specifics of their rendezvous, Mark gives us the first panel that shows them face-to-face, symbolically bringing them closer together.

9: Ricky is our protagonist. This panel not only closes out the scene and the page, but also reinforces his role by giving him a nice close-up.

Page Three

1: Script description here was deliberately spare. Artists need room to breathe – especially in panels that can wind up banal. Mark added the wine-opener, the angle and the finer points.

2: Heavier panel description here – the couch, the cat, the art – aspires to set the scene. Mark takes it to another level by giving us a low angle that showcases it all.

3: Sometimes, simplicity is all that's required. Note how the art mimics the script. Not every panel needs to be some crazy angle.

4: Celine's position on the couch wasn't dictated by the script, but perfectly accentuates her current state and enriches the dynamic of the scene.

5: This high-angle viewpoint – coupled with a lack of dialogue – provides a strong focal point for the page, while also incorporating all the elements of the scene.

WHAT THE EXPERTS SAY

A Xeric Award winner, **Jason McNamara's** comic titles include ***Less Than Hero***, ***First Moon***, ***Continuity***, ***The Gastometrist***, ***Short Hand***, ***Sucker***, ***The Martian Confederacy*** and its sequel, ***From Mars with Love***. He recently co-created the PIE Theory Alternate Reality Game and co-adapted the animated graphic novel ***Project Ajax***. He's a redhead, a Pisces and looks great in a Spider-Man suit. Look out!

WRITING FOR AN ARTIST, BY JASON MCNAMARA

When writing a comic script, it's essential to remember who it is you're writing for. Sure, you want your story to be appreciated by as wide an audience as possible, but before that can happen you're only truly writing for one person: the illustrator.

I try to keep my scripts lean on artistic direction and fun to read. You want to include enough information that the artist can follow the story and understand the characters, but leave enough breathing room for them to contribute their own vision. A two-paragraph description of a panel is exhausting to the eye; who's going to be excited about drawing someone's dissertation? Unless I'm introducing a new character, I keep the description to one to three lines, just when and where the story is taking place and what the characters are going through emotionally.

PAGE ONE
Panel One: On flat windswept plains, lights from a trailer park sparkle in the Martian night.

Panel Two: In the foreground a shadow closes in on a trailer that has a lone ray of light emitting from a window.

CAP: Do you know what happens to bad little boys and girls who stay up past their bed time?

Panel Three: From the point of view of this figure, we're closing in on the trailer as a child's face, Garcia, presses up against the window of the dimly light trailer and screams.

CAP: The blanket monster comes to eat you.

Page one

USE OF LIGHT

Notice how the light is a focal point in each panel, and helps lead the reader's eye throughout the sequence.

Most of all, you want to inspire your artist, get them personally involved. They are going to visually present your story to the world; you want them to be as invested as possible. 'She walked across the room' is an accurate description of a scene but 'Heartbroken, Alice fumbles to put one foot in front of the other as she leaves her former lover's home for the last time' is infinitely more compelling. The action may be the same, but getting your artist interested and involved with your characters will result in much richer illustrations.

Below is the script I wrote for illustrator Paige Braddock and her finished art pages for ***From Mars with Love***. You'll notice my panel descriptions are clear and brief, but provide enough emotional detail that Paige can really get to know the characters. Looking at the finished artwork, you can see how Paige interpreted the script and made it her own. She even combined two panels without losing the narrative. After receiving the finals, I lay down the lettering and take a final look at the dialogue combined with the finished artwork. I think it's important to do my own lettering, as I often discover that not everything I wrote is necessary once combined with the art. You'll notice not all my dialogue made it to the final page, and lettering offers me the opportunity for one last editing and tightening session.

When I get artwork back from a collaborator I'm always surprised at how it looks. 99% of the time it's better than how I saw it in my head, and that is the magic of a collaboration. It's a give and take, and while it's not always easy, as far as arranged marriages go, I've had worse.

Page two

PAGE TWO

Panel One: A lumbering creature with a blanket over itself chases the four Wimmer children inside the trailer. From inside the blanket a single ray of light shines on Suzie. Suzie is the dark-haired girl from Vol. 1. Garcia is the dark-haired boy, and Lucas is the blonde boy. The baby will remain nameless until end of book.

SUZIE: Ah, it's the blanket monster!
LUCAS: Run!

Panel Two: Garcia steps on the blanket as the monster closes in on Suzie.

LOU: First he'll eat your feet, unless they're dirty, then he'll start with your arms. But if you've got scabies...

Panel Three: Lou emerges, crouched and grinning, from inside the blanket, stalking her prey, and emitting a powerful light from her palm. The children smile.

LOU: The default limb would be... Hey! You're violating my rights as a monster.

LOU: Wait! Do you hear that?

PACING ESSENTIALS

As you're writing your story, keep in mind that you should have only one major important action per panel.

You do not want to give the same character more than one action per panel. For example, you want the Incredible Hulk to pick up a tank, throw it at the soldiers attacking him and run off into the jungle. Now, that would be one incredible panel! Your artist may take the main action to be the Hulk throwing the tank at the soldiers, while the other two actions appear as smaller panels on the page. At the very least, you need three panels for this action, possibly even four, in order to include a close-up of the Hulk, or a soldier's face in horror, for emotional impact.

The exceptions to this rule would be if you have a scene with a variety of characters all doing something. In this case, make sure your script emphasises the action that drives the story visually. This action should act as the focal point within the panel that leads the reader's eye.

THE ART OF ACTION

ASK YOURSELF, DOES THE ACTION . . .

By Aristotle:

» Reveal the moral quality of the character?
» Work as a unified and complete part of the whole, such that if it is shifted it makes a perceptible difference?
» Serve a necessary or probable function?

By Syd Field:

» Come in peaks and valleys to give the audience time to breathe?
» Provide quiet moments and contemplative rest points between strong action scenes?

By Bernard Grebanier:

» Constitute dramatic action and not merely physical movement?
» Result also from dialogue alone, if the dialogue presents the evolution of an emotional involvement (or the resolution of one) on the part of the persons speaking?

By Richard Walter:

» Move the story and expand character?
» Complement the scene's elements and overall purpose?
» Weave elegantly into the fabric?
» Give the actor something to do?
» Reach beyond the merely serviceable to the truly exquisite?
» Avoid static situations, e.g., telephones, cafés, offices?

VISUAL RHYTHM OF PACING

The writer sets the pace for a sequence of events to occur with the featured character. The first panel establishes a setting, the next panel revealing who was responsible for the gunshot. The following sequence happens quickly, to move the story forward, implying that this part of the story is not as important as the next sequence, which has a slower pace and reveals more about this mysterious woman.

PACE MAKER

Dave Stevens' **The Rocketeer** *sets the quick pace by using a series of large panels to reveal the main character in a heroic way (top) and a somewhat clumsy way (bottom left), while the crowd below watches in disbelief. Stevens' use of small panels sets up the sequence quickly using a variety of camera shots and angles.*

CONTINUES OVER THE PAGE »

Panel-to-panel transitions

The main action in comic books and graphic novels occurs within the panel. However, believe it or not, gutters play a part in the narrative flow of your story. Seconds to years can elapse between two consecutive panels. The reader can infer what happens in the gutters as unseen action, while reading into the next panel. Scott McCloud (***Understanding Comics***) calls this 'closure'. When readers infer what happens in the gutters, it gives them a complete interactive experience of the story, rather than focusing on the sum of its parts. It's your story, so strive to create smooth panel transitions – otherwise your readers will feel confused or disconnected from the action. The categories of panel-to-panel transition that McCloud has identified are illustrated on these two pages.

Subject to subject

A series of changing subjects within a single scene.

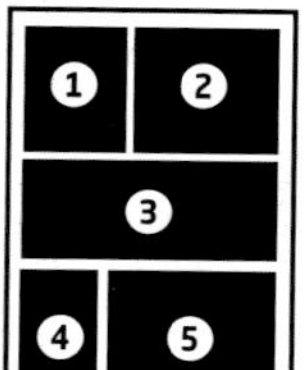

1: Panel establishes locale; dialogue balloon points out our subjects.
2: We now focus on our subjects, the previously foregrounded statue (now in the background) ties the panels together.
2-3: Shift to a low angle, to emphasise this dramatic dialogue.
4: Closing in on one character, we get the visual cue of the information he conveys, while...
5: ... this final panel gives the other's reaction to the news.

Moment to moment

A single action is portrayed in a series of moments, almost like a 'how-to'.

1: Intro to the two objects.
2: Shows what to do with each of them.
3: Shows the end result.

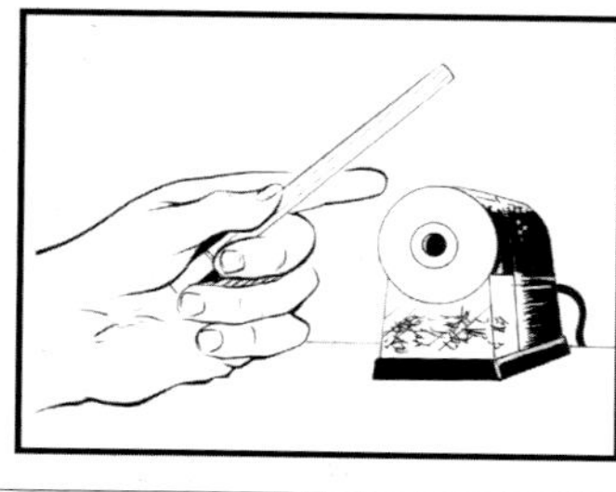

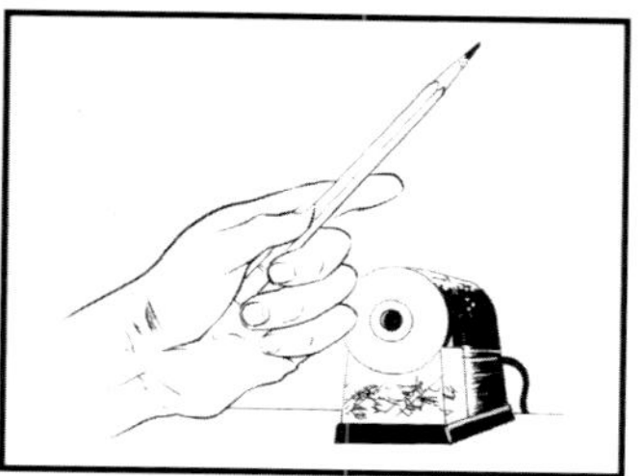

COME ON, SAM, ANSWER YOUR DAMN PHONE.
HELLO?
DINER
SAM, IT'S DANA.
DANA? YOU'RE ALIVE! I CAN'T-
YEAH, YEAH. NINE LIVES. LISTEN, I NEED A FAVOR...
NY
YOU HAVE THE DISK? HOW? AND YOU TRUST THIS CIA GUY? HARPER?
NO, BUT HE SAVED MY LIFE. IN MY BOOK, THAT COUNTS FOR SOMETHING.
JOHNNY, COULD YOU DRIVE ANY SLOWER?
LIZ, COULD YA JUST SHUT UP?
THE DISK HAS HIGH LEVEL CLASSIFIED INTEL THAT YOU CAN USE--
-- TO CLEAR YOUR NAMES. ONLY... YOU HAVE TO GO--
-- DOWNLOAD THE INTEL FROM MY PLACE. IT COULD BE RISKY SAM.
GOT IT MAN.
WE NEED TO GET TO DANA'S PLACE ASAP, JOHNNY.

SCENE TO SCENE

Transitions across significant distances of time and/or space.

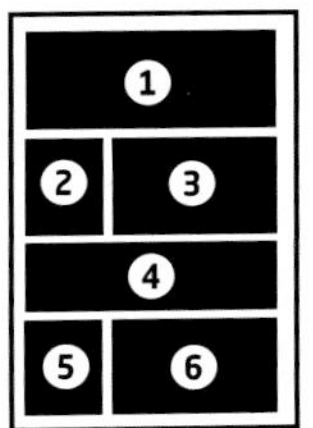

2-3: This transition takes us from the character in the phone box to the location of her conversation partner – a moving car.
4-5: We shift from the inside of the car and one side of the phone conversation, to the exterior of the phone box and the other end.
6: We again jump back to the action and dialogue in the moving car.

ACTION TO ACTION

A single subject (person, object, etc.) in a series of actions.

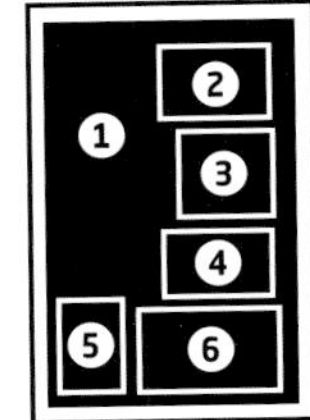

1: The character loads her weapon...
2: We experience her POV.
3: She's now inside her car, shifting gear to drive.
4: The camera pans down to reveal a cinder block.
5-6: An up-close and pulled-back exterior shot of the car from behind as it speeds off to the house.

CONTINUES OVER THE PAGE »

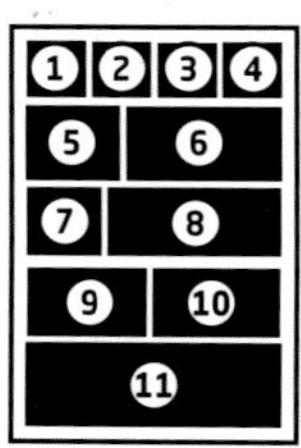

ASPECT TO ASPECT

Transitions from one aspect of a place, idea or mood to another.

1-4: Panel transitions that divert from the body narrative; intended to give a sense of place or atmosphere.
5-6: Illustrate a contrast to the cold, wet weather outside by giving way to a candlelit bathroom in which the woman is enjoying a bath.
7-8: The rubber duck surrounded by suds implies a light-hearted feeling that transitions into the woman reclined and enjoying the tranquil moment.
9-10: Aspect to aspect as a panel transition to set up a relaxed, peaceful moment that changes in an instant when the candles suddenly go out.
11: The foreshadowed danger in panel 10 is revealed here as the intruder enters the woman's home.

NON SEQUITUR

These are all panels that are seemingly out of sequence and unrelated. The only relationship these panels have with one another is being abstract. Author Scott McCloud of **Understanding Comics** *further underscores the point and proposes a counterpoint to non sequitur in comics as 'alchemy at work in the space between panels which can help us find meaning or resonance in even the most jarring of combinations'.*

WAYS TO PICK UP AND SLOW DOWN THE PACE

To slow down the pace...

Use horizontal panels
The reader's eye moves slowly across a page-wide panel.

Use more panels per page
It takes more time for your reader to absorb nine panels with dialogue than it would for the same scene visualised in three panels.

Use more words per panel
A densely written story consisting of dialogue, captions and sound effects can be overwhelming.

Use a large amount of detail
The more detail you put into a panel, the longer it may take for the reader to process.

More conversation, less action
For those of you writing drama and suspense stories, you may want to slow the pace where the characters are driving the story at a slower but intense pace, then reward your reader with a satisfying ending.

In Chapter 4 of ***Understanding Comics***, Scott McCloud details five different ways of slowing the pace during a conversation:

1: Insert a 'pause' panel.
2: Lengthen the pause by devoting several panels to it.
3: Lengthen the pause by widening the gutters between panels.
4: Lengthen the pause by widening the panel.
5: Lengthen the pause by removing borders, suspending the panel in time and space.

Nine-panel page
The sequence here depicts a slow pace for the action to unfold. The panel with the woman firing the gun is used three times to punctuate the effect of her revenge before drawing to a close. An additional panel of the pilot and the villain was illustrated to show how they were both hit by the woman's gunfire.

Five-panel page
The same situation and outcome as above are depicted here, but the pace is accelerated by using only five panels to illustrate the action sequence instead of nine.

To pick up the pace...

Use vertical panels
Vertical panels imply action and that things are happening quickly.

Use fewer panels per page
The less the reader has to absorb, the quicker the pace of the story is for them to read.

Use fewer words per panel
Give the reader less to read, so they have mainly artwork only.

Use little to no detail
If only a few characters and little background are shown, the reader can move quickly through.

DIALOGUE

In all narrative writing, the trick is to simulate real speech. Your dialogue has to move the plot along, convey surface and deep characterisation and express the characters' (and the writer's) point of view.

In comics, you have a tough challenge. You have static art and limited space to get your words and meaning across. Your dialogue must be believable, but not meandering and repetitive. How do you do this?

- Practise dialogue by writing different approaches to the same scene. Try letting your hero do most of the talking, then let the villain dominate.
- Listen to people talking in the world around you, then adapt how they speak into literary speech. The goal is a simulation of real speech. In life, people rarely speak in complete sentences, and rarely say exactly what they mean. People leave it to facial expression and tone of voice to get their point across.
- Carry a notebook with you and write down the cool things that people say. You'll one day find a place to use them.
- Recite your dialogue out loud. Does it sound convincingly realistic to you?
- When writing dialogue, ask yourself whether each character has a distinct personality. For example, a college professor might say: 'I propose we initiate aggressive action.' A longshoreman might say: 'Let's trash the bums!'
- Practise all of the above on a regular basis.

WORD COUNT

What's the optimum number of words to include on a page or in a panel? The answer is pretty flexible and depends on the aim of your story. If you want a longer read with a lot of insights, then go for dialogue-heavy scripting. If your aim is to let the visuals carry the story with a minimum of yack, then you will obviously need to keep the dialogue sparse.

There's a rule-of-thumb – attributed to Stan Lee – to be applied to dialogue when starting out.

WORDS PER PANEL IN AMERICAN-STYLE COMIC BOOK WRITING

Comic book authors have come up with their own guidelines for word counts, based on their own experience and preferences.

BILL WILLINGHAM

The author of ***Fables***, amongst other things, uses this guideline:

'As a general rule, unless there is a very good reason, I never let a single word balloon exceed more than two full lines of text in a Microsoft Word document, set at 12-point type, Times New Roman font.

'And I try to keep it at no more than two such word balloons per panel, but sometimes that can be fudged a bit, if there are three very small word balloons, for example.

'Captions can occasionally exceed the two-lines-per-caption rule, because, a rectangular-shaped caption is easier to fit in a panel than an oval-shaped balloon - generally speaking.'

ALAN MOORE

The author of ***Watchmen***, ***V For Vendetta***, ***Killing Joke*** and many other works, uses this guideline:

'Mort Weisinger, DC Comics editor, said that if you've got six panels on a page, then the maximum number of words you should have in each panel is 35. No more. That's the maximum. 35 words per panel. Also, if a ballon has more than 20 or 25 words in it, it's going to look too big. 25 words is the absolute maximum for balloon size.

'This gives you somewhere to start - you sort of know, OK, so six panels, 35 words to a panel, that means about 210 words per page maximum... [so] if you've got two panels, you'd have 105 each. If you've got nine panels, it's about 23-24 words - that'll be about the right balance of words and pictures. So that is why I obsessively count all the words [in my scripts], to make sure that I'm not going to overwhelm the pictures. I've seen some terrible comic writing where the balloons are huge, cover the entire background... '

DIALOGUE BASICS

As the writer, it's your job to get into the characters' heads, to understand their personalities through dialogue.

Dialogue should flow naturally
Dialogue should flow naturally from the characters that you have either created or that have been given to you.

Dialogue should not be interchangeable
If you've written a line of dialogue that could literally have been spoken by one of several characters, it's not a good line of dialogue. Dialogue should be informed by individual personalities.

Listen to people around you
You will find that most people have certain catchphrases or verbal repetitions that they use all the time. Feel free to adapt these little verbal tics into your characters, or even create some of your own. Remember, once you establish a voice for a character, you have to maintain it for consistency.

Hold yourself down to a maximum of twenty-five words per panel. That's twenty-five words for everything; dialogue and caption. (Alan Moore still uses twenty-nine words per panel as his guide.) Try it out and see how it works for you. Once you're comfortable with it, and you've got it working, start playing with variances, but not until you can first make the rule work.

Dialogue as a narrative tool

At one time, comic books were a combination of dialogue, thought balloons and captions. Over time they have tended to imitate television and film in terms of their execution. Captions are now usually only used in cases of first-person narrative ('I'm Wolverine. I'm the best there is at what I do. And what I do is fill up page after page with my internal thought process, so I can be strong and silent and yet still never shut the hell up.'), while thought balloons have largely been relegated to the dust heap.

So dialogue is no longer simply one of several narrative tools in comics, but to all intents and purposes it is your only narrative tool (after all, narrative captions are just running monologues, like something out of an old crime drama). That being the case, I'd advise you to master it thoroughly.

REVEALING CHARACTER

The conversation between the two girls in biology class reveals something about each of them. The blonde girl doesn't have the stomach to dissect a frog, whereas the brunette has no problem with it. In fact, as a kind gesture on the brunette's part, she gives her dissected frog to the blonde.

WHAT THE EXPERTS SAY

Dan Wickline is a published writer and photographer. A California native, he currently resides in Los Angeles with his wife, Debbie. Dan has written for Image Comics, IDW Publishing, Humanoids Publishing, Zenescope Entertainment, Avatar Press and Moonstone Books. In 2010, Dan is writing the re-launch of ***ShadowHawk*** for Image Comics.

Depending on the type of story you are writing, the amount of space you have to establish characters and their relationships may be very limited. The dialogue you choose, how it's grouped together and the emotions of each panel as it's illustrated, when done right, can quickly convey a lot of information without having to slow down an action/adventure tale with tons of exposition. You have to convey your characters and their relationships to others without it feeling like a speed bump in your story.

1001 Arabian Nights: The Adventures of Sinbad is supposed to have the feel of a classic Saturday matinee action story but still have the depth that readers want today. To make that work, the script needed to be at a quick pace with limited dialogue. Every sentence needed to service the story, so having a character seem dark and brooding one moment when talking about his past, then wide-eyed and smiling the next panel when looking at a woman he loved told a lot about the character with only a few sentences instead of having to go into details about his past and actually stating his feelings for the woman. These two pages establish a lot about the character of Ashcroft and his relationship with others, as well as give an ominous clue to the future… all in 18 sentences.

From '1001 Arabian Nights: The Adventures of Sinbad #8' Written by Dan Wickline, Art by Eduardo Ferigato, Published by Zenescope Entertainment.

PAGE FOUR

Panel One: Ash standing by the table as Shon'Du walks away.

ASHCROFT: Old Man said you wanted to see me?

SINBAD: Have a seat.

Panel Two: Sinbad pulls a folded letter out of his shirt or belt.

SINBAD: There is someone in Baghdad I need to get this message to. I would like you to be the one to take it.

Panel Three: Ash seems disappointed.

ASHCROFT: So you're heading into the desert to face unknown dangers and you want me to run an errand?

Panel Four: Sinbad slides the paper across to Ash who is looking at the front of it.

SINBAD: Look at who the recipient is and tell me who else I can trust to get it to Baghdad?

ASHCROFT: Oh… yeah. I'll go.

Panel Five: Sinbad looks at Ash very seriously.

SINBAD: There is one other thing I wanted to ask you.

SINBAD: Why were you with Orland? The gems controlled the others; but you weren't wearing one.

PAGE FIVE

Panel One: Ash looks down at the table.

ASHCROFT: When I first hooked up with Orland, I had nowhere else to go. Figured I would make some money and then move on.

Panel Two: Ash looks over his shoulder at Samelia who is joking with Old Man.

ASHCROFT: But I found something worth staying for…

Page four

Page five

COMMENTARY

Page Four:

1: By having Ashcroft stand and get permission to sit we establish the subordinate relationship to Sinbad.

2: Sinbad uses 'need' to stress the importance of the note but 'would like' Ash to take it, showing how Sinbad chooses to lead.

3: His reaction tells the reader that he worries Sinbad doesn't think he's good enough and that he may have his own doubts.

4: Who the note is to and Ash's reaction illustrates quickly the importance of the task over having Sinbad having to explain it.

5: When someone comments about wanting to ask a question it raises the importance of the question. Here Sinbad shows there is an issue that's been bugging him.

Page Five:

1: Having Ash look down shows his dark past without actually commenting on it. Eduardo's including Old Man and Samelia was brilliant here. Ash seems detached.

2: When her mood turns to laughter, Ash brightens and we see his love for her, but he is still not part of her life in the way he wants.

3: Here it was important to show Sinbad not only accepts Ash's answer, but has himself done things out of love. Also we needed to bring the scene back around.

4: Having Ash on his feet brings it full circle. By blacking out the background Eduardo helps emphasise the ominous nature of the last sentence.

WHAT THE EXPERTS SAY

A Chicagoland native, **Matt Silady** taught eighth grade for six years before pursuing a career in comics. In 2007, he published his first graphic novel, ***The Homeless Channel***, earning an Eisner nomination for Special Recognition. He is now an Adjunct Professor at the California College of the Arts.

I love the challenge of translating the spoken word to the written page. I get a kick capturing the way people say one thing, but tend to mean another. It's always fun pulling off a scene where someone says just the wrong thing at just the right time, making everyone in the room cringe.

For such a visual medium, comics have a knack for throwing the spotlight on great dialogue. And by great dialogue, I mean the kind of dialogue that reveals character, advances plot, creates conflict and crackles with the energy with which we really speak. And yet, there are times when great dialogue is not the best thing for your scene.

In this two-page sequence from ***The Homeless Channel***, television executive Darcy Shaw learns that her sister has tragically died while sleeping on the city streets. The cop's dialogue fills us in on what happened, adds a bit of levity to the moment and makes the sadness of the situation seem all

PAGE 130
Panel 1: A police OFFICER and MIKE, a cameraman for The Homeless Channel, stand watch over an alley marked off by crime-scene tape. DARCY steps out of the cab.
OFFICER Mary?
MIKE: Mary Shaw. This isn't just anyone-
OFFICER: Well, no. She's got a name. And that saves me a lot of time and paperwork.

Panel 2: We've switched POV and now look back at the OFFICER and MIKE from within the alley. MIKE notices DARCY has arrived as the OFFICER continues to speak.
OFFICER: It may be sad-
OFFICER: But your boss's got herself here first bumsicle.
MIKE: That's her.

Panel 3: DARCY looks over her shoulder at MIKE and the OFFICER. She addresses them in a calm, but direct manner.
DARCY: Mike, you can go home.
DARCY: Blue – go find out why there isn't an ambulance here yet.

OFFICER: (off-panel) I'll see what I can do.

Page 130

the greater. Instead of taking the cop to task for calling her dead sister a bumsicle, Darcy somehow maintains her composure.

In the end, we see that the emotional climax of the scene isn't between Darcy and the cop. It's between Darcy and her sister. So, when the two are momentarily alone, the best thing I could do for the scene was slowly back away from the keyboard.

Because sometimes saying nothing, says everything.

Page 131

PAGE 131

Panel 1: MARY is huddled against a dumpster. She clutches her bag. Although she has been dead for hours, the subzero nighttime weather has frozen her solid. To the reader, she looks like she is peacefully asleep. DARCY stands above her.

DARCY: Jesus.

Panel 2: Close-up of MARY clutching her bag. DARCY reaches out and gently touches MARY's hair.

No Dialogue

Panel 3: We see only DARCY and MARY lit by a streetlight from above.

No Dialogue

PANEL ORIENTATION

The decision to use wide or horizontal panels gives the sense of time passing slowly. Aesthetically, it takes the reader's eye longer to travel across each panel than it would if Silady had decided to use vertical panels, which implies the sequence happens quickly.

ARTISTIC STORYTELLING BY CHAD HARDIN

WHAT THE EXPERTS SAY

Chad Hardin graduated from Southern Utah University with a Bachelor's in Illustration in 1999. Chad has worked with large publishers as well as independent publishers such as: Marvel (***Web of Spider-Man***, ***Antivenom***), DC Comics (***Zatanna***, ***Warlord***), Boom Studios (***Farscsape***, ***Traveler***) and Digital Webbing (***Fists of Justice***, ***Bloodrayne***). Currently Chad resides in Enoch, Utah, with his wife and four children. During his spare time, he takes art courses through AAU online to obtain an MFA in Illustration.

It is a comic book illustrator's job to tell a story visually. Whether drawing the main protagonist, the environment or even a lowly prop, comic artists must tell the story with each panel.

Visual characteristics within each panel allow the reader to distinguish the setting, mood, emotion and action contained on the page. It is the artist's job to 'act' out the story visually. When the artist is unsuccessful at getting their characters to 'act', the suspension of disbelief is broken and reading the comic becomes drudgery. The better the artistic storytelling the more immersive the experience is for the reader.

The example

These sequential illustrations from ***Digital Webbing Presents #30*** are pages from my early comic career. They are important to me personally because they were samples that caught the attention of editors from large publishing companies. These pages were the catalyst that brought me from being a comic hobbyist to a comic professional.

The story revolves around the aged Marc Mason, a patient who believes he is the ancient alter ego of the golden-age superhero Fists of Justice. His dementia has earned him a stay in the Charm City Psychiatric Ward. After several cruel and torturous treatments, Mark fears that holding on to what he believes is true is costing him his ability to reason. While on the brink of his sanity, Mark is visited in his dreams by Professor Mistyk, who tries to help him uncover the truth of his identity.

Making your players act

If you have ever gone to a portfolio review and wondered why the editor breezed past your pinup shot and focused intently on your sequential pages, it is because they are looking for your storytelling ability. Many people can draw pretty pictures, but being a comic artist means that your drawings cannot just look good, they have to act as well.

While comic artists must be proficient in drawing every subject in existence – and some that don't exist at all – mastery of the human form is paramount to storytelling. Human gesture, posture and emotion are the vehicles in which plots are driven and stories acted out. It is not enough to know the anatomy of the ideal body type. Sequential illustrators must master the human form in all its diversity of shape, age, size and gender. They must know how bodies move, rest, sleep, eat, fight, cry, laugh and love, and they must represent this with such authority that it captivates the reader into coming back for more.

When looking at my own work, I ask myself the following questions to see if I have successfully acted out the scene with my characters on the page: Without the aid of text, can the reader establish what is happening by the acting from visual characterisation? What are the environments telling the reader? Can the audience tell what the characters are doing, thinking or feeling by their gestures, postures and facial expressions? Can the reader tell who the heroes and villains are? Are the actions clear enough to easily read what is going on? If the answer is yes, then I have done my job. If not, then a rework of the page might be in order.

Seekng honest feedback

Sometimes when I am in doubt about my storytelling I seek the opinion of a small child (usually from six to nine years old). If the child can accurately tell me what is going on in the story simply by looking at the pencilled pages, then I know I have been successful. Children are brutally honest; they will not hesitate to point out flaws in drawings or storytelling. Peers, on the other hand, might sacrifice truth in lieu of loyalty, etiquette or some other well-intended but not-so-honest opinion.

ZOOMING IN ON DETAIL

When you want a drawing full of emotional impact, zoom in close enough to see these body parts and the expressions the characters are displaying. A close-up shot often has more of a focus on the character's emotion than a long or full shot. The close-up detail in the finished art gives a sense of integrity to the character of Marc Mason – we want to follow his story.

RECOMMENDED READS

Drawing The Head & Figure **by Jack Hamm**
A how-to handbook that makes drawing easy. Offers simplified techniques and scores of brand-new hints as well as step-by-step procedures with hundreds of illustrations.

Dynamic Figure Drawing **by Burne Hogarth**
Figure drawing is the most essential - and the most difficult - of all skills for the artist to learn. In this book, Bruce Hogarth, one of the founders of the School of Visual Arts in New York, introduces his own revolutionary system of figure drawing, which makes it possible to visualise and accurately render the forms of the human body from every conceivable point of view. 300+ drawings and diagrams.

Vanishing Point: Perspective for Comics **by Jason Cheeseman-Meyer**
Vanishing Point shows you how to conquer the fundamentals of perspective drawing and then equips you with technical tricks and tools that make dynamic and complex scenes a snap. This complete guide helps you build your understanding of perspective to an intuitive level so you can draw anything you can imagine. Complete instruction on drawing in one-, two- and three-point perspective and four- and five-point curvilinear perspective (where 'straight' lines are drawn as curves). Shortcuts and tips show you how to create believable perspective in no time flat.

Facial Expressions **by Mark Simon**
Facial Expressions includes more than 2,500 photographs of 50 faces - men and women of a variety of ages, shapes, sizes and ethnicities - each demonstrating a wide range of emotions and shown from multiple angles. Who can use this book? Oh, only every artist on the planet, including art students, illustrators, fine artists, animators, storyboarders and comic book artists.

DRAWING TECHNIQUES

'I feel that talent means little unless coupled with an insatiable desire to give an excellent personal demonstration of ability…'

FIGURE DRAWING

Regardless of what kind of story you want to write or draw, whether it's a superhero or social drama, you need to draw people from real life. Your book's going to have people in it. Ordinary people, extraordinary people, but people.

10 PRINCIPLES OF FIGURE DRAWING

Consider trying these exercises when practising pencilling figures for comics.

1: Loosely sketch the figure with a pen or pencil, then accentuate it by emphasising the line weights of the main action lines.

2: Sketch the figure while moving the pencil quickly, searching for personality and attitude through body composition.

3: Use as few lines as possible to sketch the figure's composition and body pose.

4: Talk some friends into letting you sketch them, and try out various poses.

5: Draw close-ups of a range of different expressions.

6: Stick with one expression, but alter the lighting. See how the light can apparently change the meaning of the expression.

7: Find a building near you and sketch it from a variety of perspectives, distances and lighting conditions. See how its character alters as the way it is presented changes.

8: If you are going to be sketching in one site for some time, pick a place where there's plenty of activity, such as markets or docks, or anywhere with lots going on.

9: All figure action should be based on a distribution of the weight of the body.

10: Try building figures without using a model or copying from a photograph.

The Chinese say that the longest journey starts with a single step. Even the strangest tale begins with people doing ordinary things – a young couple having a screaming match; a policeman dealing with an aggressive drunk late at night; an old man at the supermarket checkout finding he doesn't have enough cash to pay for the groceries. All mundane events, sure, but it's seeing how the people in each drama react that's important – the couple oblivious to anything except their anger; the policeman calm and professional; the old guy flustered and embarrassed. You can put them all together in the same supermarket at the same time, then spin out their imaginary lives from that moment in time, or rewind and show how they ended up in the same place.

EYES PEELED

Artists should always carry a sketchpad, as a few simple sketches of interesting buildings or striking landscapes can be used later in your artwork. As for observing people, nothing beats taking down a bit of real life now and then. If you've got the nerve, sketch a few faces while you're at it, especially the more unusual ones. It will not only improve your technique, but it will help you to develop a repertoire of figures, faces and expressions.

LAYING THE FOUNDATIONS

The aspiring comic book artist must learn the principles of figure drawing before thinking about the cosmetic details of what a character is going to look like or what clothes they're going to wear. Artists that can master the foundation skills of drawing the figure and apply it in a realistic and dramatic way in comic books are the ones who'll succeed.

This book alone will not teach you everything you need to know to develop and hone your comprised of the flashiest costume or special ability they have; it's how well you compose the figure structurally that gives a character a dynamic and convincing look in comics.

Making your drawings dynamic

The idea when sketching out a figure for your story is to stay loose and aware of who your characters are and what they are doing. This applies especially to movement and motion of a character. Even characters that are standing still or sitting in your story have to be brought to life through convincing composition and linework. Drawing a 'pose' is not storytelling. A pose may express a character's personality, but still has to have a sense of movement to it.

Balanced action

When you're sketching out compositions of your characters in action, bear in mind that balance keeps them in control of their actions. This may sound a bit silly, but think about it. A figure skater can lead with their head pointing in the direction they want to go even though their body is moving in amazing ways on the ice. It's all about control. A simple line drawn at a slant is the 'centre line' that is the basic action movement. Centre lines give balance and suggest how your figure will move: standing still, twisting, turning, forwards, backwards, sweeping, leaping, charging all contribute to more fluid and graceful movements in your figure work. Turn over the page to find out more.

FIGURE PROPORTIONS

As you can see from the figures lined up in this well-composed and well-drawn illustration, proportion is crucial to good figure drawing. A suggestion would be to observe people in real life and draw a 'proportion wall' for figures of different body types and height.

CONTINUES OVER THE PAGE »

5 ACTION POINTERS

1: When action is important to the scene you're drawing, emphasise vigorous movement.

2: Overemphasise your character's attitude and exaggerate their poses.

3: Avoid stiff and inactive figures – try to have your characters doing something at all times.

4: Don't have your characters stand or sit in the same position during a series of panels. Even if they just scratch their head or move their hands while they speak, it keeps them moving.

5: Speed or motion lines can help your character perform its action.

DYNAMIC FIGURES

Dynamic figure drawing works well for illustrators seeking to draw heroic figures based on realistic proportions. The slightly exaggerated proportions enable this figure to feel as though it is leaping off the page.

WEIGHT DISTRIBUTION

When you draw a figure standing on two feet, the weight is distributed within a rectangle. For your drawing to be a convincing pose, understand the principles of balance. If your pose looks awkward, try referencing a model to pose for you to understand how the figure balances itself. The weight of the body will support itself through a number of poses. Observe the human figure in action and render what feels and looks right to you.

CENTRE OF GRAVITY

Balance keeps control of your figure's actions. A simple line drawn vertically or horizontally implies the movement of your character. The figure shown here pushes off her back foot as she leaps forward. The direction of the blue line shows where the character will move. Movement that is drawn without the use of the centreline of balance will not give the impression of forward movement.

WHAT THE EXPERTS SAY

Pete McDonnell has created illustrations, storyboards, cartoons and comic books for clients including Hewlett-Packard, The History Channel, Neiman-Marcus and Cisco Systems, and has created cover art and illustrations for ***The Wall Street Journal***, ***Weekly Standard*** magazine and ***Popular Science***. He illustrated nine graphic novels of historical subjects for Capstone's ***Graphic History*** line and Rourke Publishing. He lives in Sonoma County, California, with his wife, Shannon, and son, Jacob.

Grab a drinking glass from your cupboard. Now, look at it from above: a circle. Gradually tilt the drinking glass. You'll notice how the shape changes to an oval or ellipse as you turn it sideways. Try sketching some simple household objects from various angles to see how their shape changes. This drawing mechanic is called foreshortening, the creation of an illusion of depth, and must be carried out with confidence to effectively trick the eye.

A few tips:

- Sit up straight; no slouching! Sketching in a slouched position can drastically affect the drawing of a foreshortened limb.
- Draw what you see and not what you think it looks like out of your head.
- Elements of your drawing will appear closer to you due to seemingly larger proportions, while objects away from your point-of-view will seem further away.
- Apply the use of line weights – vary your lines from thick to thin from foreground to background. Bold lines jump out while thinner lines recede.

REALISTIC FORESHORTENING

This drawing shows a figure with arm extended towards us and fist clenched, illustrating natural, or realistic, foreshortening. The fist is correctly proportional to the rest of the figure, and even though the clenched fist is pointed directly at us, it doesn't appear particularly threatening.

EXAGGERATED FORESHORTENING

With exaggerated foreshortening of the fist, there is a more dynamic impact to the drawing. The fist is drawn at the same size as the character's head, with a greatly foreshortened arm that disappears behind the extended fist. The figure itself is tilted slightly towards us and appears to be lunging forward. This kind of foreshortening gives the figure a comic book effect.

Body language

Body language is something we've all inherited from our animal ancestors: simple signs that tell the rest of the pack how we're feeling, our status and the mood we're in. These visual clues cut through verbal language and its inherent ambiguity.

Body language is rarely ambiguous – and generally, it's subconscious, too. With a bit of practice, you might be able to control some of your unconscious signals, but the action of the pupils and blood flow under the skin are way beyond the control of mere mortals.

The best use for body language in a graphic novel is to portray gestures that everyone understands. Posture is one of the most obvious – timid people shrink into themselves, while loud, aggressive types puff themselves up. People express interest and sympathy by leaning towards another person; disinterest by pulling back. Crossing the arms is a defensive gesture, representing a shield that has been raised against the world. An even more obvious gesture is pointing at someone – this can convey a straightforward threat.

NERVOUSNESS

A young girl, sitting, wearing a short skirt. Her arms are rigid, her hands clasped together and clamped between her thighs. She's obviously uneasy.

PROTECTIVENESS

Although this woman is cuddling her baby, holding him safe and close to her, her eyes are watchful.

CONCERN OR ATTRACTION

Two people, sitting together (different sexes). One is leaning towards the other, touching him or her lightly.

CONFIDENCE

Man sitting in a low chair. He's thrown back, arms resting along the chair's back. One leg is crossed carelessly over the other.

STANDOFFISHNESS

A figure standing, arms folded across his chest in a classic stance. To bring the point home, his head is slightly turned away, and the expression is stiff and indifferent.

AGGRESSION

A man pointing, his whole arm rigid. It seems like he's aiming a weapon of some sort. His face is angry, too.

DEFENSIVE

A figure huddled up, bent in on itself, arms wrapped around the vital parts of the torso.

LACK OF CONFIDENCE

A figure standing with shoulders hunched. He is wearing a long coat to add to the droopy feeling.

AT EASE

Two people, standing. Their stances are almost identical – one is imitating the other, either to fit in or because he feels close.

SHOCK OR FRIGHT

Hands thrown over the face or eyes to protect vision, or simply to blot out whatever scared the figure.

DRAWING HEADS, HANDS AND FEET

Drawing heads, hands and feet is critical to drawing convincing characters and it is often these details that separate the good comic book artists from the great. Your formal training begins here, with expert John Keebink.

The key to drawing a thing well is having a workable simplification of it in your mind.

Over time you must develop the ability to hold a simple three-dimensional shape – a foot, for example – in your mind. The alternative is to have a conventionalised way of drawing a thing for each of several angles. That may not sound bad, and it worked for years for John Byrne, but the unhappy truth is that, even for pros, the little unglimpsed errors that cling to your work consist almost entirely of shapes and juxtapositions from one view being misapplied to another. All mediocre artists are accidental Cubists.

Look at ***Fig. 1***. It's a fairly credible-looking drawing of a foot seen directly from the side. Maybe the instep (the middle top of the foot) swells upward a bit too much, but it's not bad. Then, looking at a respectable drawing of a shoe (***Fig. 2***), we can see the correctly observed fact that the sole of the shoe rocks up, off the floor, in front.

The trouble comes when you try to take this flat understanding of the foot into a different view. Let's go to, say, a more frontal view, from a higher angle (***Fig. 3***) – one more typical of the way we usually see shoes. The need to foreshorten the foot for this view seems to call us to increase the curviness of that S-curve on the top edge of the original foot. A curious innate human urge to represent the front ends of shoes as puff pastry has given the shoe a distinct echo of Mickey Mouse's bulbous brogans. Moreover, the very slight curving upward of the sole has morphed into the entire front end of the foot hooking mysteriously, painfully, outwards.

Compared with a photo or better drawing, this is clearly disastrous, yet it is typical of what we all do before we learn to deal with 'form'. This is done through what I call 'SRSs': simplified rotatable solids.

Heads

The need to draw an attractive, dimensional human head – in any style – makes it essential to start with a 'simplified rotatable solid'. Consider for a second the fact that few drawings of appealing, believable heads have ever begun with a charmless, sloppy, skewed or ugly underdrawing. The need to start building a mental library of those simple solids should be getting increasingly plain.

You can base your default starting head shape on an egg, or a simplified skull, or a sphere with jaw area added and the sides lopped off. These are all workable starts, however a better option is something a little more refined. This shape can be drawn from almost any angle and still keep its proportions (***Fig. 4***).

Faces

When your faces look weird, and you keep having to redraw the features, it's usually because you've lost your artistic connection to that solid, or didn't make it well in the first place. Without realising,

THINK IN 3D

These three images show the basic evolution of a basic foot into three-dimensional shoe. Imagining your subject in three dimensions is critical to your comic drawing skills.

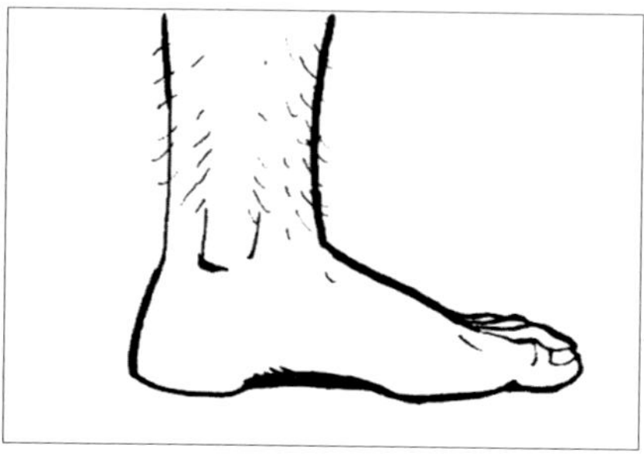

Fig. 1

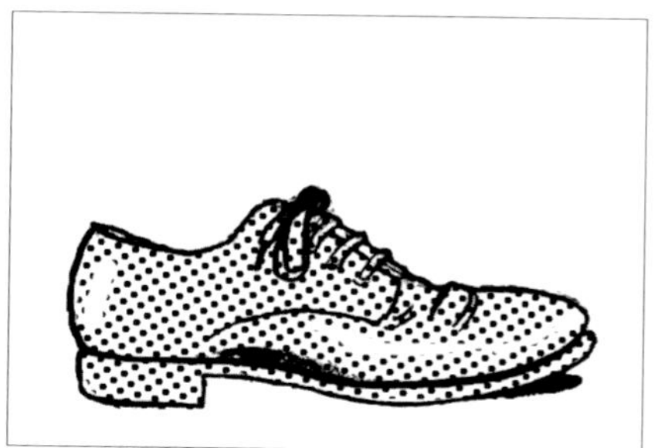

Fig. 2

Fig. 3

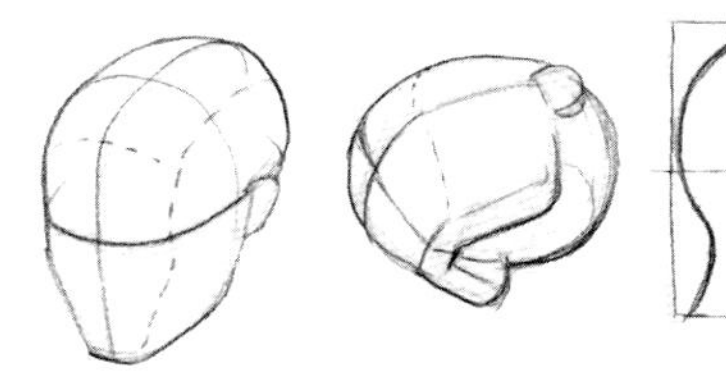
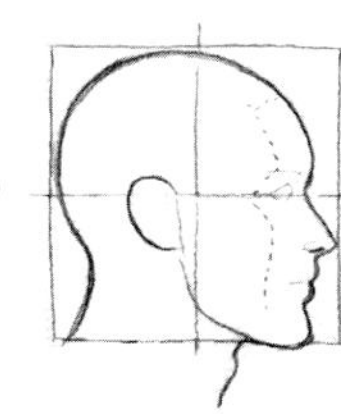
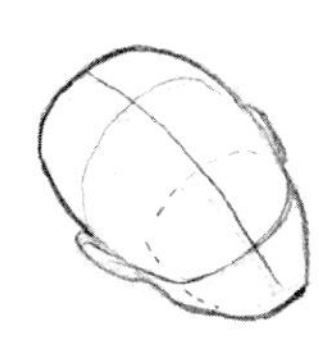

Fig. 4

HEAD SRSs

Heads are just a little taller than deep, on average. There is a slight flattening of the front and side planes, as is visible in the faint squarishness of the horizontal centreline. The ears are already in place (before the nose even), just a little behind the vertical centreline for the side planes of the face.

THE QUASIMODO EFFECT
I WAS ONCE HUMAN

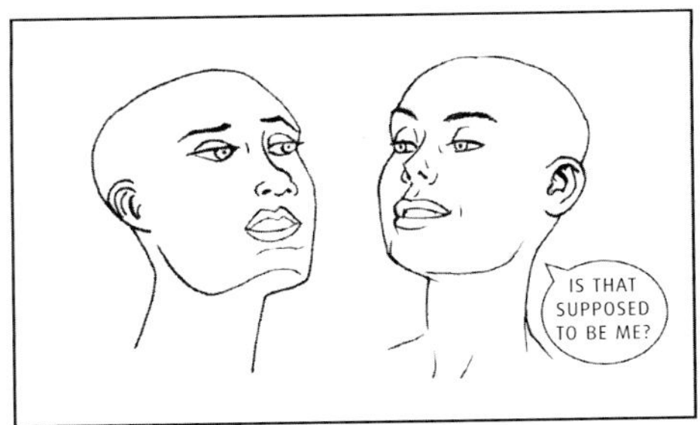
IS THAT SUPPOSED TO BE ME?

Fig. 5

THE QUASIMODO EFFECT

This can happen when you draw each feature in its entirety and without regard for the angle each is seen from. Handling a somewhat difficult view like this (attempted) down-angle can have a monstrous result.

you are likely presenting an impossible hybrid view: the different facial features are drawn as if seen from a variety of directions. No wonder that when attempting to draw difficult angles on faces, we get something along the lines of ***Fig. 5***: a Quasimodo effect.

Erase back to that underdrawing stage, grab your blue pencil and make that head shape work, in its simplest, cleanest form, with centrelines that really hug and define that solid – centrelines done in a hasty, perfunctory way are not worth the time they save. When you return to drawing the features, locate them very, very softly and vaguely at first with the blue pencil before you refine them.

Aligning the eyes is key (see 'Drawing eyes', right). Remember that the eyes are pushed back a little in relation to the eyebrows and the bridge of the nose. Drawing the nose after the eyes can help you make sure you have them placed, aligned and spaced properly. If it's still not working, look for a photo reference.

DRAWING EYES

Up-shot or down-, it is imperative to always visualise eyes as spherical. When you do a down-shot, think of the lower lids as semicircular balconies hugging that sphere of eyeball, for example. Then you won't draw the eyes like they were painted on a flat surface. The lines of the eye opening will only ever appear straight where they come between your viewpoint and the core of the eye's sphere. As they retreat from us towards the 'horizon' of the eyeball, they will curve more and more, due to the progressive foreshortening imposed by the eye's spherical shape. So if you always draw the eye opening as a leaf shape regardless of one's angle of view, you need to refine your approach.

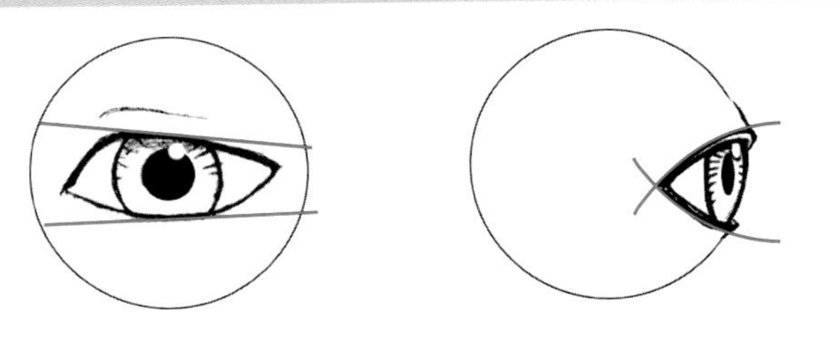

EYE LINES

The lines of the edges of the eye opening are partly straight when the eyeball is aimed at us (left), especially near the centre. These lines curve like crazy when they are moved over to the edge of the eyeball (right), because of foreshortening and their wrapping around to the other side. Watch for this in profile and near-profile views.

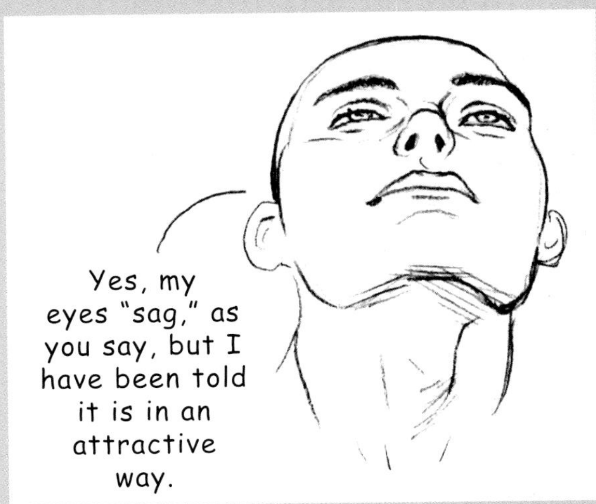
Yes, my eyes "sag," as you say, but I have been told it is in an attractive way.

UP-SHOT EYES

When the face is shown in extreme up-shot – as when the jaw takes on a W shape or the nose breaks the top line of the forehead – the eyes appear to 'sag' slightly at their outer edges.

CONTINUES OVER THE PAGE »

When we forget that the bridge of a nose can overlap the inner corner of an eye, when we fear to draw an eyebrow that wraps around to the unseen far side of the head or forget that eyebrows are mostly ahead of the eyes, we can easily create little dead, flat zones in our drawings – and we can be the last to recognise them. One solution is dutiful, analytical attention to the far side of the face, in photos and life.

Three-quarter view

When we see a face in three-quarter view (see ***Fig. 6***), especially in close-up, the far eye is just a little foreshortened, a little closer to a side view. Thus it looks a tiny bit shorter, less wide across. A little of this is due to the fact that our sightline to the far eye necessarily runs a little more across the eye and a little less at it than the near eye. This difference is greater still when the viewer or camera is close up, and when the bridge of the nose is strong enough to cover a little of the far eye. Intriguingly, this is something that some of the very simplest anime and manga styles exaggerate. This gives animators the ability, even in styles of Pokémon simplicity, to draw in a way that heightens the feeling of form, conquering the limitations of two dimensions. Ironically, this is something that most anime imitators totally miss, at least at first.

The three-quarter view does not excuse you from spacing the eyes properly. In your blue-pencil underdrawing, place that far eye. Keep it a little shorter on its horizontal axis than you might think is right. Forget the nose for now. Draw a space-keeper 'third eye' right next to the far eye. Because it's a little closer to us and facing a tiny bit more towards us, you draw the third eye a little longer. Finally, the near eye, longest and biggest of all. The far corner of the far eye will be very blunted by the foreshortening of the eye opening and the sphericalness of the eyeball. But the near corner of the near eye will be extended, displayed to our eye at nearly its full length and pointiness.

Draw in the bridge of the nose. However, don't draw it as a line; it's a three-dimensional shape. Sketch it as a wedge with a flat base. 'Glue' that base between the eyes, right on the third eye. The bridge of the nose itself will tell you whether it's deep enough to cover some of the far eye. No need to guess. And no compulsion to half-blindly cram the eye onto the visible area past the bridge of the nose, which often results in the far eye being too forward or far out.

Now make sure that the forehead and thus the eyebrows are a little ahead of the eyes. If you halve the space between eyebrows and find that the mark is directly above the centreline between the eyes, you need to adjust: the centreline of the eyebrow must be shifted towards the outside, moved out into a wider orbit around the centre of the skull.

Look for this unequal eye length in photos of three-quarter view faces. You will always see it, even when the bridge of the nose is too shallow to cover any of the far eye.

Weird-looking facial detail is also very noticeable in profile. See ***Fig. 7*** for some important dos and don'ts.

Feet

Feet are extremely important. It takes a long time to get feet to touch the ground believably, and in perspective, and longer to get them to look like they are supporting weight.

Flexed toes will point to the outside, away from the other foot, a bit more than relaxed or extended toes. When the heel is raised, and the foot flexed (see ***Fig. 8***), the ball of the foot and toes will be pressed firmly down. Study how the smaller toes react to the stress of having weight put on them.

Avoid 'bow-tie' feet. Beware any foot that seems to have a waist.

FLEXED FEET AND TOES

The 'cutout' area of the arch can make the foot look like it narrows at the middle from some angles. It doesn't, so avoid overgeneralising this to other views. Focus on the overall form, and the long, continous shape of the instep. When the heel is raised and the weight rests on the ball of the foot and the toes, as in these views, you will often see wrinkles across the tops of the toe and sometimes the toes will each take on the S-curve shown on the right. Don't be too quick to hide farther toes behind nearer ones. From most views you will see at least part of all of them.

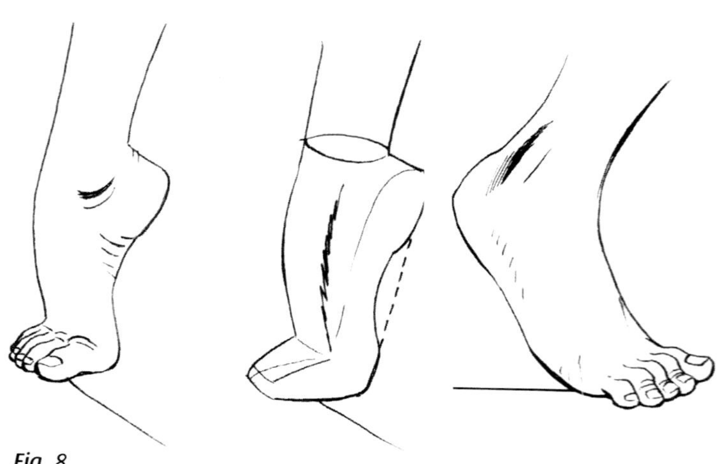

Fig. 8

FACIAL CONTOURS

Some people (left), from some angles, have strong changes in their facial contours. When the same contour is wrongly generalised and applied to other facial types and angles (middle), unappealing errors creep in. In fact, the contour of this part of the face is very often quite subtle and smooth (right), especially on women and especially in more frontal views.

Fig. 6

COMMON PROFILE MISTAKES

The head on the right illustrates a compendium of common profile errors: dropped ears; sloping forehead; pro-wrestler brow; overly deep-set eye and eyebrow; and coloured contact-lens eye (the pupil should be centred in the iris). The dreaded mullet nose – perky in the front, angry at the back – also makes an appearance. In reality the nostril and the bottom of the nose are roughly parallel as a rule, and the nostril shouldn't be pushed back onto the face like this, but live more on the nose. Are you doing any of these?

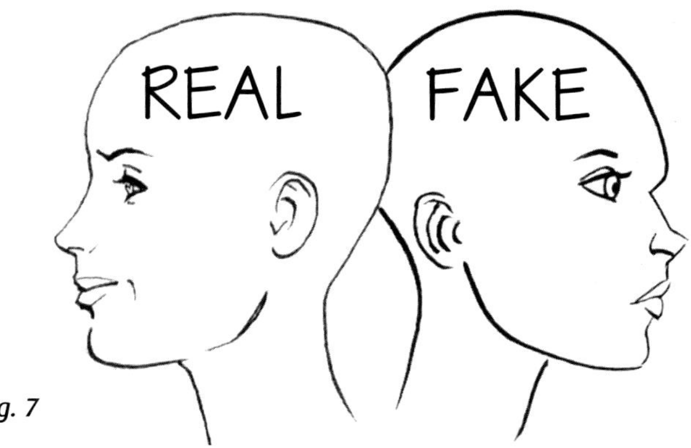

Fig. 7

DRAWING HAIR

Drawing hair is not all that difficult but it does take quite a bit of time to make the result look real and natural. In fact, it usually takes two to three times longer to do the hair than it does to do the rest of the portrait. So, do not get frustrated and know that you will have to spend the time. Here are some pointers to help you succeed at drawing the best hair possible:

Line drawing
As always, the first step is to produce a line drawing that shows the overall shape of the hair and maps out some of the main value areas. At this stage, you should look at the hair as a shape and ignore all details, such as strands. Do observe however how the hair flows, i.e., take note of the growth directions of the hair.

Values
Next, using the map you created on your line drawing, start laying in the major values, i.e., the major darks and lights. Make sure you always follow the growth direction of the hair. This is very important. Follow the flow.

Blending
At this stage, you can blend the darks out towards the lights. Then, reapply the darks and pull them into the light areas using a tortillon or a pencil (if there is not enough graphite on the paper). Work from the dark areas into the light areas. After that, use a pointed putty eraser as a drawing tool to pull the lights into the darks. This process should be repeated several times until you reach the desired fullness.

CURLS

If your subject has curls, you should treat each curl as a separate object with its own darks, lights and highlights. At the same time, make sure that each curl fits into the overall layout of the hair. This means, for example, that a particular curl should flawlessly connect to its neighbours.

CONTINUES OVER THE PAGE »

Hands

When it comes to drawing hands you won't get much use out of SRSs, because hands are too flexible. Instead we must resort to a more situational set of observations. Let's get back to basics to review what we know about drawing hands.

- Half the length of the hand is palm, half is fingers.
- The outer edge of the palm is straighter in women and children, but fully curvaceous in dangerous, muscular men (***Fig. 9***).
- The palm is a wedge shape (look at its outer edge) (***Fig. 10***).
- No set of knuckles exists in a straight line. All are arrayed along curves, with the middle finger's knuckles most advanced.
- The middle finger is the longest of the four, and because its knuckle is above and ahead, its length appears even greater.
- The fingers only taper in the outermost two bones (towards the fingertips). This is seen most clearly in a fist, where the base bones of the fingers – the punching surface of the fist – are parallel (though of unequal length), and the last two bones of the fingers crowd together near the centre of the palm (***Fig. 11***).

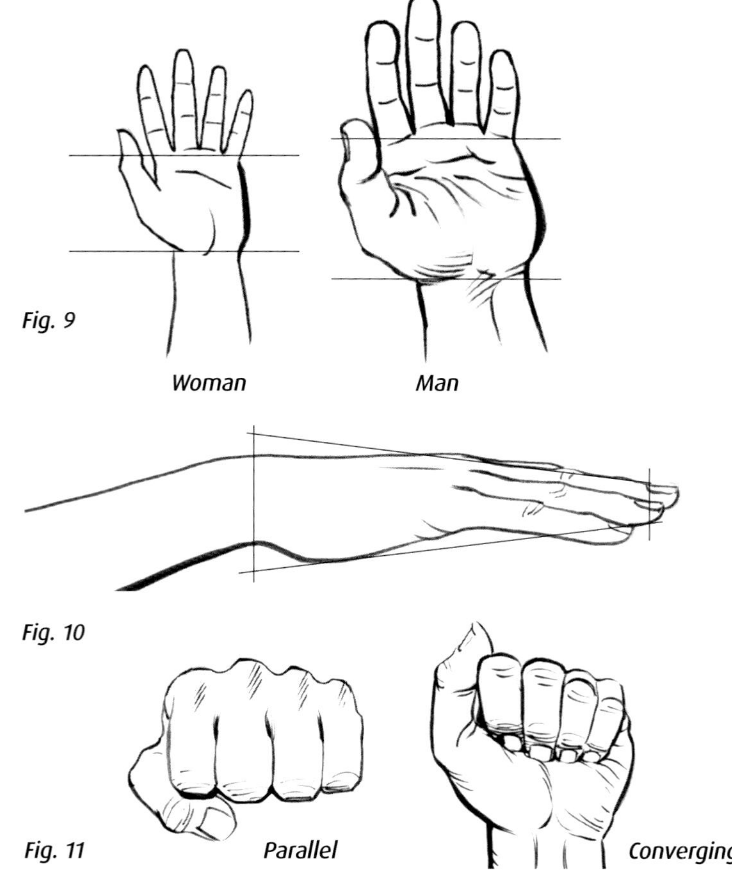

Fig. 9

Fig. 10

Fig. 11

Parallel converging

- The knuckles are hinged so as to cause that crowding. A closed finger doesn't close straight down, but touches nearer to the centre of the palm.
- Straight wrists and straight fingers make poor gestures for talking characters. The result is a distracting 'spear hand'. Great for the Silver Surfer firing a bolt of energy, pretty awful for a conversing human. It is much more natural to have the wrist bent a little and each finger bent

Fig. 12

HANDS AND FACES

There is a limit to how close to the face you can put an open-handed gesture, but fists and pointing hands seem to do fine near the face.

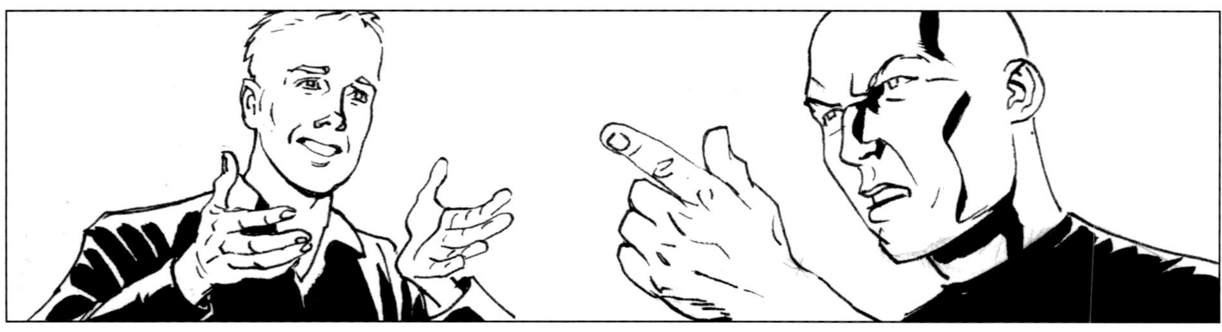

Fig. 13

a little more than the one next to it. Usually the index finger will be the most extended, the little finger the most closed (***Fig. 12***).

- The poses of each of the four fingers should be closely related in a progression. The centre two fingers are the most passive, echoing the index finger. The little finger is more of an outlier, naturally bowing out the most and sometimes posed in a way that's more extended than its companions, especially in feminine poses.
- Smoking poses are natural and graceful.
- Don't bend the outermost knuckles more than a little, as this suggests arthritis.
- To place a hand believably, quickly sketch the whole arm, even outside the panel. Does it look like the upper arm and forearm are proportional? Is the elbow in a natural position, or is it in front of the torso?
- It does not look natural to have someone gesturing with their hands close to their own faces, though pointing hands may work there. Most of our gestures are in the general vicinity of our chests (***Fig. 13***).
- GOOD: Drawing fingers with a mix of curved and straight lines and really deciding where the knuckles are.
- NOT SO GOOD: Drawing fingers with all curved lines, which makes them look pudgy and soft.
- KINDA BAD: Drawing female hands that are too angular, that lack a graceful, continuous 'flow'.
- BAD: Drawing fingers whose individual poses are unrelated to the closest finger(s) and whose knuckle spacing and fingertip shape vary. Fingers should look like they are shaped the same, and cooperating – imitating each other a bit.
- Please don't skip the lines between fingers to give them that fused look. This is a silly affectation, not a cornerstone of your style.
- To draw hands better, source photo reference or use a mirror.

HEADS, HANDS AND EMOTION

Hands are fundamental to compound the facial expressions of a character and to convey emotion in your drawings. The use of hands further communicates the specifics of an emotion the character is expressing: for example, happy, sad or angry as shown respectively below.

PERSPECTIVE

Things appear to get smaller the further away they are. Linear perspective is simply a tool that will allow you to create a sense of distance and scale in your images, to show objects overlapping, getting smaller or converging in an orderly way.

Perspective follows a number of rules; like all rules, they must be learned and understood thoroughly, so that you can break them with surety and confidence when you need to. Gradually, as you become more confident with perspective, you will be able to plot out a few key lines and estimate the rest. This will work only if you know the rules well enough to use them in your head.

Perspective is built upon rectangles and 90° angles. In all the examples, it should be understood that the structures drawn must either be built of 90° angles or placed inside an imaginary box.

ONE-POINT PERSPECTIVE

In perspective drawing, every set of parallel lines has its own vanishing point. One-point perspective is a very useful system for rendering the illusion of depth on a two-dimensional medium. Here's how:

PLOTTING A CUBE

Look at ***Fig. 1*** opposite. From the vanishing point, mark off three points equidistant from each other – two on the horizon line (A and B), and the third straight down from the vanishing point (C). Point C is where you are viewing the object from, and the triangle ABC represents your cone of vision – the area you can see without distortion.

High horizon line provides a large foreground area for action.

Mid horizon line gives a regular viewpoint.

Low horizon line allows for dynamic upward views of figures or buildings.

PICTURE PLANES

Each of these three picture planes shows a different position for the horizon line. You'll notice how positioning the horizon line higher or lower within the picture plane changes your point of view. Ask yourself: Which horizon line placement would be best for a composition of New York harbour? How about a plane taking off? A helicopter flying over rush hour traffic? A horizon line in the middle of the picture plane that divides the space above and below equally might suggest your background has no emphasis in your story.

Draw the leading edge of your square or cube, and from each end of this line (D and E), extend the sides of your shape back to the vanishing point. Then, from each of the forward corners, draw a line to the opposing point (A or B) on the horizon line. Where these lines cross the sides of your object, draw in the back edge (F). This will give you a perfect square in perspective. To make the cube, simply add the vertical lines (the same length as your horizontal leading edge) to the leading edge, plot out the back edge of the plane facing the vanishing point, and it becomes the depth of your cube.

Dividing a plane into a grid

Create a triangle as you did in ***Fig. 1***, and draw your plane as in ***Fig. 2***. Along the leading edge (D/E), mark off the number of units you need (F), and extend each one to the vanishing point. Then, draw a line from a front corner to the opposing back corner. The points where this line crosses the lines from F to the vanishing point are your horizontal dividers.

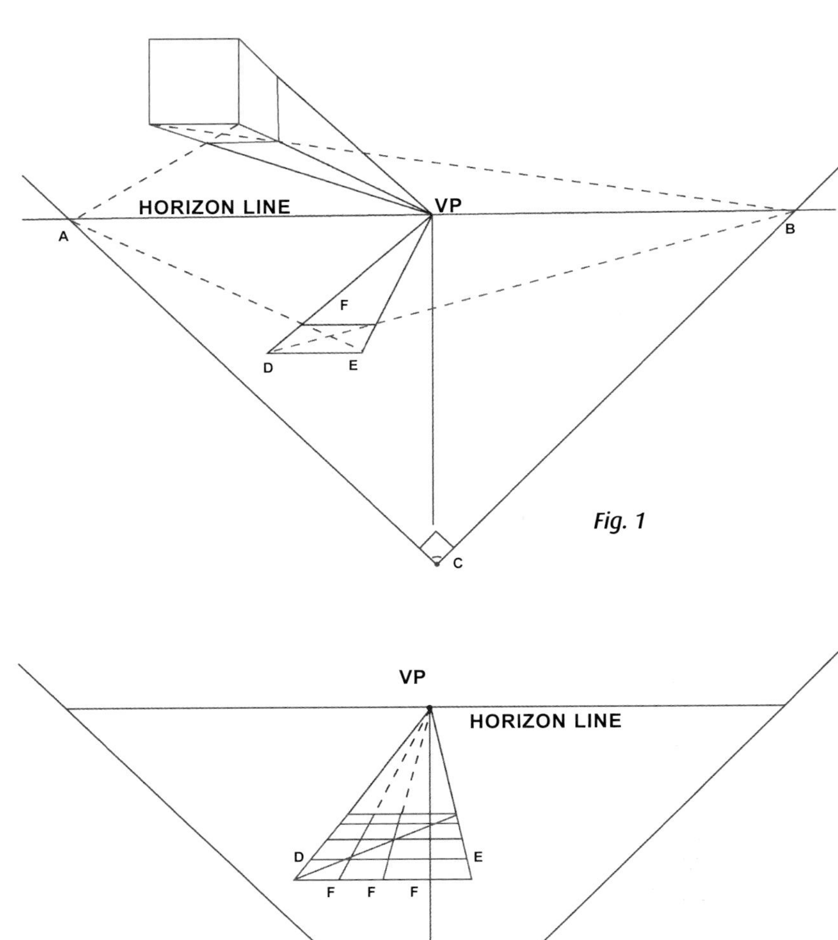

Fig. 1

Fig. 2

COMMON DEFINITIONS

Horizon or eye line
Represents the height from which you are viewing the object or scene. Outdoors, this will actually be the horizon; indoors, it will be a line which represents your eye level. The only exception would be if you were outside, viewing from a very high or wide vantage point, in which case the slight curve of the Earth would be noticeable.

Vanishing point (VP)
The point on the horizon line at which parallel lines of an object seem to converge. There may be only a single VP, or there may be multiple ones. These points are not fixed, but are determined by what you are seeing and where you are seeing it from (your viewpoint).

One-point perspective
This occurs when you and one side of the objects you see are on parallel planes. There will be a single vanishing point, so it is called one-point perspective. Think of the way a road, a row of power poles and a fence often all seem to converge at a single point on the horizon.

Two-point perspective
This occurs when the objects you see are at an angle to you. There will be one edge or corner that is closest, called the leading edge. Both sides of the structure which recede from this leading edge will have their own vanishing points; hence the term two-point perspective.

Three-point perspective
This is very similar to two-point perspective but with the addition of a third vanishing point located either above or below the horizon line at which all vertical lines converge. Three-point perspective is most often used when depicting tall buildings or wide panoramas.

Vanishing trace
This is a point above or below a vanishing point. Vanishing trace is used to determine the correct angles on things such as sloping roofs, as well as to determine how to keep the distances between a row of objects uniform.

CONTINUES OVER THE PAGE »

One-point perspective in practice

Once you've drawn a grid layout for one-point perspective and decided on where the horizon line should lie, create another layer of your drawing on a separate piece of paper. A light box is recommended during these steps to help you understand how these steps work best. You have an idea for a man driving a convertible into a busy San Francisco street full of cars, a cable car and pedestrians.

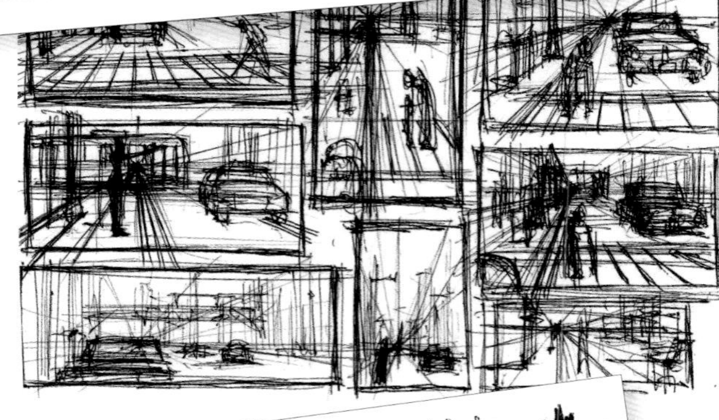

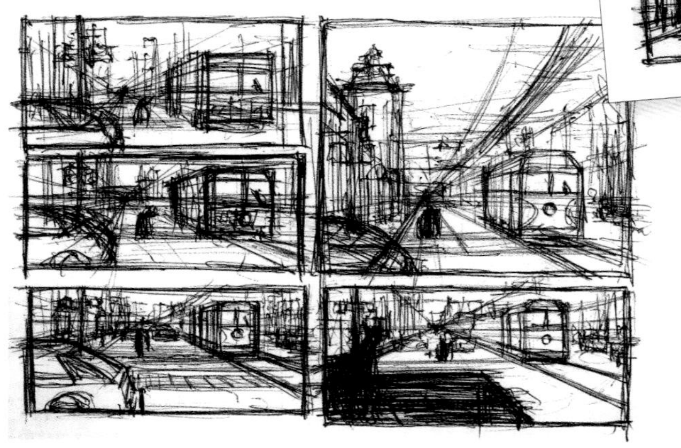

1

SKETCHBOOK THUMBNAILS
Artist and Educator Joko Budiono starts out his one-point illustration with a series of thumbnails. Joko explores various compositions of his subject matter before deciding to go with the darkened sketch of the convertible in the foreground with the cable car for the city street scene.

2

CONTOUR LINES
Begin to draw in your contour lines to help define the objects in your composition. Use your vanishing point to sketch in light grid lines (or construction lines) to help keep the proportions in proper perspective.

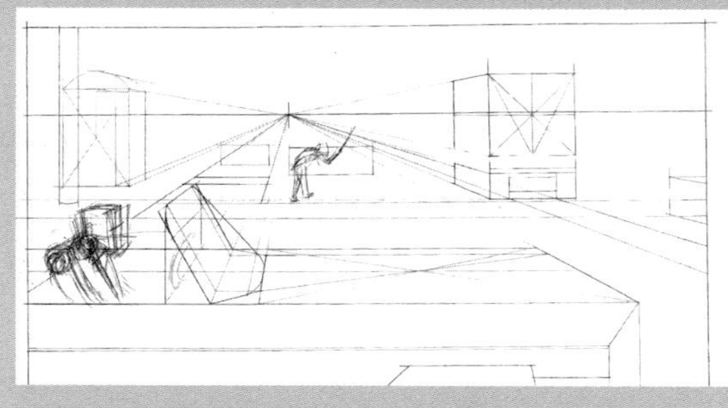

3

ESTABLISH YOUR PLANES FOR DEPTH
This includes the foreground, middle and background. Determine your light source (if you're using one in the pencil stage of the drawing) and lightly pencil in shadows.

4

ADDING DETAILS
Objects in the foreground should have the most detail (variation in line weights, bold lines, higher contrast) while images in the background will have lighter lines and softer contrast of values.

SCENE ANALYSIS

The cable car, buildings, cars, people and the driver of the convertible all converge on a single point. All vertical lines are vertical and horizontal lines are parallel with one another. If they are not, your objects may look distorted and buildings may begin to lean. Offsetting the vanishing point from the centre creates movement in the action scene here and prevents the composition from being stagnant and uninteresting.

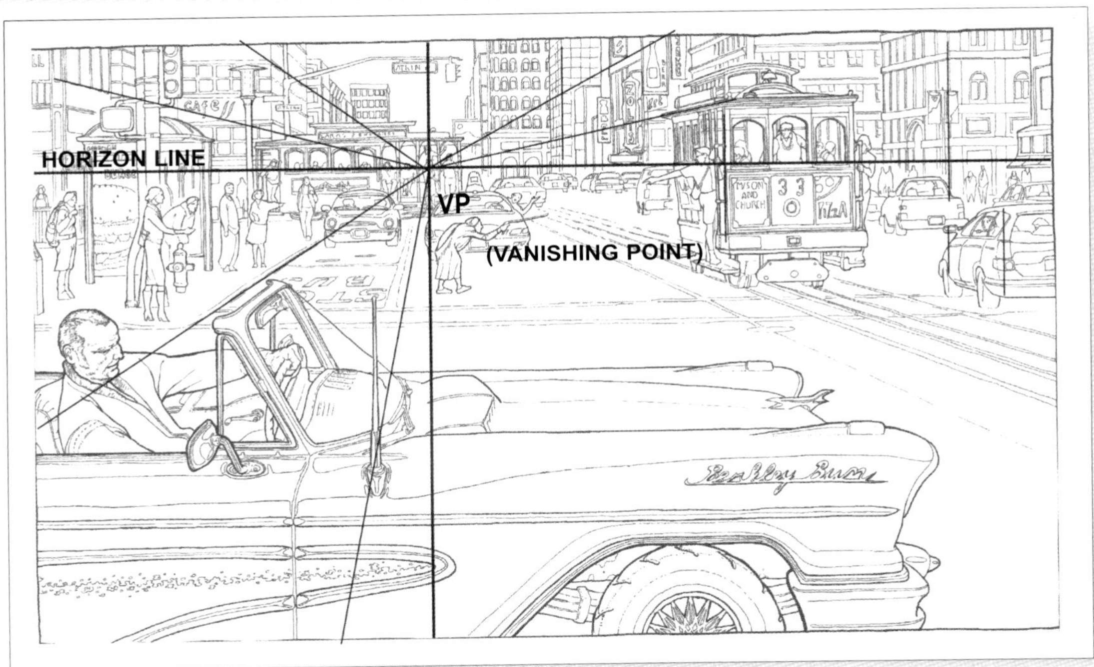

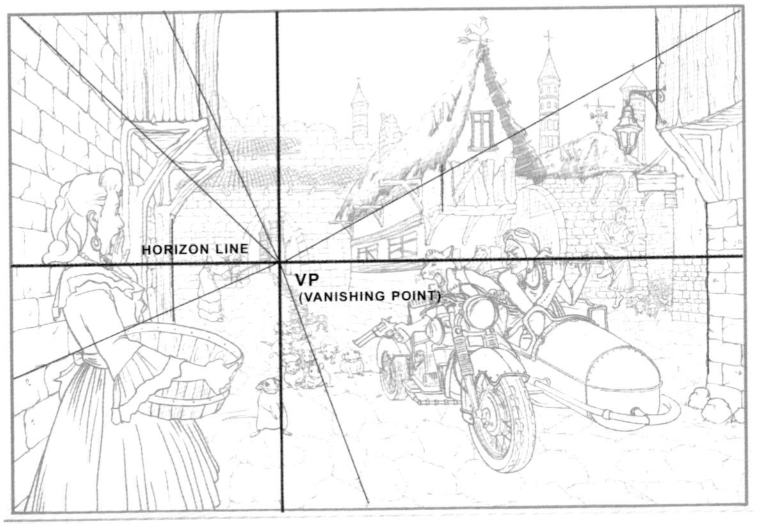

VARIATION

The horizon line established here is closer to the POV of the woman on the left in the foreground. All construction lines converge to one vanishing point on the horizon line. The action in this composition originates from the vanishing point as the woman reacts to the character on the motorcycle riding into the scene.

CONTINUES OVER THE PAGE »

DYNAMIC COMPOSITION

No matter what type of perspective you use, dynamic layouts should be composed with the emphasis of leading the reader's eye throughout the panel and page.

As you can see in the image on the left, the composition is well drawn but not well composed for narrative eye flow. The objects and the women in the image mimic the panel frame itself feeling uninspired. The image on the right has lines and shapes in the composition leading the eye throughout the scene. The women, chairs, shoes, etc. are much more interesting because they contrast against the horizontal and vertical framework of the composition. Overlapping objects creates an illusion of depth and, placed strategically, they create a more natural, kinetic scene.

Avoid boring compositions like this...

...Compose dynamic layouts like this.

TWO-POINT PERSPECTIVE

Two-point perspective can be used to draw the same objects as one-point perspective, rotated: looking at the corner of a house, or looking at two forked roads shrinking into the distance, for example. One point represents one set of parallel lines, the other point represents the other set of parallel lines. Looking at a house from the corner, one wall would recede towards one vanishing point; the other wall would recede towards the opposite vanishing point.

Two-point perspective has one set of lines parallel to the picture plane and two sets oblique to it. Parallel lines oblique to the picture plane converge to a vanishing point, which means that this setup will require two vanishing points.

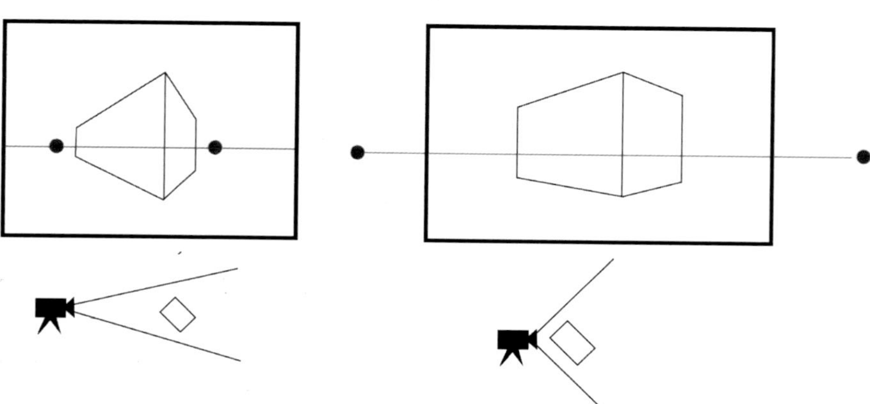

A narrow FOV with vanishing points too close together results in a distorted composition of your scene.

A wide FOV with vanishing points established with a right angle station point results in a more relaxed, realistic-looking composition.

ZOOM LEVEL AND FIELD OF VIEW

Field of View (or FOV) determines how much we can see by how close or far apart the vanishing points are on your horizon line. To understand how the zoom level works, imagine looking through a camera lens to bring in your focal point closer without distorting your point of view. The vanishing points appear to close in as you zoom in and then appear to get further apart as you zoom out. The composition doesn't change, just your proximity to the scene.

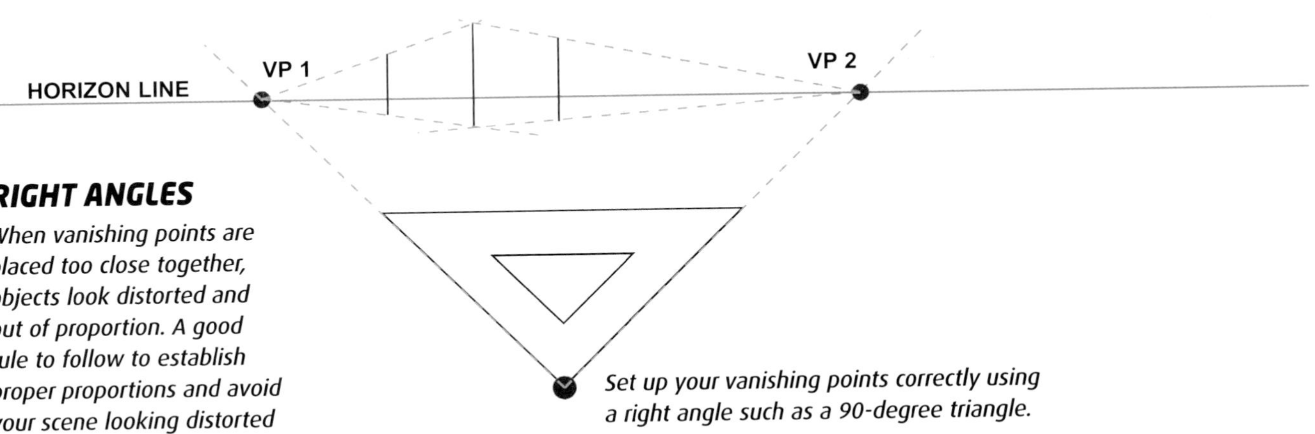

RIGHT ANGLES

When vanishing points are placed too close together, objects look distorted and out of proportion. A good rule to follow to establish proper proportions and avoid your scene looking distorted is to use a right angle to set up your vanishing points.

Set up your vanishing points correctly using a right angle such as a 90-degree triangle.

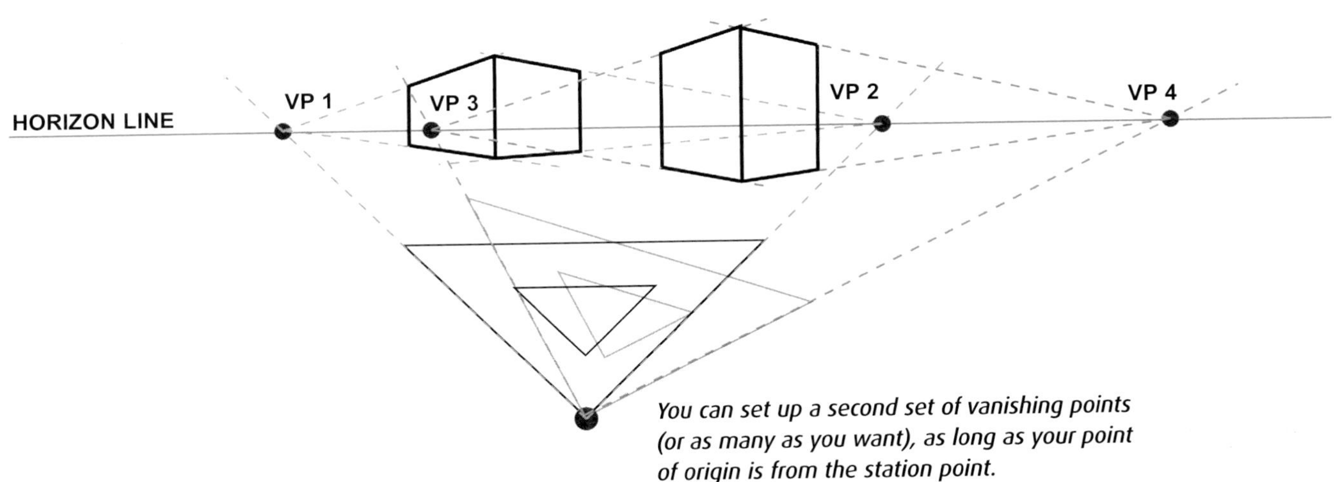

You can set up a second set of vanishing points (or as many as you want), as long as your point of origin is from the station point.

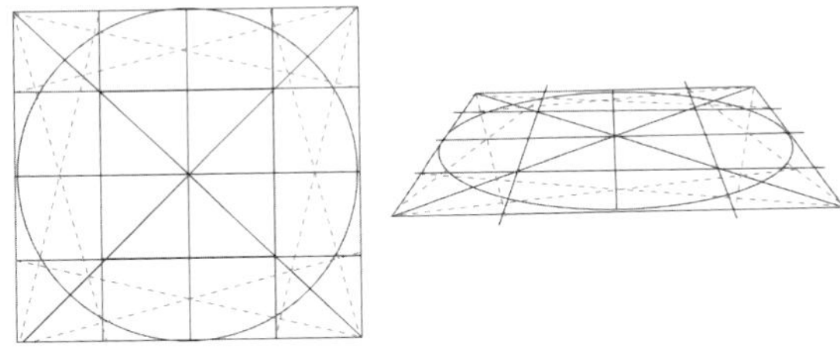

ELLIPSE

An ellipse is really a circle in perspective. While you will often have to draw your ellipses freehand, you can give yourself a few guides to help out. The flat square shows the points at which the circle and square connect. Simply draw the square in perspective, and then freehand draw the ellipse, using the points of contact as your guide. Note that the widest part of the ellipse is not the mathematical centre of your square but slightly in front of it, as you are not looking at a flat ellipse but at a circle in perspective.

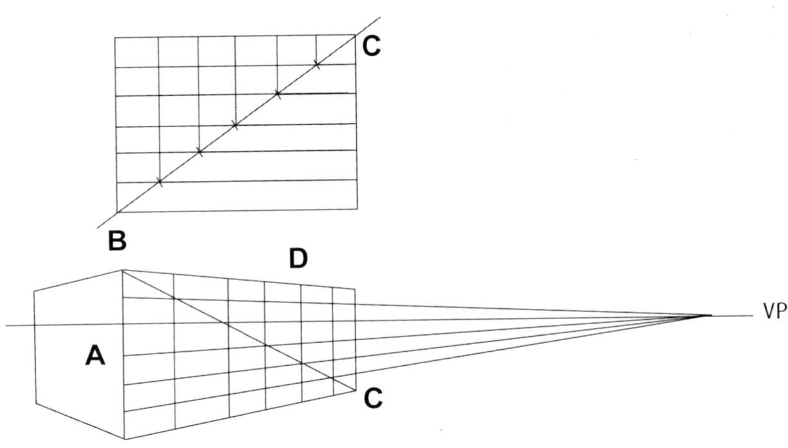

DIVIDING A PLANE INTO EQUAL UNITS

Just as in one-point perspective, you can divide your shape into any number of units along the vertical leading edge (A) and extend these points to the vanishing point. A diagonal from corner to corner of the shape (B/C) crosses these lines and indicates where the vertical lines must be (D).

CONTINUES OVER THE PAGE »

Two-point perspective in practice

Once you've worked out your composition, you can begin laying out your fine line drawing on a new sheet of paper over the finished sketch on a light box. Each stage of the drawing uses a pair of vanishing points based on a right angle station point.

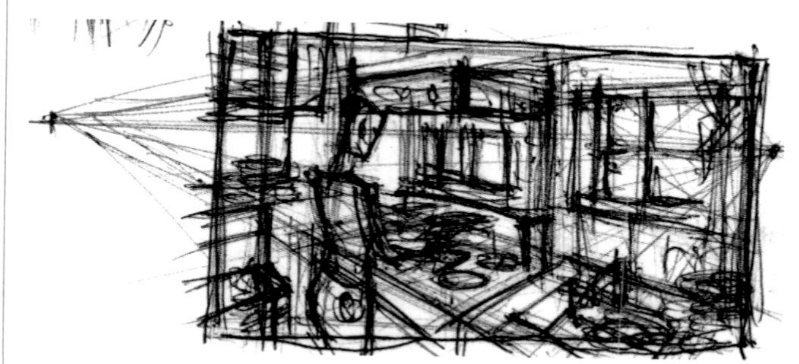

1 THUMBNAILS

It's good to get into the practice of placing your vanishing points outside your scene. Again, you don't want the vanishing points too close together, creating a distorted composition of your scene. Sketching out roughs (thumbnails) in pencil or pen is a good way to figure out your proportions before committing to the details of a line drawing. You can problem-solve your composition, and placement of your figure and objects in the early stages before you're too far into your drawing to make corrections.

2 CONTOUR LINES

Draw in your contour lines to help define the objects in your composition. Use your vanishing point to sketch in light grid lines (or construction lines) to help keep the proportions in proper perspective.

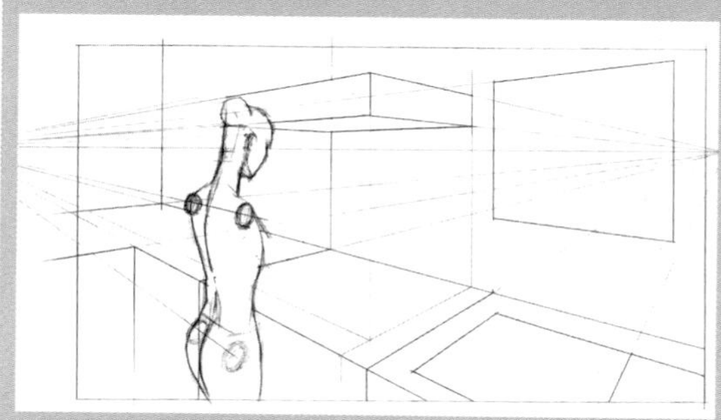

3 ESTABLISH YOUR PLANES FOR DEPTH

This includes foreground, middle, and background. Determine your light source (if you're using one in the pencil stage of the drawing) and lightly pencil in shadows.

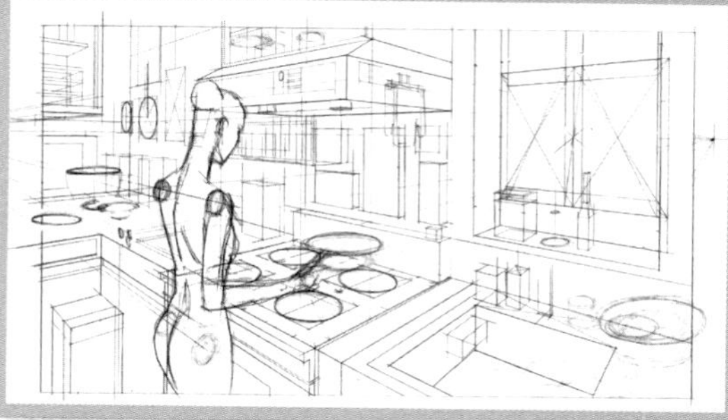

4

ADDING DETAILS

Again, consider the planes for depth; objects in the foreground should have the most detail, variation in line weights, bold lines, higher contrast, while images in the background will have lighter, thinner lines, less variation in line weights, few details, softer contrast of values. This illustration uses a composition much closer to the camera, thus the depth is only a few feet as opposed to the one-point drawing lesson on pages 74-77. The finished illustration shows the horizon line at the subject's eye level. You can see how both vanishing points are close together and the image looks realistic, with no distortion. Keep in mind that using a right angle to establish the two points will result in a realistic composition.

SCENE ANALYSIS

The kitchen scene has a horizon line that lies higher in the composition, resulting in your point of view looking down. This is also known as a down shot. The dressing room (below) has a lower horizon line that changes your point of view looking up. This is also known as an up shot. By changing the horizon line you dictate the point of view of your reader.

VARIATION

As you can see in this illustration, vanishing points don't always have to be close together. The vanishing point on the right is further away than the one on the left. The picture looks realistic and in proportion because the station point to create the vanishing points was drawn at 90° (right angle).

CONTINUES OVER THE PAGE »

THREE-POINT PERSPECTIVE

Three-point perspective is a development of two-point perspective; none of the planes of an object are parallel to the picture plane. Like two-point, your object has two VPs somewhere on the horizon. But three-point perspective also has a VP somewhere above or below the horizon.

Low camera angle

The diagram to your right illustrates how three-point perspective works from a low camera angle looking up at the object. Notice how the horizon line lies below the object which is positioned closer to the VP to its left. Keep in mind, the closer you position an object to its VP, the more distorted that plane of the object becomes.

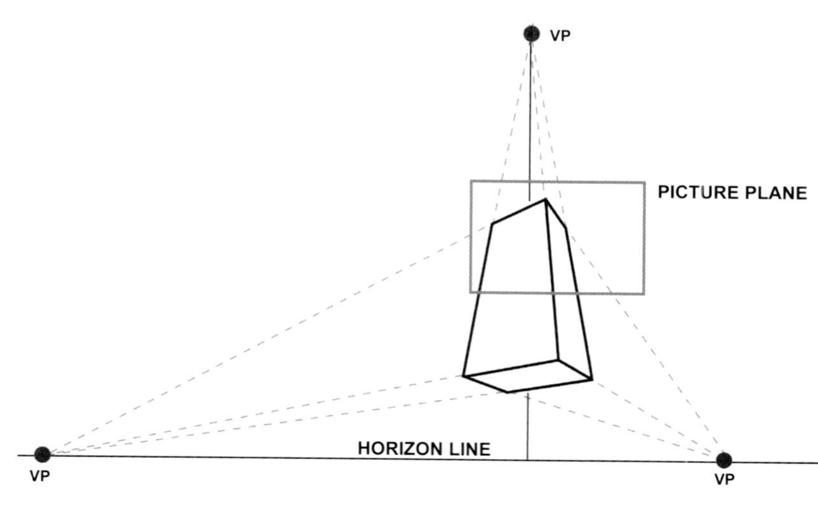

Moving the 'picture plane'

The object can be imagined as a skyscraper, and using a picture plane can help determine the most effective composition for storytelling. As a suggestion, you should work in layers of tracing paper first. This way, you can move your drawing under the picture plane for the best placement, as you can see in the examples, right. If the first image were a comic book panel, a caption box could be placed to the right of the skyscraper indicating some details about the story or a narrative panel from a character's POV.

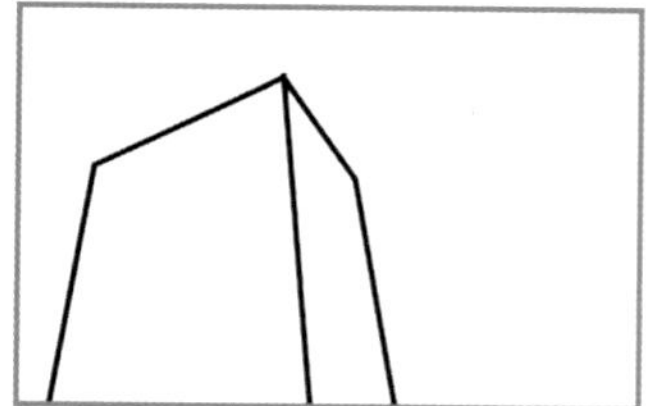

Moving the picture plane around your three-point drawing gives you options for an effective composition to best serve your story.

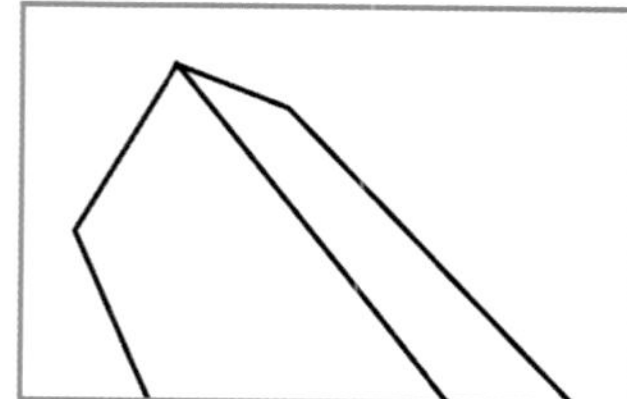

Consider 'tilting' your subject matter within the picture plane of your comic panel. Sometimes, you'll be surprised at the results it may bring to further impact your story.

Three-point perspective in practice

As you can see from the steps illustrated by Joko Budiono below, well-composed structure trumps the cosmetic details every time. A good artist will render pencil roughs (thumbnails) until the best one successfully directs the eye, rhythm and story flow.

CONTOUR LINES
Draw in your contour lines to help define the objects in your composition. Use your vanishing point to sketch in light grid lines to help keep the proportions true.

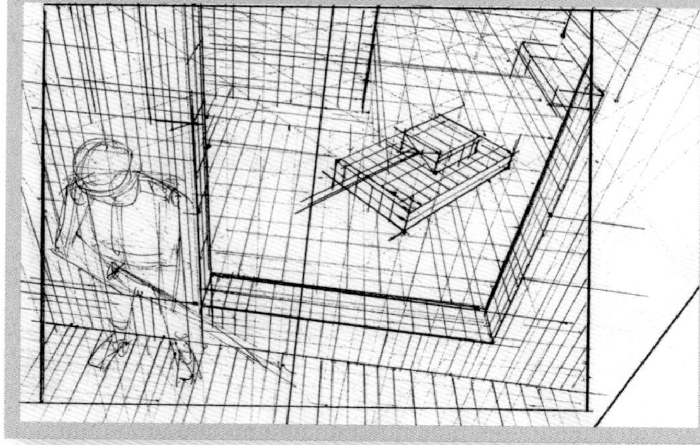

ESTABLISH YOUR PLANES FOR DEPTH
This includes foreground, middle and background. Determine your light source (if you're using one in the pencil stage of the drawing) and lightly pencil in shadows.

3

ADD DETAILS
Details start to emerge and line weights begin to give depth to the illustration.

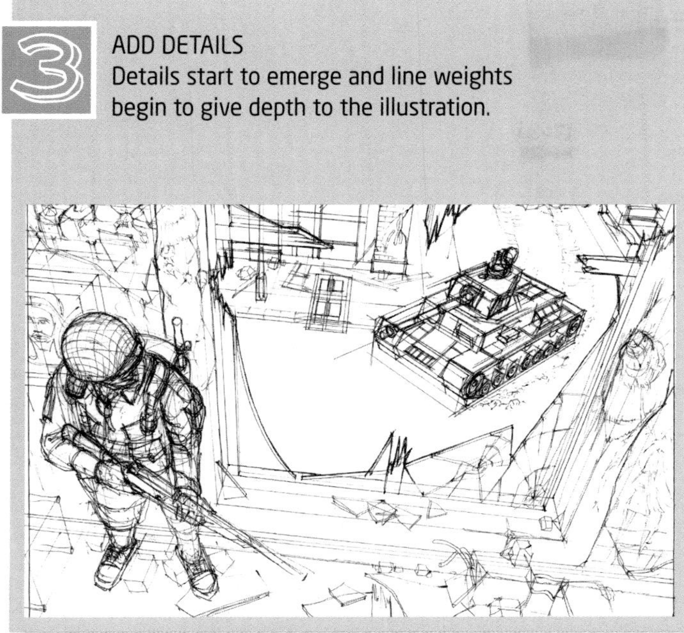

4

FINISHED DRAWING
Three planes of depth have been established: foreground, middle and background using varying line weights, overlapping objects and detail.

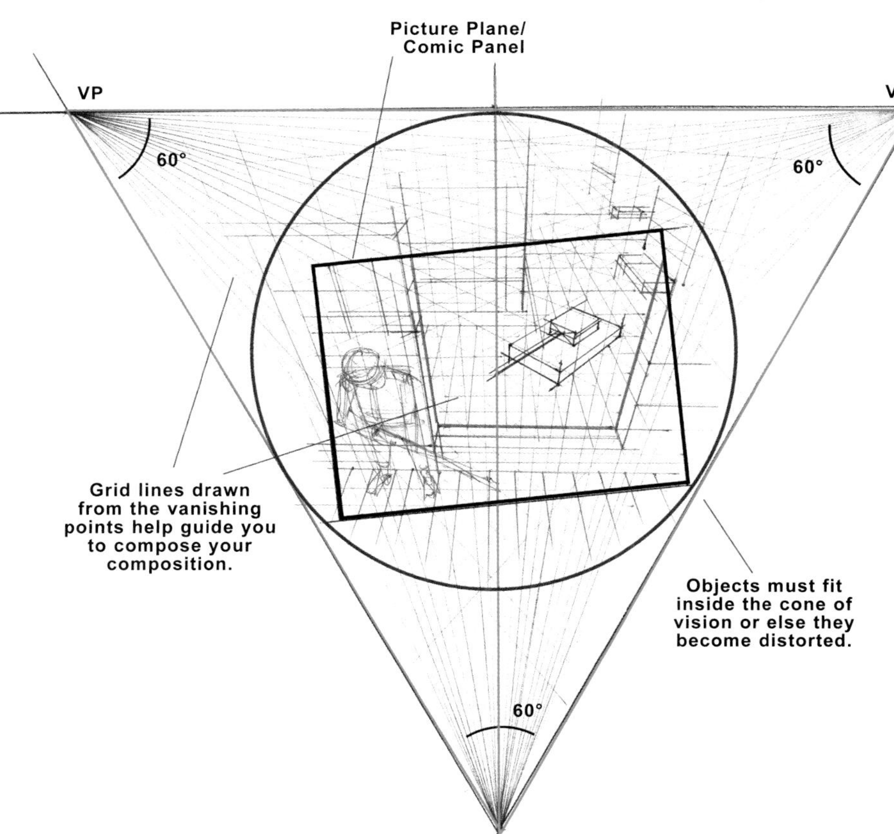
Picture Plane/
Comic Panel
VP
VP
60°
60°
Grid lines drawn from the vanishing points help guide you to compose your composition.
Objects must fit inside the cone of vision or else they become distorted.
60°
VP

SCENE ANALYSIS

The vanishing points in this grid layout over the composition go far beyond the picture plan to achieve a realistic look. The illustration is drawn within the cone of vision to avoid a distorted image. Grid lines (or construction lines) to the vanishing points help establish line work for the composition to keep the objects in perspective. The composition still resides in the centre of vision and the dynamic camera angle adds to the heightened drama of the scene. What makes this composition effective is the slight tilt that impacts the emotional tension.

USING PHOTOGRAPHIC REFERENCE

As you sketch out a scene, your world will begin to take shape. But how do you make your idea visually realistic?

Leonardo da Vinci famously noted: 'You cannot draw what you cannot see.' In order to have a convincing background, you want to develop your backgrounds using references from real life and practise drawing them every day.

TAKE PHOTOGRAPHS

Illustrator Andrew Loomis once said: 'Never guess when you can find out.' As an artist, this is your governing philosophy – and the camera is your governing tool.

The tricky thing about using photos for reference is not to depend on them and all the details that photos capture, otherwise your drawings tend to look stiff and 'look' like a photograph. This breaks away from the drawing style of your comic book.

Remember to use photo references as a tool and for inspiration to enhance your drawings and composition. In other words, using photo references should spur creativity, not stifle it. That's what it's all about: using photo references without being a slave to them.

BUILDING YOUR VISUAL VOCABULARY

Drawing is mostly about understanding your subject. Observing and drawing from photographs will train your visual vocabulary, so you will have a stock of mental images to call upon without having to refer back to the photos themselves. The more mental images you build, the faster you'll be at drawing for your comic book.

Imagine you're drawing from a ***Spider-Man*** script for Marvel Comics. The first page calls for our hero, Peter Parker, and his girlfriend, Mary Jane, on a date having dinner in a fancy restaurant. They're seated next to a window overlooking Central Park. Suddenly, Peter's 'spider sense' goes crazy and he looks out the window to see a mugging take place in the park.

Now, there are several images here you will have to draw well and you will need to research them well. Use books, newspapers, the internet, even mirrors to observe facial expression. When using references for drawing comic books, consider only what you need for your scenes to divulge the story clearly and in a dynamic way your readers will enjoy.

Sketch several different camera angles of the same scene and choose which one communicates what's happening most effectively. Stage your own scene with friends acting as the characters. Take photographs from the perspective of Peter and then Mary. Which works best for the story you're telling?

Apply perspective whenever possible to any picture on a page. Sketch the scene of Peter Parker and Mary Jane in the restaurant in one-, two- or three-point perspective and decide which best tells the story. Remember that photographs should only be used to help you draw what you cannot picture in your mind.

Develop several sketches first purely from imagination before taking photographs for reference. Sketching allows you to capture the shapes and various camera angles and will encourage you to trust your mental images. Choose interesting or difficult angles and poses for your character. You should have at least three to four sketches before deciding which one to work with. The easiest way to find photos from reference is the internet, but you may run into copyright issues if trying to duplicate the image exactly the way it looks. The best reference photos are the ones you take based on your concepts. Here are some common mistakes to avoid when using photo reference:

- Copying or tracing the photos exactly.
- Trying to duplicate all of the details.
- Allowing the photograph to trump your conceptual ideas.
- Being influenced by colour from the photo instead of using black and white.
- Using the photo for the final drawing when it should be used only for the comprehensive stage.

1 COPYING THE PHOTOGRAPHIC REFERENCE

Copying exactly makes your subject look flat, stiff and boring. The focal point is the assassin and her sniper rifle. The background interferes with the rifle and isn't as important as the character. The background is a setting for the character and should complement, not conflict with, your focal point. Do not centre your composition like the photograph; a foursquare composition that mimics the picture plane looks static and dull.

2 SIMPLIFY AND EMBELLISH

Take the dominant elements from the photograph that you think will work well for your composition. The brick wall has been added for the character to lean up against. The original background has been removed and replaced with buildings. The key is to simplify and embellish the image to make it feel more natural and authentic. The assassin and the sniper rifle are emphasised with ink and a brush to highlight the focal point. This is good but not great – you're getting there!

3 STORYTELLING

The illustration is now embellished with an elaborate city skyline and a rooftop ladder. As the storyteller, your job is to communicate the action of your character. The rooftop ladder has been added to suggest this is how the assassin gained access to the roof or her planned escape. When you reference from photos, make sure you embellish the storytelling aspect and don't just draw a 'portrait-style pose'.

CONTINUES OVER THE PAGE »

4 COLOURING

The illustration has been inked with a Winsor Newton Series 7 Sable brush #2 size and a Rotring Rapidograph #0.18 size technical pen (see page 11). Add screen tones for texture and shadow effects. Use added light and shadow for visual clarity to help create mood and contrast. Use only what is necessary for your background. Details are good, but don't overdo it so it looks busy and confusing to the eye, losing your focal point in the process.

PHOTOGRAPHING A MODEL FOR REFERENCE

Economy-style lighting

You'll notice that light two has been replaced by a reflector. The strength of light one being 'bounced' off of the reflector onto your subject varies based on the distance the reflector is held from the subject. For those who use photo reference sparingly for drawing, this method is the economical way to go. A decent digital camera and a foam core board lined with aluminium foil works great as a reflector indoors or outdoors.

Remember that the lighting can be adjusted to a variety of ways to find the look you want for your subject. Practice and experimenting are the keys to finding a method that yields a solution for photographing your reference subject.

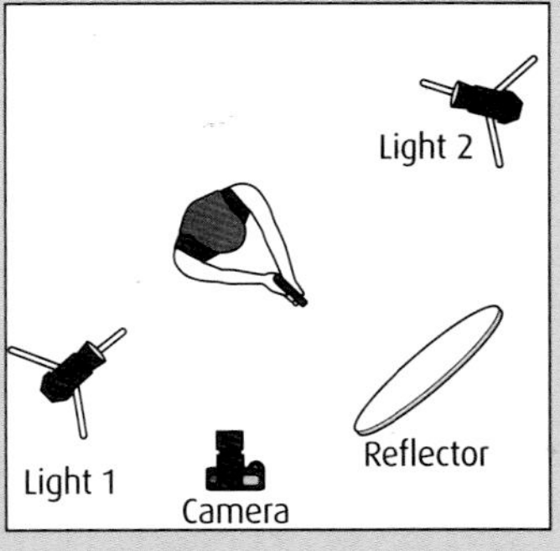

Professional-style lighting

All three lights are pointing at our model. Light 1 is called the 'key' or 'main' light. It is the main light source for the subject and provides depth by creating shadows.

Light 2 is called the 'fill' light. This light is not as strong as Light 1 and is usually positioned in front of your model while you photograph them. If you want your shadows more prominent then use less fill light. The point of having a fill light is to produce less light than the key light or you will lose the depth in the portrait.

Light 3 is called the 'hair' light. Its purpose is to separate from the background by lighting the hair. This gives a three-dimensional quality to photo references for understanding depth in illustrating comic book panels.

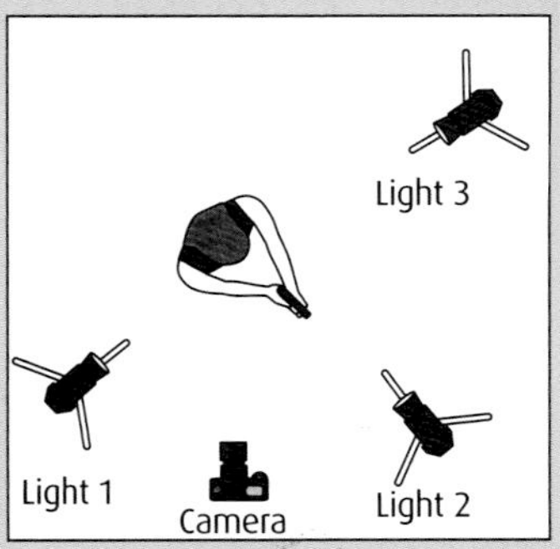

HOMEMADE REFLECTOR

In these examples the photographer and her assistant are using a homemade reflector to light the subject. The best times to photograph a model outdoors is early in the morning or later in the afternoon. The bright sunlight during the middle of the day can wash out the shadows on your subject.

FINISHED COMIC BOOK

As you can see from the various photos, the photographer shot the subject in different positions and angles. Allow for 'happy accidents' with your photo-referencing process. Your style may dictate a realistic world or a stylised one where the subject and the background are loosely gestured.

TIPS FOR ADAPTING PHOTOS FOR REFERENCE

- Start with an initial quick sketch of your character or background.
- Choose interesting to difficult angles and poses as opposed to simple eye-level 'portrait' style images.
- Sketch the general impressions of the important details for your background.
- Put the photograph away before revising your sketch.
- Tilt your composition slightly so the point-of-view is not the same as the photo you used.
- Draw your background or character using only the interpreted sketch.
- Stylise and distort the shapes that fit your style.
- Simplify backgrounds.
- Make the image feel more authentic and natural.
- Think in terms of three planes/layers of depth: foreground, middle and background.

RECOMMENDED READS

The DC Comics Guide to Pencilling Comics by Klaus Janson

The Insider's Guide to Creating Comics and Graphic Novels by Andy Schmidt

Drawing Words and Writing Pictures: Making Comics: Manga, Graphic Novels, and Beyond by Jessica Abel and Matt Madden

Panel Discussions: Design in Sequential Art Storytelling by Durwin Talon

How to Draw Comics the Marvel Way by Stan Lee and John Buscema

Making Comics: Storytelling Secrets of Comics, Manga and Graphic Novels by Scott McCloud

The Five C's of Cinematography: Motion Picture Filming Techniques by Joseph V. Mascelli

Film Directing Shot by Shot: Visualizing from Concept to Screen by Steven D. Katz

Comic Artist's Photo Reference: People and Poses by Buddy Scalera

Framed Ink: Drawing and Composition for Visual Storytellers by Marcos Mateu-Mestre

©HIMES 5-17-10

COMPOSITION AND LAYOUT

'With the plot written out briefly, the next step is to work out the series of pictures to be as interesting individually and vivid as possible and at the same time carry forward the main action. I pay particular attention to design, composition and points of view.'

LAYING OUT THE PAGE

The comic book page layout is comprised of a series of shapes, called 'panels', arranged in a narrative order for ease of reading. The layout itself guides the reader's eye, whilst the content in the panels provides a clear narrative flow.

This page details the most commonly used components found on a typical comic book page. The terms presented here represent the most basic vocabulary used in discussing the inner workings of any comic.

TERMINOLOGY

Knowing the difference between such elements as a panel and a gutter is the first step towards using these and other building blocks in highly creative fashions. Note that these are not rules, but merely definitions. For most creators, comics are a collaborative medium. As such, knowing the meanings of these words – and their general uses – allows for clear communication between all involved in a project.

GRID AND FREE-FORM LAYOUTS

There are two types of page layout used for comics: grid and free-form. The grid is the most traditional and basic page layout for creating comics.

Characteristics of a grid layout

- The panels are the same size and shape.
- The reader can easily follow the visual narrative.
- The grid helps the artist focus on the contents of the panel and not the page layout.
- The viewer immediately sees that no one panel is more important than another.
- The grid layout is considered the more difficult of the two types because the free-form design can mask certain artistic deficiencies, whereas the grid forces the artist to put the emphasis on composition within the panel.

THIS TYPE OF PAGE LAYOUT IS KNOWN AS A GRID.

TYPICALLY IN THIS TYPE OF LAYOUT, THE PANELS ARE THE SAME SIZE.

YOUR JOB AS A STORYTELLER IS TO DETERMINE HOW TO BEST INTERPRET THE SCRIPT INTO A CLEAR AND EFFECTIVE PAGE LAYOUT BY MAKING GOOD DECISIONS ON PANEL DESIGN.

Characteristics of a free-form layout

- This layout allows for more dynamic storytelling.
- Panel size, shape and arrangement indicate meaning to the reader.
- An artist can design any configuration as long as the arrangement is clear to read.
- Panel shape and size are decided by the content according to the script.
- The free-form layout becomes part of the storytelling component.

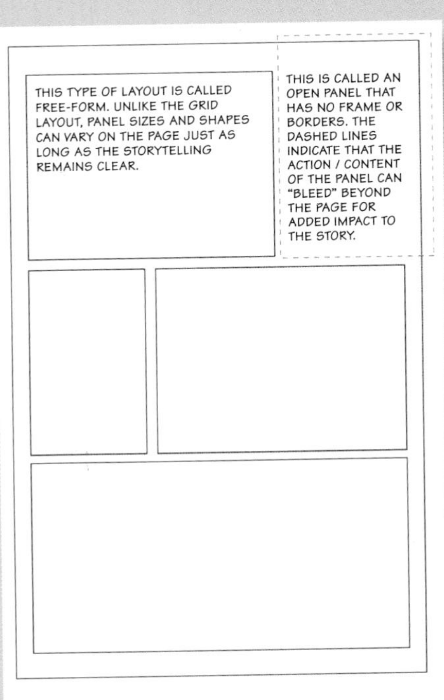

GRID SEQUENCE

This particular page uses a sequence of 16 panels that are all the same size and shape. The more panels you use on a page, the less room you have for words and pictures. It is important to make sure each panel has a clear focal point.

FREE-FORM SEQUENCE

On a page from **Valentine: Reloaded,** *Daniel Cooney uses the free-form format. There are several advantages to using this type of layout, such as being able to incorporate the design of the page into the storytelling.*

PANELLING THE PAGE

How the panels are arranged on the page has an impact on the overall layout and on the storytelling.

Ask yourself what the scene from the script is about, and decide how best to communicate the writer's words into pictures for the reader. You need to choose the type of panels that best impact the story sequence.

The shape, size and dimensions of the panels on a page dictate the pace and the focus of the given scene. In sequential art, certain shapes convey certain connotations. Page-wide, panoramic panels tend to be used for vistas, for establishing locations or for epic, dramatic actions. They slow things down for a moment. Conversely, vertical panels – particularly ones that stretch the length of the page – create a sense of both claustrophobia and speed. While a panel can indeed be any shape, the circle tends to be used as a point of focus, drawing attention to a particular detail. Slanted or diagonal panels imply speed and action, and frequently suggest that whatever is happening in the panel itself is sufficient to knock it off kilter.

Inset panels refer to panels that are situated within a larger image. When employing one or more insets, the artist must pay special attention to the overall page composition, making sure these panels do not obstruct valued story details nor impede the narrative clarity.

LAYOUT VARIATIONS

Use thumbnail sketches to try out a few different layouts in order to fully explore your options. This way, you're pencilling the page that works best to tell the story. Focus on the content of the panel and less on how 'cool' your page looks with panels arranged in a dynamic way. Keep in mind that the best compositions within a panel are the ones sketched out conceptually prior to drawing the panel box. This forces you to shortchange the possibilities of the various camera angles and shots in a composition that may be dictated by the shape of the panel. Page layout and panelling the page is a negotiation of decisions best suited for clear and effective storytelling. Here are some ideas:

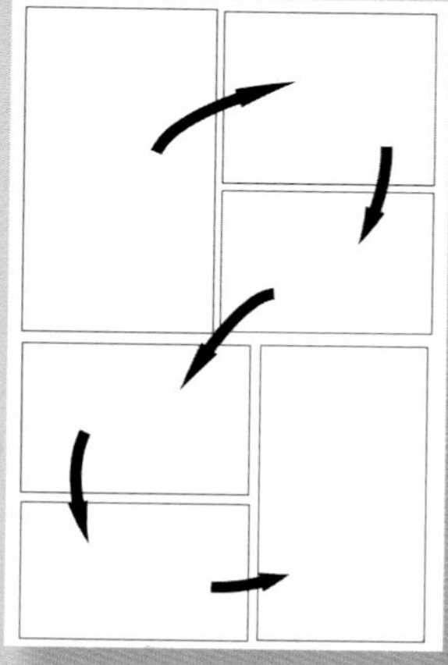

This layout could prove challenging to a reader. Try to have actions, captions or word balloons to help lead your reader's eye.

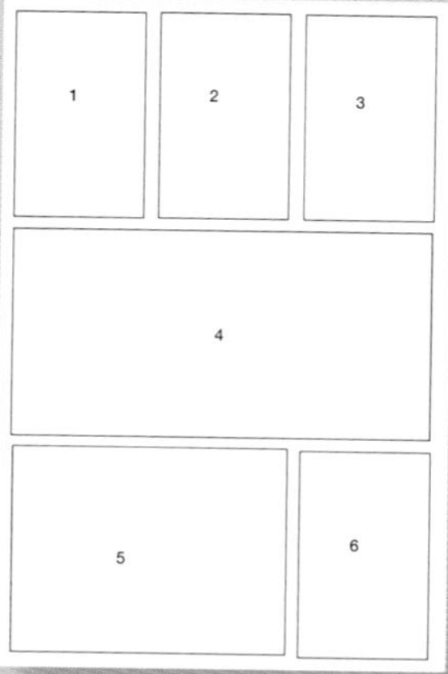

While panel sizes on a page may vary, keeping them within well-defined tiers will allow the reader to easily follow the story.

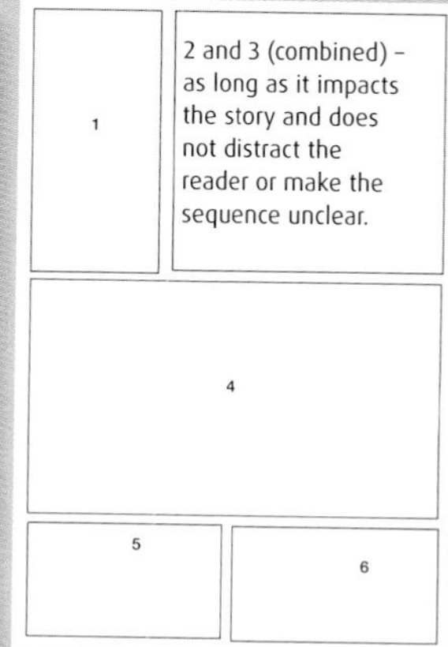

A script may call for one panel – in this case panel four – to be the largest on the page.

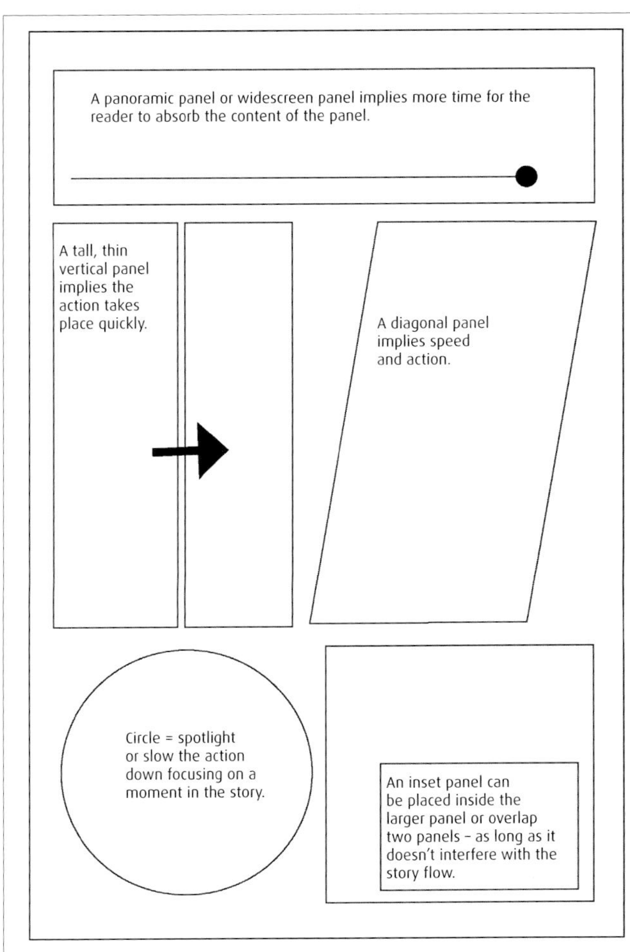

A panoramic panel or widescreen panel implies more time for the reader to absorb the content of the panel.
A tall, thin vertical panel implies the action takes place quickly.
A diagonal panel implies speed and action.
Circle = spotlight or slow the action down focusing on a moment in the story.
An inset panel can be placed inside the larger panel or overlap two panels – as long as it doesn't interfere with the story flow.

BASIC PANEL CHOICES

Panel choice plays a huge roll in conveying the pace of the scene, the focus of the action and the readability of the page. The skilled artist knows which type of panel to use and for what purpose.

BREAKING FROM CONVENTION

It's also possible to combine panel types. Here, artist Daniel Cooney figuratively rips the page in half, using a combination of diagonal and widescreen panels to freeze the frantic action.

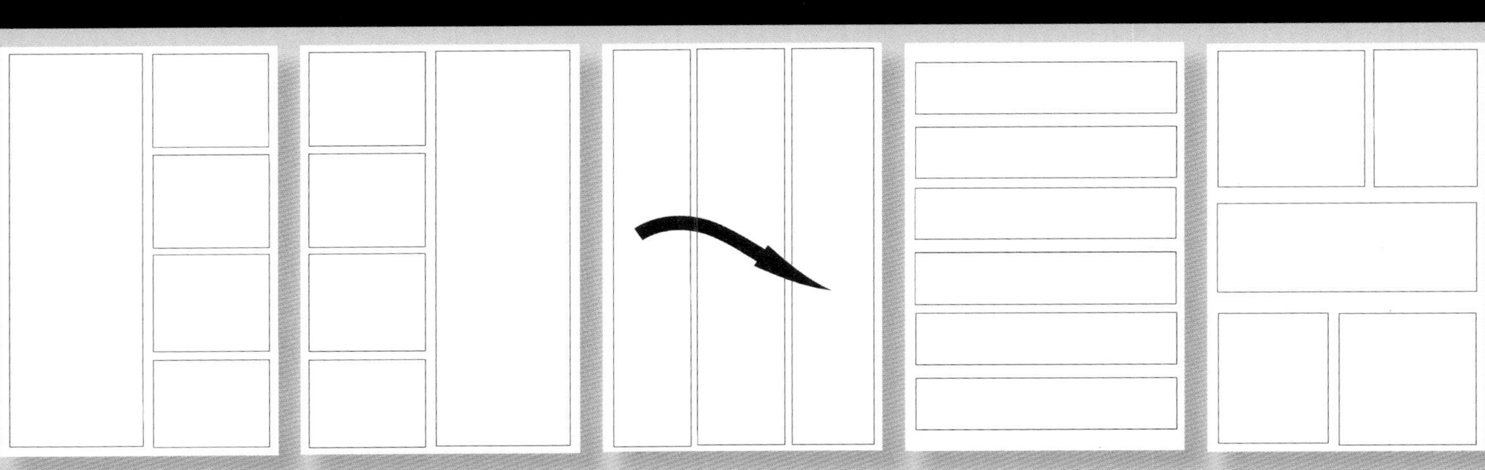

Stacking panels on the right works well because our eyes are trained to read from left to right, down, and back to left to right again.

If you place the larger panel on the right, the reader's eyes would continue across to the larger panel, foregoing the panels on the left, thus disrupting the story flow.

On this page – made up of only vertical panels – the reader again has a clear sense of action, following the story left-to-right.

Stacking page-wide panels leads one to read the story from top to bottom.

Remember that most pages call for a variety of panel shapes and sizes as befits the action and focus of the page.

PANEL BASICS

The actual size of the frame in relation to its content is an important consideration. The size of a panel, along with the size and focus of its content, contributes to the emotional impact on the reader.

If a huge, one-page frame dwarfs an object, it's going to look lost and small. If that's what you want to evoke, then fine, but if it's something you want to draw the reader's attention to, you've failed. Drawing the same object, the same size, but in a much smaller frame will instantly draw attention to it. It's all about perception. A simple optical illusion can make something seem either bigger or smaller than it really is. Even a tiny diamond, if drawn crammed up against the edges of the frame, will appear to be huge. Actually putting the object outside the frame – making the frame smaller than the object – will really make it stand out. Look at these examples and note the varying impact framing of the subject(s) has upon reader perception and reaction. Remember that what one cannot see within a panel is equally as important as what one can see.

CORRECT
The way in which the size of these panels changes is a way of cranking up tension. The sequence begins with regular panels that don't concentrate on anything specific, moves to the pivotal centre panel, where the assistant is about to push the button and finishes with rapid-fire panels.

THE STORYLINE

A couple of masked robbers enter a jewellery shop. They're dressed in black. Brandishing shotguns, they scare the handful of customers into one corner of the room, then make for the central display. A shop assistant reaches for the alarm button. One of the robbers sees what she's doing and swings a gun in her direction.

INCORRECT
If the panels are all of a similar size they will not evoke a feeling of movement or importance. What's more, there's no sense of focus; so readers will wonder just what they're supposed to be looking at. Where's the major action?

180-DEGREE RULE

The 180-degree rule is a guideline employed in motion pictures that has been embraced by most comic artists. It states that two or more characters or objects should always have the same left-to-right orientation within a scene in order to maintain narrative clarity. Crossing this imaginary line has the potential to create confusion in the reader.

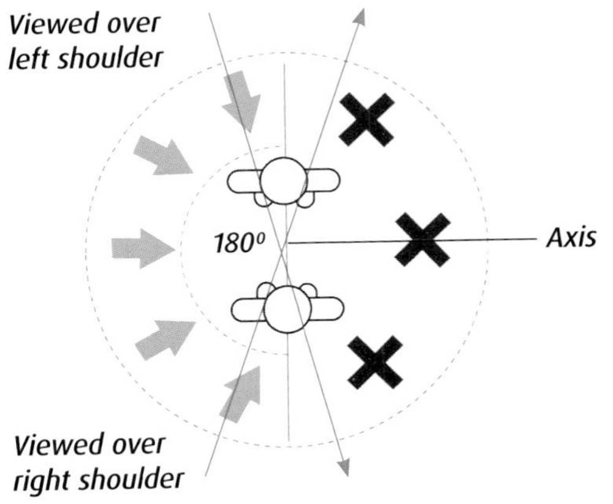

AXIS OF ACTION

Think of two characters in a scene. Draw the axis of action (an imaginary line that separates the camera from action before it). If the 180-degree rule is observed correctly, the camera must not cross over that line, otherwise there is a visual discontinuity.

THE POWER OF THE NEUTRAL SHOT

A neutral shot can be used to change the direction of a moving object, like this car, by having it come towards the reader or go away. Without the neutral shot, juxtaposing the two cars together would create the illusion of a collision and disrupt the story flow because of poor choices made in camera shots.

180-DEGREE RULE IN ACTION

Look at ***Fig. 1***. Panel one is an establishing shot of a woman on the left and a man on the right. In panel two and three, the camera has zoomed in for close-up shots of each character. The imaginary line on one side of the axis has not been broken. In order to change the direction of the action, a neutral shot must be used (see below). In panel four, the woman and the man are profiled before crossing the imaginary line of action to the other side of the axis, as we see in panel five. Without a neutral shot, your story's visual continuity may be disrupted and cause confusion to the reader.

WHAT HAPPENS WHEN YOU BREAK THE RULE

Now look at ***Fig. 2***. As before, panel one is the establishing shot, but in panel two, the man crosses over the imaginary line. This confuses the reader, creating a pause in the storytelling, and wrongly suggesting that the man and woman are talking to someone else in the room that we cannot see. In panel four, the line is broken again by the camera moving to the other side without using a neutral shot. You can see how confusing this page is compared to the page illustrated the correct way.

Fig. 1

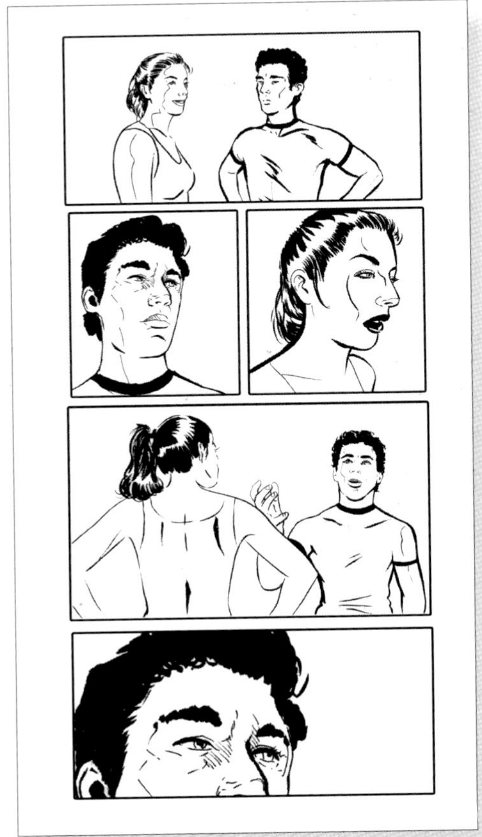

Fig. 2

CONTINUES OVER THE PAGE »

Inside a single panel

Comics tell their stories through a combination of images and text. The clarity of such storytelling relies heavily upon the composition of the elements within each frame. The goal of any artist should be to create an image within a panel that is both aesthetically appealing and easily comprehensible. Striking this balance, the artist will fulfill his or her mandate to convey the story in visual terms, thus not only forwarding the narrative, but also sustaining reader interest through a variety of compositions. Most rules of visual design that apply to similar disciplines – such as motion pictures and advertising – hold equally true for comic panel composition.

Rule of threes

A simple rule to follow when laying out your page begins with dividing each panel into thirds horizontally and vertically (shown right). Where the lines cross are the points of natural focus within that frame. It is important to be aware of your focal point from panel to panel for the sake of clarity in story flow.

Two shot

The two shot is a visual solution for when two or more characters give one another information that is happening off-panel. This device gives the reader the desire to continue reading to find out what it is that the characters see that they cannot. Look at page 97 for some key examples of the two-shot.

Finding the focus

Note the intersections of the horizontal and vertical lines above. At these junctions, our eye is naturally drawn to such details as the characters' faces and the book being produced by the female character. In the panel on the right, the image is arranged to draw the reader's focus to her eyes – by way of her sunglasses – and her beverage. Note that not every intersection of imaginary horizontal and vertical lines needs to contain important visual material.

OFF-PANEL ACTION AND GESTURE

In this panel the man in the background is pointing to something off-panel that the captain in the foreground sees, yet is not revealed to the reader at this point.

OFF-PANEL ACTION AND EYE-CONTACT

The woman in the foreground is clearly distracted by action happening that hasn't been revealed to the reader.

OFF-PANEL ACTION AND PANELS

This two-shot composition has both characters looking at something the reader cannot see, while the inset panel reveals what the woman is pulling out of her concealed sheath under her sarong.

BREAKING BORDERS

A characteristic that many comic book artists feel the need to do is break panel borders with their subject matter. Breaking the panel border can add a visual dynamic to the page layout, as long as it does not interfere with the story flow. If your design choices are poor, without any regard for the visual narrative, you will not succeed at illustrating sequential art that reads clearly. This example is slight, but enough to give pause to a reader, who may go directly into the next panel, missing the transitional panel and thus disrupting the story flow.

PUTTING IT ALL TOGETHER

This example showcases logical use of maintaining the 180-degree rule, keeping the two characters on consistent sides of the imaginary line in each panel. Also, note the variety of panel sizes and framing choices, and how they combine to create a dynamic page. Furthermore, each of these panels adheres to the rule of threes, focusing reader attention upon the most pertinent information and actions.

ANGLING THE CAMERA

Graphic novels succeed because their pictures give a visual clarity for the reader to understand, supported by a sound story structure. Your job is to communicate clearly what the script calls for in each panel, using a variety of camera shots and angles.

Top to bottom: Point-of-view shot, close-up shot, long shot.

The comic book panel is simply a window you choose to best frame the character, place and situation of the story. Every panel in a page layout has to contain at least one of these aspects that make the story work visually.

Character is the 'who' in your story, and the focal point. Place is the 'where' in your story, establishing a setting, while situation is the 'what' in your story. These three aspects are essential for keeping your reader involved with the story you're illustrating. The camera shots and angles you choose are how you intend the reader to see the story unfold through their eyes.

The worlds of cinema and comics have some similarities and differences. Both tell stories through words and pictures, all the while using technology to achieve the end result. Film terms apply to the use of storytelling direction in comics, so let's take a look at some examples for one of the most important storytelling devices you'll use for making comics and graphic novels.

Camera Shots

Establishing shot

A mandatory shot that is essential for establishing the setting of the story. The establishing shot can be used for any location, just as long as you give enough visual information for the reader to understand where the action occurs. Usually, a rule of thumb would be an establishing shot for every scene change, each time a new element is introduced in the scene or when a character moves through a scene.

Long shot or full shot

Imagine a figure illustrated in full from head to toe with an emphasis on the background the character occupies. Distance is key here, with the camera far enough away to show the location and who's involved in the scene.

Medium shot

A panel featuring the subject from the waist up with a background that may be very detailed or not detailed at all.

Close-up

A panel that emphasises the subject and can include a facial expression, with or without hand gestures. Close-ups can be used to frame an object a character is holding for a detailed look, or visualise the object up close itself.

Extreme close-up

The eyes or the mouth of a character fill the entire panel.

Over-the-shoulder shot

This is a shot of someone or something taken over the shoulder of another person. The back of the shoulder and head of this person is used to frame the image of whatever (or whomever) the camera is pointing towards. This type of shot is very common when two characters are having a discussion and will usually follow an establishing shot that helps the reader place the characters in their setting.

Point-of-view

This shot is as if the reader were looking through the eyes of a specific character.

CAMERA ANGLES

There is a great variety of camera angles to choose from, any of which can add an interesting perspective to the content of the panel. Sometimes the camera angle can greatly influence the reader's interpretation of what is happening on the page.

THE TILT ANGLE OR DUTCH TILT

This is a cinematic tactic often used to portray the psychological uneasiness or tension in the subject matter. A Dutch angle is achieved by tilting the camera off to the side so that the shot is composed with the horizon at an angle to the bottom of the panel.

LOW-ANGLE SHOT

Also known as the worm's-eye shot, the camera looks upwards towards a subject, and can make the subject look powerful, as above and right.

HIGH-ANGLE SHOT

Also known as the bird's-eye shot, the camera looks downwards, generally shot from just above head height. This angle can make a subject – in this case the woman at the table – look vulnerable.

CONTINUES OVER THE PAGE »

FROM CONCEPT TO COMPLETION

A well-composed page does not spring into being overnight. Every comic book goes through a series of steps before reaching its final form.

Whether a solo project or a collaborative effort, the creation of a comic book follows a sequence of stages. As all stories begin with the word, so too do comics, each having as their foundation a clearly written script, a blueprint to guide the artist and provide the narrative. Working from this document, the artist then creates rough drawings – known as thumbnails – as a tool for translating the script into its visual form. These thumbnails become the basis for more refined pencil drawings, which in turn will be ultimately finalised in the inking stage.

1 USING THE SCRIPT

This script is written by Tim Andrick and illustrated by Jeff Himes. The full script used here gives the artist all the visual information needed to draw the three-to-four page sequence. Here, the full script includes visual descriptions of the character, background and situation. Sound effects and captions are applied if needed.

COUNTRY GAS STATION, DUSK
The sun barely peeks over the horizon. We see a gas station with a glass front and two 'analogue' gas pumps sitting along a narrow country highway. A small one bay service garage attaches to the right hand side of the station. The station has a classic 'Vee' shaped canopy, with harsh yellow sodium lights.

SUPERIMPOSE: 'JUNCTION POINT'

REBECCA pumps gas. She replaces the gas nozzle, and walks into the gas station.

We see a dingy gas station with aisles of snacks. A wire-frame newspaper rack sits behind the station attendant SKEETER, who reads the paper while he talks on the phone with CARL. REBECCA approaches the counter...

2 THUMBNAILS

The artist first sketches out pencil roughs or 'comps' of the pages near the size of the comic book page. The format chosen here is a landscape one versus the more traditional portrait page orientation. Drawing thumbnails allows you to establish all the important story points from the script to ensure clear and effective storytelling.

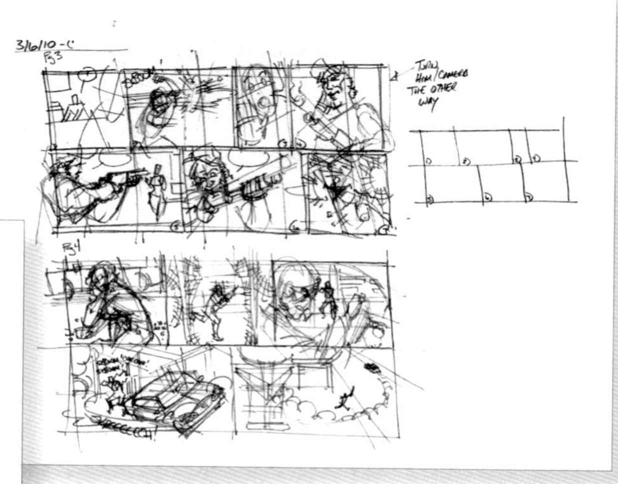

EXPERIMENT

This is when the artist first interprets the script, looking for the best combination of framings, panel choice, camera angles and the like. The thumbnail process allows the artist to both experiment and develop the best possible visual narrative. Note the varied framings of the same panel in the examples here.

3 PENCILLING

The next step is to photocopy the thumbnails to the size of your 28 x 43-cm (11 x 17-inch) art board (or another size suitable for pencil and ink – your choice) and tape each page to the back of the board. Use a light box to trace through the thumbnail sketch to your clean art board. This stage allows you to revise elements in your panels that impact the story and add details necessary for the drawing. Light and shadow should be considered at this stage as well, before you refine the linework, to ensure the narrative works well with the script. In this particular example the artist used pencil, fine-point markers and a Sharpie to refine the sketched-out thumbnails.

4 INKING

The artist then finishes the pencilled pages by inking them, adding variation to the contour lines for depth, texture and lighting. It is important to point out that mistakes do happen along the way, and they allow you to improve on the original and give you invaluable experience of problem solving during the process. Your goal when working from a script is to work out all the problems early, before you commit too much time to details. Focus on the important elements of the story and how they might fit together on a page before getting caught up in the style and all the flashy details. Remember, well drawn doesn't mean a well-composed story. If your storytelling is not clear from panel to panel on the page, your well-drawn pictures will be just that: pictures with no story to tell.

GRID OR FREE-FORM LAYOUT? BY MARK SIMMONS

WHAT THE EXPERTS SAY

Mark Simmons graduated from the Academy of Art University in 2009 and is currently working as a storyboard artist, comics writer and illustrator and giant robot expert. You can see his work in the ***SIREN*** comic anthology and on his website at ***www.ultimatemark.com***. By the time you read this, he should be able to talk about his latest projects, but for now he's labouring under a code of silence like that of the deadly ninja.

As the name suggests, '24-Hour Comics Day' is an annual event in which cartoonists are challenged to create a complete 24-page comic in 24 consecutive hours. Like many other strange ideas in the field of comic art, it's the brainchild of Scott McCloud, author of ***Understanding Comics***. Although the 24-hour comic is obviously something of a stunt, and the conditions are fairly arbitrary, you might be surprised at how much you can produce in a single marathon session.

One piece of advice I found particularly helpful when I took this challenge was to complete each page before starting the next one, rather than pencilling and inking them in batches. This makes it a lot easier to tell how much time you're spending on the average page, and I doubt I'd have been able to finish on schedule otherwise. I also decided to work at a fairly small size – 17 x 28 cm (7 x 11 inches), roughly the dimensions of a printed comic book page – so I'd only have to cover half as much surface area. As a result, these felt more like deluxe thumbnails than 'real' comic pages, which helped encourage me not to spend too much time fussing with them.

Beginning with grid

When you're working under such tight time pressures, using a grid really saves a lot of time, as you don't have to waste precious minutes pondering how to lay out each page. I've picked out a few pages from my 2009 entry, ***Commedia***, to illustrate the grid's flexibility and some of its useful characteristics.

These opening pages establish a simple six-panel grid that continues throughout most of the story. If it was good enough for Jack Kirby, it's good enough for me! These pages are devoted mainly to a parade of petty indignities suffered by our narrator in his daily life, and I think the metronomic consistency of the square panels adds to the comedic effect. Each event is equally weighted and interchangeable, going nowhere and building up to nothing. It's interesting to consider how the feel of this sequence might be subtly altered if these panels were taller or wider, rather than inert little squares.

The sequence is bookended by a pair of double-wide panels. These are both intimate close-ups, given greater impact and immediacy by their larger size. If we're thinking of these pages as glorified thumbnails, then perhaps these images might become full-bleed panels in the 'final' version, giving us an even stronger contrast with the detached tone of the little boxes in between. Even then, the grid would still serve as the basic framework of the page.

Camera shots and angles

The shot choices for the remaining panels are pretty straightforward. The overhead establishing shot is carefully composed to save me the trouble of drawing the whole restaurant, and the wider dimensions of the final panel give enough horizontal space to show the two characters interacting. I'd like to say that I deliberately staged this to show the hero's love interest turning away from him, as her doubts about his character increase. At this point, though, I'd been jamming out pages for more than 12 hours straight, and I'm honestly not sure how much of this was conscious decision-making.

Moving forward in free-form

Then, inevitably, the romance comes to an end. Now it's all over except for the giant puppet rampage.

As the story enters the home stretch, the layouts become increasingly free-form, with more and more dramatic splash panels. (This was also a good choice in terms of time management, since the big action panels were a lot quicker and easier to draw.) Unless you're making a deliberate point of sticking to the same grid all the way through your story, ***Watchmen***-style, I think it's perfectly reasonable to stretch it and squish it and even discard it as your storytelling needs dictate. In this case, the narrative clearly called for verticality.

Unless you plan to draw all your comics in frantic all-night marathons, you normally won't be facing time pressures this extreme. But the classic grid is always a very useful tool to have in your cartooning arsenal, and in situations like this, it can be a real lifesaver!

FINISHED ARTICLE

The results of a 24-hour comic writing competition illustrate how grid and free-form layout styles can be used to good effect.

I ALWAYS WANTED TO THINK OF MYSELF...
AS A GOOD PERSON.

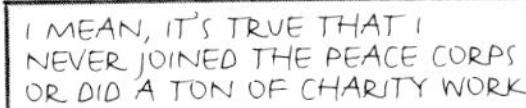
I MEAN, IT'S TRUE THAT I NEVER JOINED THE PEACE CORPS OR DID A TON OF CHARITY WORK.

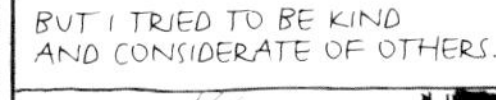
BUT I TRIED TO BE KIND AND CONSIDERATE OF OTHERS.

THAT'S NOT SUCH A COMMON THING IN THE MODERN WORLD.

WHICH SEEMS TO BE FULL OF EVERY KIND OF RUDENESS.
I SAID LIGHT FOAM.

I TOLD MYSELF THAT, IF I COULD RETURN KINDNESS FOR UNKINDNESS...
PLEASE GIVE UP THIS SEAT

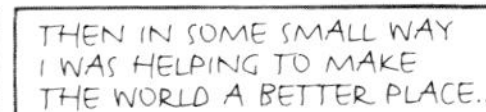
THEN IN SOME SMALL WAY I WAS HELPING TO MAKE THE WORLD A BETTER PLACE...

AND THAT MY HARD WORK WOULD, IN THE END, BE ACKNOWLEDGED.

I WAS A REAL SUCKER...
NO
NO REPLY

...UNTIL I MET MR.PUNCH.

THIS WAY, SIR! MA'AM!
WOULD YOU LIKE TO SEE THE WINE LIST, SIR?
ALL ON THE HOUSE, OF COURSE!

WHEW! I'M SO GLAD WE FINALLY FOUND TIME FOR A NICE DINNER.

HUH. DOESN'T ALL THE FAWNING GET OLD, THOUGH?

EH, ITS STILL AN IMPROVEMENT. YOU SHOULD SEE HOW SNOOTY THIS PLACE USED TO BE!
THEY'RE NOT ANY NICER, YOU KNOW. THEY'RE JUST AFRAID OF YOU.
IS THAT REALLY WHAT YOU WANT?

WITH THE BENEFIT OF HINDSIGHT
I THINK THAT MAY HAVE BEEN THE POINT
WHERE THINGS STARTED GETTING OUT OF HAND.

WHAT THE EXPERTS SAY

Nate Piekos graduated with a BA in Design from Rhode Island College. Since founding Blambot Comic Fonts & Lettering in 1999, he has lettered comics for Marvel, DC, Oni Press and Dark Horse, has become type designer to Harvey Award Winner Mike 'Madman' Allred, and has had his designs licensed by such companies as Microsoft, Six Flags Amusement Parks, ***New Yorker*** Magazine, The Gap and many more. His work has not only been utilised in comics, but on television and in feature films as well. He's been drawing fantasy heroes, giant monsters and buxom women since adolescence and now that he works in the comics industry full time, he can be less embarrassed about continuing the hobby as an adult. Nate lives in rural Rhode Island with his lovely wife.

TYPICAL COMIC STRIP TEMPLATE

This is the generic three- or four-panel strip you see in your newspaper. The goal is a little different here. You just want the panel border. Your original art size for strips is 10 x 33 cm (4 x 13 inches). With an 28 x 35-cm (11 x 14-inch) pad of Bristol, you can fit two strips on one sheet like you see here.

Formatting your work properly will make your art instantly attractive to a potential publisher when you showcase your portfolio. Presentation takes patience, but the results are worth every minute. Here are a few items you might find useful.

Bristol board

Comic book artists typically use 28 x 43-cm (11 x 17-inch) sheets of heavy, high-quality art paper called Bristol board. Bristol board comes in two 'tooths' (surface texture): Plate (which is smoother) and Vellum (which is rougher). Check them out and decide which is best for you. You can find Bristol in your local art supply store typically in 35 x 43-cm (14 x 17-inch) pads. Just trim off the extra 8 cm (3 inches) with a T-square and an X-acto knife – or you can leave that 8-cm (3-inch) gutter on and use it to do quick little sketches of things you're trying to work out. What brand you use is up to you. Most people swear by Strathmore. It's a nice high-quality name. It's a little more expensive, and it is very good. Utrecht is another good brand if you can find an Utrecht shop. It's almost identical in feel and costs a little less. You can often get name-brand Bristol pads cheaper at craft shops than at art supply shops. So look before you buy! Comic strip artists also use Bristol board, but comic strip art is smaller than comic book art. 28 x 35-cm (11 x14-inch) pads work perfectly and let you fit two strips on one page.

T-square

You can probably pick a T-square up at the art shop for £7 to £10. It will save you loads of time when you're drawing 90-degree angles for not only your original art guides, but for panel borders as well. It's a must-have. An 45-cm (18-inch) or larger T-square is ideal.

Pencils

This should be obvious: When you're ruling off your original art, use a pencil. You're going to erase these lines once you've inked your panel borders.

Measuring the Bristol board

Fig. 1 shows you how to measure an 28 x 43-cm (11 x 17-inch) piece of Bristol for typical comic art. There are a few slight variations, and the sizes have changed a little through the years. What we have here is an 28 x 43-cm (11 x 17-inch) sheet with a 25 x 38-cm (10 x 15-inch) bleed and a 22 x 34-cm (9 x 13.5-inch) panel border. The purpose for ruling off the sheet is to give you an idea where your panel borders are and where your 'safe zone' is outside the panel border. When the art gets reduced and then trimmed digitally for final print size (which is typically 16.8 x 26 cm/6.625 x 10.25 inches these days), you're going to lose the art outside your bleed area.

Ever notice in comics when the art goes right up to the edge of the cut page? That's called 'full bleed'. In this case, the artist drew a little beyond that so that when the art was trimmed down, there was some play in case it wasn't exact.

'Safe zones' and 'Danger zones'

Fig. 2 is the bottom right hand corner of your sheet. On any page there are 'safe zones', where you can scribble safely without risk of your picture being cropped, and 'danger zones' (or full bleed), an imaginary line that your pencil must not cross. We'll use this for reference.

1: This is your 'safe zone' where the majority of your art will be. Go nuts. Draw until your hand bleeds!

2: This is your panel border. Most of your panels will butt against this rectangle.

3: This is your 'full bleed' line. Anything outside your full bleed is no-man's land. Just tumbleweeds out here. Anything you draw there will almost certainly not be seen in the final page.

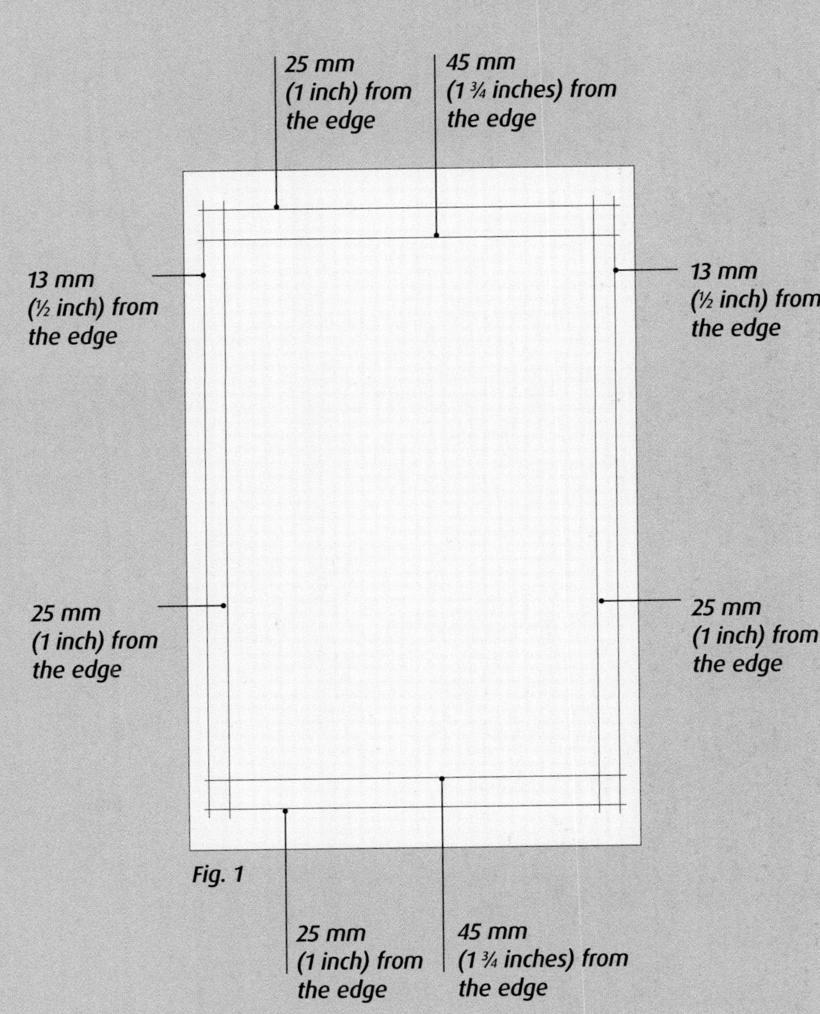

Fig. 1

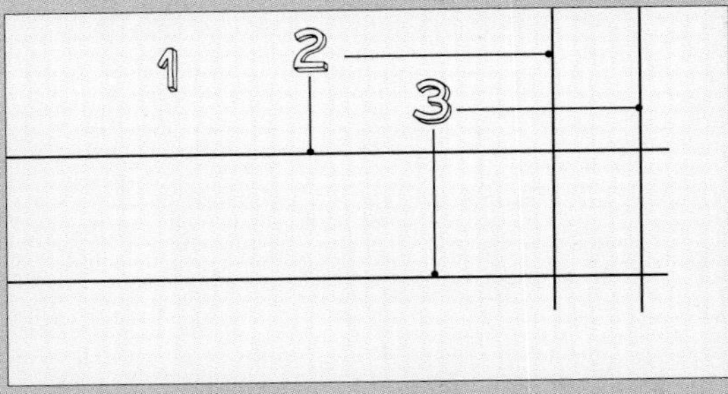

Fig. 2

RECOMMENDED READS

***The Art Of Comic-Book Inking* by Gary Martin**

The Art of Comic-Book Inking has become the industry-standard manual for aspiring inkers seeking to take their work to the next level or for working professionals looking to broaden their skill set.

***The DC Comics Guide to Inking Comics* by Klaus Janson**

Legendary comic book inker Klaus Janson uses DC's world-famous characters - including Batman, Superman and Wonder Woman - to demonstrate an array of inking techniques, covering such topics as using textures, varying line weights, creating the illusion of three-dimensionality and working with light and dark. Janson's lively step-by-step instructions are informative, exciting and clear enough for beginners to follow.

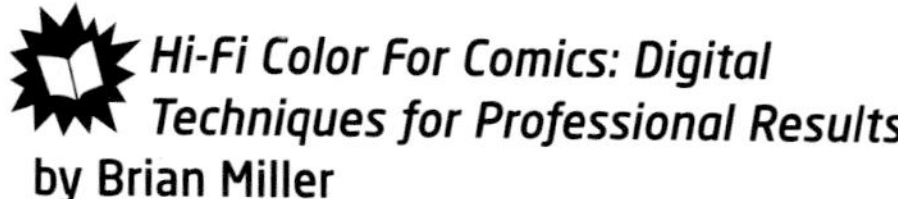

***Hi-Fi Color For Comics: Digital Techniques for Professional Results* by Brian Miller**

Readers will get instruction on equipment, scanning, setting up pages, and colour theory, flatting, rendering, special effects, colour holds, colour separations and even details on the business of becoming a professional colourist.

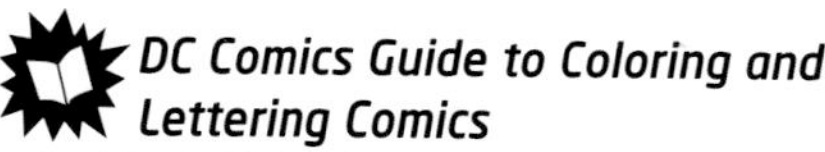

***DC Comics Guide to Coloring and Lettering Comics* by Mark Chiarello & Todd Klein**

Acclaimed comic book illustrator Mark Chiarello and award-winning letterer Todd Klein demonstrate dozens of surefire strategies, practical techniques and professional secrets for dynamic comic book colouring and lettering.

INKING, COLOURING AND LETTERING

'I will throw all my best efforts into it, my thoughts and political observations, but ultimately I want to create a narrative that keeps you turning the pages and leaves you with a sense that this thing has a reason for being there.'

Frank Miller

THE ART OF INKING

A page of pencilled artwork can be revised for corrections, but a page with ink cannot. So rule number one is to make sure you're totally satisfied with the artwork before you start inking.

THE INKER

Inking comic book art originally meant that another artist would trace the penciller's work with pen and ink. The inker was simply just another cog in the machine. Over time, inking comic book pages developed into more of an art form, and inkers introduced new techniques to bring the art of inking to another level. As comic books matured, the work of the inker increased with the demands of the improved, detailed work of the comic book penciller.

Technology has now taken the place of the inker in a growing number of books by publishers, and software programs such as Photoshop and Painter, with a colourist hammering the keys and clicking a pen or mouse, now create effects that are similar to or have improved upon the hand-skilled labour of the inker.

REASONS FOR INKING

This chapter will introduce you to the traditional skill sets and tools of an inker for comic books and graphic novels, as well as other mediums such as newspaper strips, storyboards and illustrations. The purpose of inking a page is to make it more visible to the scanner. When graphic novels first started, photographic films and emulsions weren't as sensitive as they are today. They needed a good, black image to capture all the details. It is possible now to scan in pencils and work from a high-quality digital image, but the printed image may not be as good.

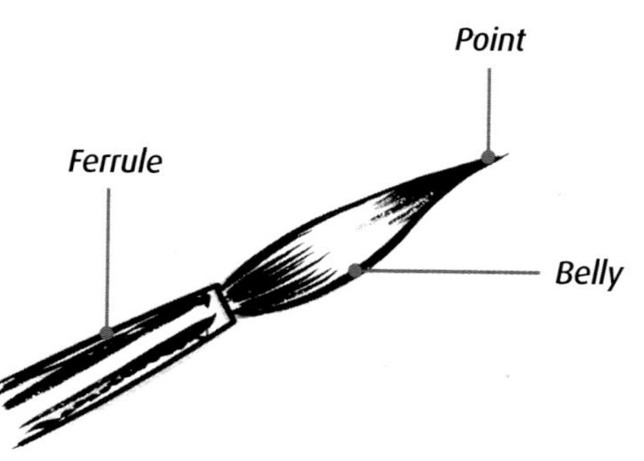

Another reason for inking is to add depth and greater contrast to the pencils. (Some artists deliberately use pencils for grayscaling after inking, instead of ink washes.)

Ways of getting all that ink onto the page vary with the artist. Some prefer brushes (take a look at some completed artwork – the pages where lines thicken and taper smoothly is brushwork), others work with crowquill and dip pens (often texture, detailed work) and others use whatever is at hand for finishing and effects.

INKING WITH A BRUSH

The first time you pick up a brush, you'll immediately notice it feels different from holding a pencil. Inking with a brush at first can be frustrating, until you get a feel for how a brush behaves and what it can do for you. If you can master the use of a brush for inking, you'll be happy with the versatility and results that the brush can bring to your work.

CHOOSING A BRUSH

Selecting a good brush for inking comic book pages can make all the difference in the results you expect to achieve. As you take out your brush, make sure that there are no single hairs sticking out from the belly of the brush, that the belly of the brush doesn't bulge out and that the brush snaps to a point when you flick it on your wrist.

The brushes that are considered the industry standard are Kolinsky red sable round, Raphael 8404 size 4, and Winsor & Newton Series 7 sable brush size 2 or 3.

BRUSH CARE

Always clean your brushes after each use by rinsing them in warm water. You can also rub bar soap or hair conditioner through the bristles of the brush and rinse. You want to avoid ink buildup near the ferrule of the brush, which can shorten its life span.

HOLDING THE BRUSH

Ink with your shoulder and elbow for smooth, consistent lines and not with your wrist. Hold the brush between your thumb and forefinger while resting it on your middle finger. Relax the side of your hand and wrist on the paper you're inking on.
Keep the brush firmly in your grasp and move only your wrist at the pivot point.

BRUSHWORK TIPS

Getting comfortable inking with a brush takes patience and hard work. In order to utilise the versatility of the brush, practise various warm-up techniques, observing the results you achieve with your grip and wrist and forearm movements.

Thick to thin brushstrokes

This approach hinges on two variables for inking smooth, varying lines. First, determine your light source, as objects closer to the light have thinner lines and objects that are further away have heavier, thicker lines. The second consideration is the direction in which you work. Some will start away from the body and work in towards it, and others from the body out. You want to ink away from wet areas to avoid smearing.

Feathering

When you pick up the brush and practice ink strokes from thick to thin, observe which way you start: your starting point is near you and you brush away from your body, or you start away and brush towards you. Think about it. The feathering method, with ink lines close together, creates the illusion of a darker value, while some brushstrokes are further apart for a lighter look. Whatever method you prefer, the line weights consist of thick to thin throughout.

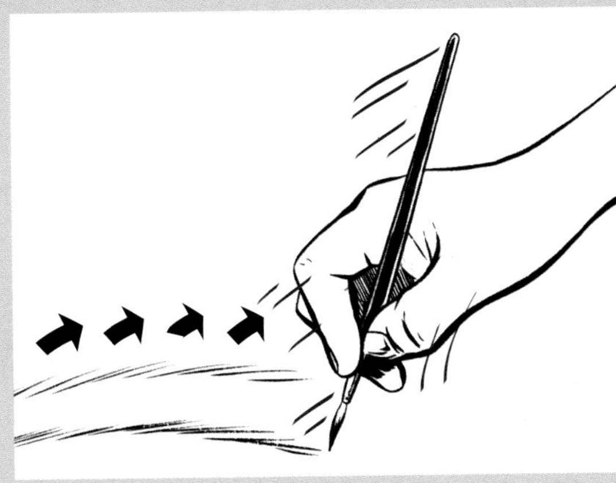

WORK QUICKLY

This example shows quick, short brushstrokes going from left to right. Brushing away from wet ink develops a good habit of avoiding smears while working.

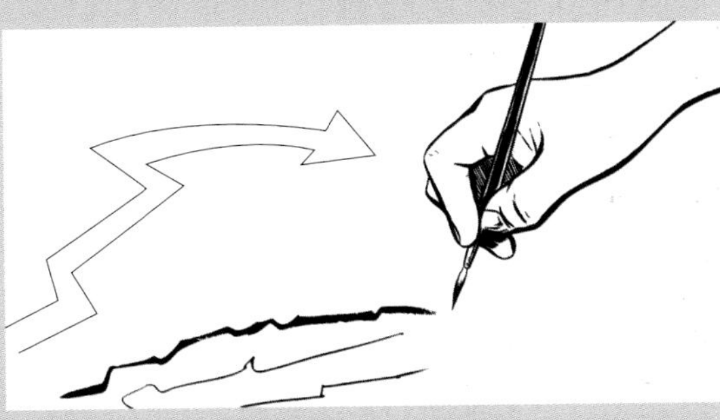

ZIGZAG METHOD

This method is useful for achieving varying line weights with sharp shifts in the brushstroke. Hold the brush in a way you are comfortable with. Keep your fingers, wrist and forearm as a single unit as you move the brush across the paper. Like a spring, push down for a thicker line and pull up for a thinner line.

EXPERIMENT

The brush is much more versatile than the crowquill pen. Practise brush techniques to get familiar with the brush: feathering, crosshatching, dry brushing, thick lines, thin lines, bold to light lines, smooth to jagged lines and more.

CONTINUES OVER THE PAGE »

Nib pens

Mastering the use of a brush to produce fine, consistent lines takes time, and you have to be very disciplined with your execution. The nib pen can strike fast and give you those thick to thin strokes with a flexible tip, and straight hard lines with a stiffer tip. Think of the nib pen as your 'nicks and scratches' tool. You can use it to add texture to a boulder or details to a face or landscape. Once you get a feel for nib pens, you'll find they are expressive in their own right, and great for producing distinct linework.

Handling the nib pen

Hold the pen as you would a pencil, making sure the top of the nib with the imprint side is facing up. Before you dip your nib in ink, press the nib pen down onto paper, applying some pressure, to reveal the two tines splitting apart. The amount of ink dispersed depends on the pressure you apply to the pen.

For fine-point penwork use flexible nib tips, such as Hunt 100, Hunt 102, Hunt 108, Gillot 170, Gillot 290 and Gillot 659. For coarse pen lines use stiffer nib tips, such as Gillot 404, Gillot 1068A, G-pen and Bowl-Point/Saji.

Pigment liners

These pens are basically felt-tip pens with permanent ink that won't bleed when mixed with India ink. These are ideal for inorganic objects such as buildings, cars and other structures that require precision lines and detail using a template, triangle or ruler.

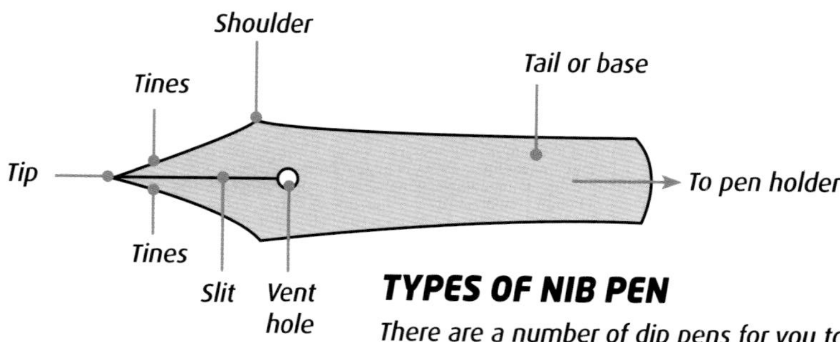

TYPES OF NIB PEN

There are a number of dip pens for you to choose from. Try a few different types of nib tips, ranging from flexible to stiff. Industry-standard brands include Hunt (Speedball), Gillot, G-pen and Deleter.

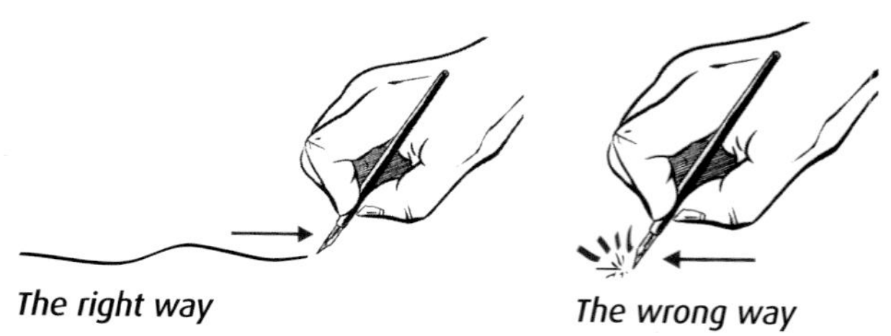

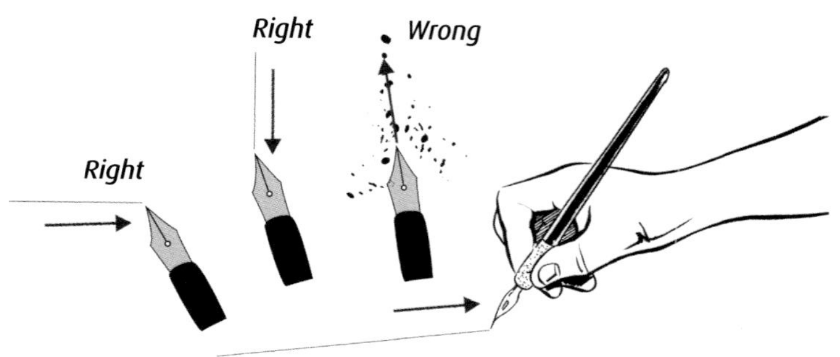

HOLDING THE PEN

Holding the pen nib upside down and going 'against the grain' will allow the nib to skip and snag the paper, resulting in splattered ink and tearing of the surface of your pencil work. Move your entire arm when inking long horizontal or thin lines.

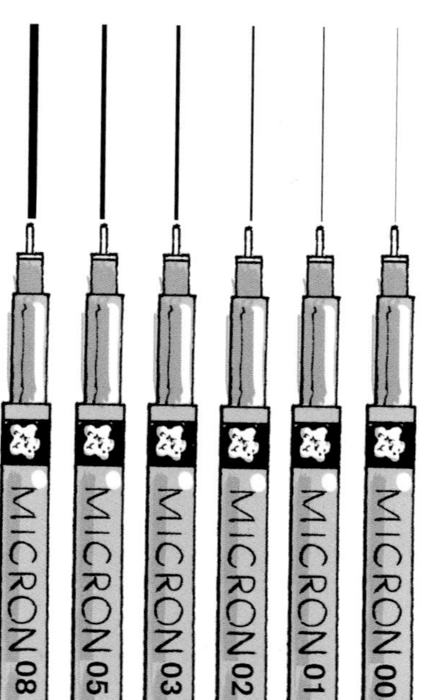

TYPES OF PIGMENT LINER

There is a variety of pigment liner brands to choose from, ranging from Sakura's Micron pens (illustrated) to Copic's Multiliner steel-tip pens.

RENDERING USING BRUSH AND PEN

Inking is all about decisions to make involving what type of line weights, contour styles, solid blacks, textures, lighting and other choices that factor into inking comics. Above all else, inking varying line weights epitomises what comic book inking should be mastered to establish the illusion of depth in your work. Keep in mind that controlling the brush means to control the amount of ink flowing from it onto your paper. The illustration here exemplifies the qualities of comic book inking.

The eclipse around the fist was created with an elliptical template with a Sakura Micron 01 pen.

The white stars were created with a brush and Pro White by dabbing over the ink.

The white splatter effect was created with a toothbrush and Pro White. With the bristles facing down, move your thumb, applying pressure to release the ink over your work. The more pressure you apply, the greater the splatter.

The falling stars and meteor shower were created using a Pentel Presto! correction pen by moving the pen quickly over the finished inked areas. The pen will skip, producing broken-up lines for a cool lighting effect.

The black splatter effect is created with a toothbrush and Pelican India ink. With the bristles facing down, move your thumb, applying pressure to release the ink over your work. The more pressure you apply, the greater the splatter.

The 'Kirby Krackle' is an inking technique made famous by the artist Jack Kirby. Dip the back of an eye dropper, or the eraser at the top of a pencil, in ink and tap it onto the surface of the paper.

The starbursts were created with an X-acto blade. Chip away at the paper, holding the blade firmly between your thumb and index finger. It takes practice, and be careful not to cut yourself.

The curves were pencilled using a French curve and then inked with a Sakura Micron 01 pen.

The white streaks of light were drawn with a Pentel Presto! correction pen by moving the pen quickly over the finished inked areas. The pen will skip, producing broken-up lines for a cool lighting effect.

The figure, planet and outer space were all inked with Winsor & Newton Series 7 sable brushes, sizes 2 and 3.

The radiating black lines were inked with a crowquill Hunt 108 nib pen, and the straight lines aided with a ruler.

CONTINUES OVER THE PAGE >>

Compare and contrast

Here is the same page in pencil and then inked, with initial pencils and finished inks by artist Brandon Pike. Some of the best inkers are the ones who have the ability and talent to draw, such as Wally Wood, Dick Giordano, Kevin Nowlan, Joe Sinnott, Sal Buscema, Alex Raymond, Leonard Starr and Stan Drake.

Pencilled page

The pencilled page establishes everything the reader needs to know about this sequence: the characters, the setting and the situation. However, some corrections will need to be addressed by the inker. For instance, it is difficult to achieve varying line weights and textures with pencil, but easy to achieve with a stroke of the brush or crowquill pen.

The establishing shot is clearly drawn and given a sense of depth with varying line lengths.

The artist has defined the time of day using light and shadows on the windows and architectural surfaces.

In the second panel, a foreground element is introduced in an interior room. The contour line is noticeably thicker than in the background.

The panel frame is broken by the woman's head, which in this case works well because it leads the reader's eye into the next panel.

Contrast plays an important part in visual clarity, making sure the focal point is clear. The shaded areas on the hair of the figures and on the curtains help separate the planes in this panel.

A close-up shot shows the woman's attention being directed towards the window. The curtains are now alive with movement, indicating that something has changed.

A new element is introduced that is visually very effective for two reasons. First, the direction of the gun points towards the woman and her child, helping direct the reader's eye from the previous panel. Second, the thick contour lines around the gun and the hand indicate that this is closest to the camera, while the woman and child are clearly in the background.

Inked page
Inking with a brush and pen, giving careful consideration to details and rendering, helps define the narrative flow and gives a mood to the sequence. It is important that you are aware of the light source in every panel while inking, and that you are mindful of the varying contour lines separating the planes to produce the illusion of depth.

It is important to be aware of negative space. The thin, light and broken lines are the furthest parts of the image from the foreground.

Here we can see how the inkwork can define depth in a drawing using varying line weights and light and shadows that overlap to establish the foreground and backgound.

The line weight of the woman's shoulder is thicker to indicate she is in the foreground. Notice the change made from the pencilled drawing, the strap is no longer here.

The areas behind the child have been inked in with solid black, defining the contrast between her and the background.

The woman's hair is separated by an outline using negative space, giving the illusion of a line.

Shadows are clearly defined now in the background on the window frame and curtains.

You can see how white gouache or Pro White can distinguish features such as hair strands, and outline the figure to give contrast against the background. Brandon chose to fill in the area behind the woman with ink instead of inking the brickwork. The decision makes the panel less busy and keeps the focal point between the woman's eye and the moving curtain.

The weapon is clearly defined using a combination of line weights and shadows. The composition is effective in framing the woman and her child and depicting that a threat has entered the room.

SCANNING YOUR ARTWORK

This article explains how to scan black-and-white line art. The purpose of scanning your artwork is to end up with a very clean, high-resolution digital file of your line art suitable for colouring either for web or print.

In this section, you'll learn how to scan your artwork using step-by-step instructions for configuring your scanner, saving your art to a digital file, cropping and sizing the page, fitting segments of oversized art together and troubleshooting crooked artwork. You'll be introduced all of these steps by using Adobe Photoshop, the industry standard for scanning artwork and colouring comics.

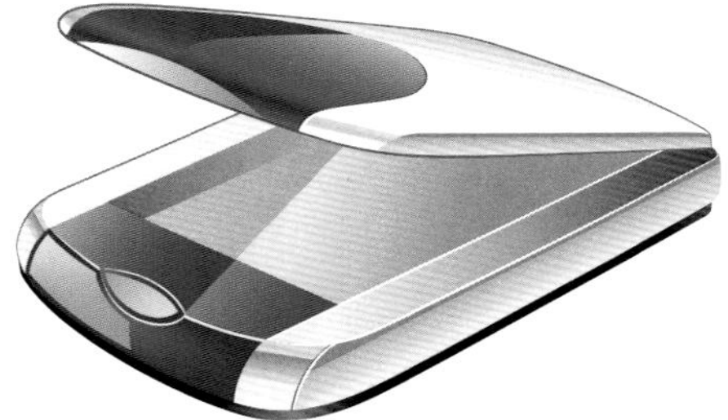

The majority of reasonably priced scanners will scan an area of 22 x 28 cm (8½ x 11 inches) but requires scanning your 28 x 43-cm (11 x 17-inch) artwork in two pieces. The Mustek 30 x 43-cm (11¾ x 17-inch) scanner is one of the more affordable large, flatbed scanners available on the market.

When it comes to determining which platform is best for you – Apple or PC? – it's really down to personal preference. Photoshop files are compatible with either. There are certainly other graphics programs available, so do try them and find what you're most comfortable with. However, Photoshop is the industry standard, so the steps that follow refer to that.

Here's a list of the hardware and software used for this lesson (you'll need these or an equivalent):

- Mac Pro desktop computer
- 3 gigabytes of RAM
- Two 2.4 GHz Intel core 2 duo processors
- 20-inch widescreen monitor
- Graphics tablet
- Large flatbed scanner
- Large-format inkjet printer
- Adobe Photoshop CS2 or higher

SCANNING AND SETTING UP THE PAGE

1 PREPARATION

If your scanner is a standard size, you may need to make reduced photocopies of your line art to fit your scanner. Or you may choose to scan your art in two parts and make them into one file in Photoshop. Open Photoshop, and find your scanner under the 'File/Import' menu. Click on the correct driver for your scanner.

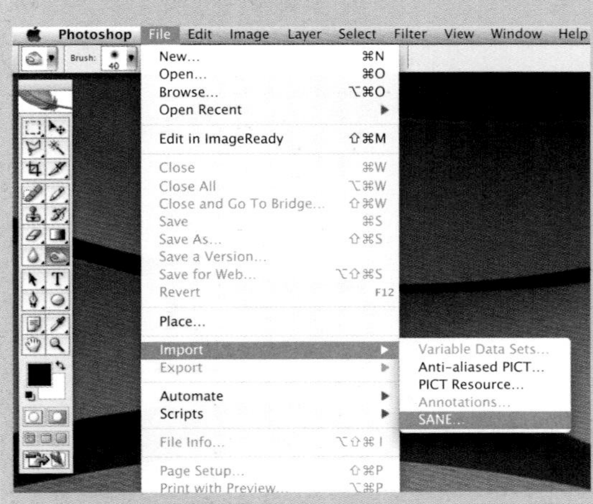

2 SCANNING

On your screen, you'll find a variety of options for scanning your artwork. For pencilled artwork, choose Grayscale, 300 dpi. For inked artwork, choose Black & White (or Bitmap), 600 dpi. If your scanner has an option for sizing, select 100%. Once your settings are selected and the artwork is placed on the glass, select 'Preview'. Set the scanning area to cover the entire page, and once you are satisfied with the preview, click on 'Scan'.

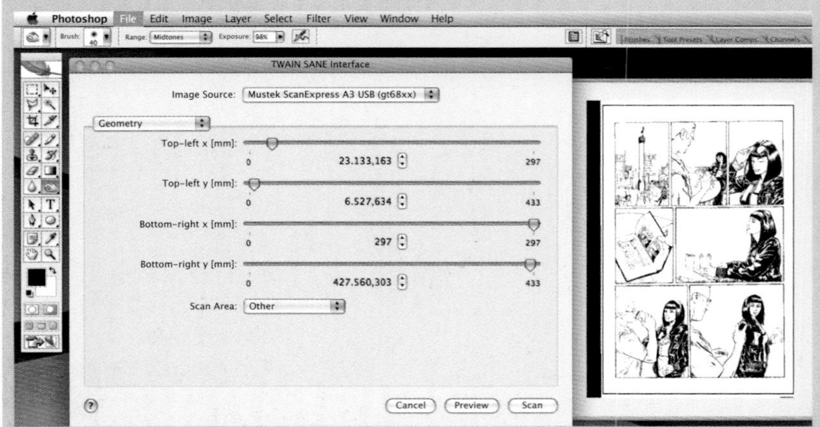

3 SAVING

Save your scan immediately to your desired location with a file name suitable for the job. If your computer is prone to crashing (or even if it's not!), it's a good idea to save your work before going any further. Save your file as a TIFF ('.tif'). A TIFF is a type of uncompressed file format that won't discard any important information, as opposed to a JPEG file ('.jpg'), which loses information that is vital for printing in order to make a smaller file size.

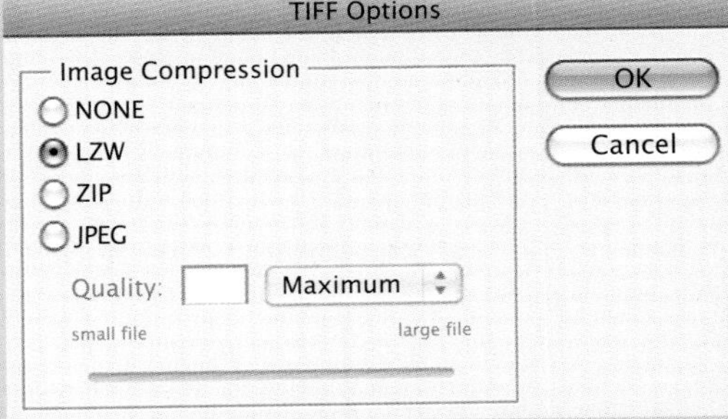

When saving your work as a TIFF, select the LZW button in the 'TIFF Options' box before hitting OK. This will reduce the file size without compromising image quality.

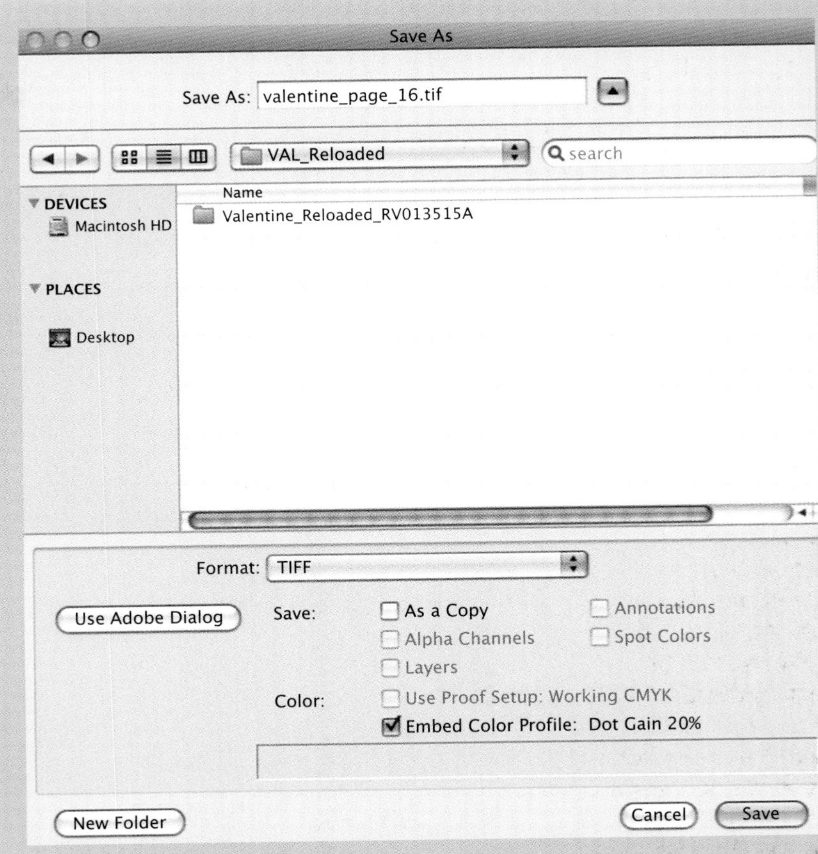

4 CROPPING AND SIZING THE PAGE

After you've scanned and saved your art, crop the page to the correct specifications for the printer. (Image > Image Size.) Make sure the boxes for 'Resample Image' and 'Constrain Proportions' are checked before you size the image. Change the width of the image to 17.463 cm (6.875 inches) and save the image.

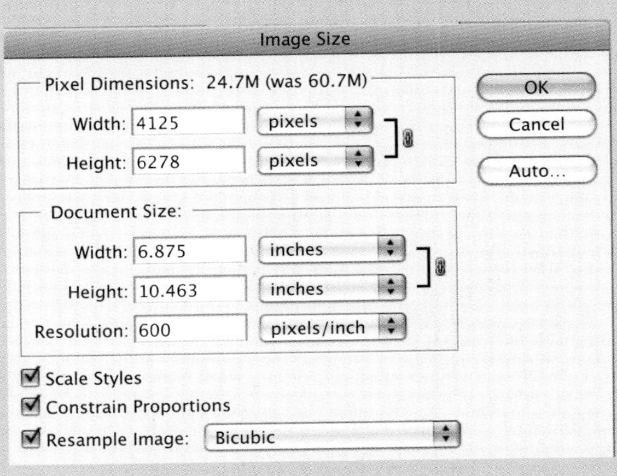

CONTINUES OVER THE PAGE »

SCANNING OVERSIZED ART

You're probably using a standard-sized scanner that scans an area of 22 x 28 cm (8.5 x 11 inches). Most comic book artwork is drawn at 28 x 43 cm (11 x 17 inches). If you can't reduce the size of your page to fit your scanner on a photocopier, the alternative solution is to 'stitch' together your page by scanning it into two parts.

1 ALIGNING AND SCANNING THE TOP SEGMENT

Line up your art as evenly as you can on the scanner bed. Keep the page flat on the glass by weighting the top of the scanner down with some books. Repeat Steps 2 and 3 from the previous lesson.

2 ALIGNING AND SCANNING THE BOTTOM SEGMENT

Align and scan the bottom segment of your artwork in exactly the same way as the top segment. Thus, ensuring that you include all the areas that weren't visible when scanning the top segment of your artwork.

3 'STITCHING' THE SEGMENTS TOGETHER

Before you can stitch your art together, open your top segment and go to Image > Canvas Size. Change the canvas size to the dimensions of your original page size or slightly larger.

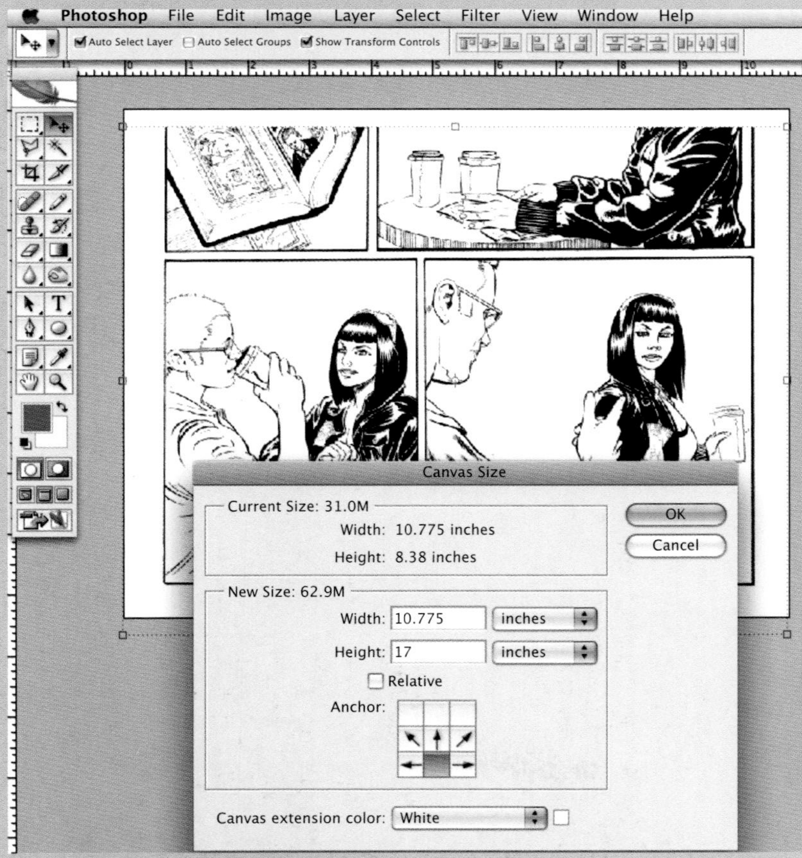

4 COPYING AND PASTING

Open the bottom segment and Select All (Command + A, or Control + A) – then copy and paste your art into the main file (the one you just changed the canvas size of).

Here's what your file should look like on your screen now.

STRAIGHTENING CROOKED SEGMENTS

» If you're having trouble stitching your segments together, one of them might be crooked. To straighten it out, go to Edit > Free Transform. Move the cursor to an anchor point and rotate the art until it lines up with the other segment.

5 MULTIPLY LAYER 1

Go into the Layers menu and select Layer 1. Change the Mode (at the top just below the Layers) from Normal to Multiply. In this mode, you'll be able to see both layers.

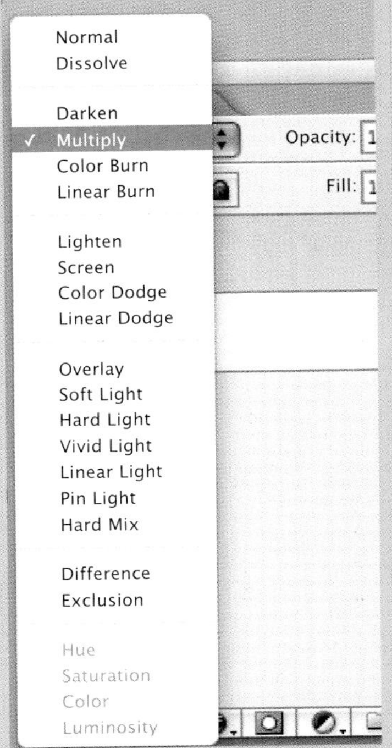

6 FITTING THE SEGMENTS TOGETHER

You'll now be able to adjust your layers to line up as one. You can remove the overlapping art using the Marquee or Polygonal Lasso tools. After you delete the overlapping art, change the Mode back to Normal on Layer 1.

Select Flatten Image (from the Layers menu). Repeat this procedure for every layer if there are more than two segments to your page. When you are finished, save the file with an appropriate name. It takes some practice to master this process, but you'll soon have it down and will move through stitching your pages in no time!

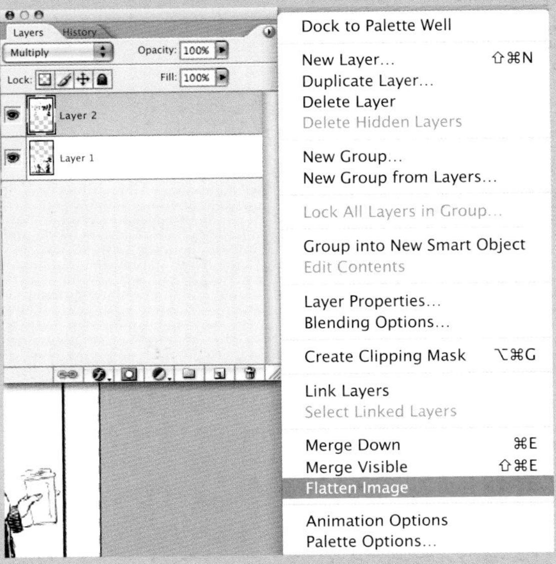

WHAT THE EXPERTS SAY

Mark Simmons graduated from the Academy of Art University in 2009 and is currently working as a storyboard artist, comics writer and illustrator and giant robot expert. You can see his work in the ***SIREN*** comic anthology and on his website at ***www.ultimatemark.com***. By the time you read this, he should be able to talk about his latest projects, but for now he's labouring under a code of silence like that of the deadly ninja.

This page was originally created for an inking class I took with Mick Gray. Mick is one of the very best inkers in the business – not to mention a tough grader! – so I tried to apply as many inking tricks as possible in the hopes of impressing him. In particular, I wanted to use solid blacks to tie the elements together into distinct foreground, middle ground and background planes.

Thumbnail

As you can see from this thumbnail sketch, I was thinking about the arrangement of the blacks from the very beginning. The composition of the main image, with the heroine framed by a roughly L-shaped arrangement of tree trunk and cast shadows, is inspired by one of Wally Wood's aptly named '22 Panels That Always Work'. The cast shadow under her leg connects the middle ground occupied by the figure to the foreground represented by the tree. Well, that was the theory, anyway!

Pencil

In the final pencils, the blacks are now fully defined. In addition to the foreground elements, I put a lot of solid black on the heroine's upper body and on the dodo perched on her knee. This creates a middle plane with lots of strongly contrasting black-and-white areas, adding interest to what's meant to be the most important part of the image. The fact that the human character and the bird are both rendered in the same style also helps tie them together in the same plane.

Technically, these black shapes represent the shadow cast by the dodo, the dark fabric of the heroine's top and the shadows cast by the unseen foliage overhead. But they're actually arbitrary shapes inserted for design purposes, rather than any kind of rigorous realism, and so I didn't feel the need to obscure the character's face with similar shadows.

Speaking of shadows, you'll notice that I indicated a grey shadow across the character's face in the inset panels at the top of the page. I hadn't yet decided how I wanted to create this grey value, and I wasn't happy with the idea of putting a lot of hatching on her face. Mick suggested doing it with screentone, and I used this method in the final piece.

Ink
When inking, spotting blacks is always a special treat with an image like this, as your page suddenly transforms from a bunch of sketchy lines into a dramatic composition. In terms of impact gained per unit of inking time, it's a much bigger payoff than painstakingly drawing frilly fern leaves.

I did a lot of tinkering with line weights at this stage, doing my best to ensure the right amount of weight on each part of the heroine's body, as well as establishing a nice thick line along the left side of her arm to separate her clearly from the background. I inked the foliage in the distance with a Micron pen so as not to create a lot of interesting – and distracting – line weight variations.

I was pretty happy with the page at this point, pending the addition of screentone shadows over the heroine's eyes in the inset panels. Her jeans, however, weren't meshing very well with the rest of the middle ground. I could have worked in some more spot blacks, drawn in a bunch of texture or left it in the hands of a hypothetical colourist. But since I was already planning on adding screentone, there was another obvious solution.

Digital inking
One round of Photoshop tinkering later and the image is complete. In addition to the shadows over the heroine's eyes and on her jeans, I ended up putting some simulated screentone on the close-up of the dodo and on the foreground tree as well. It was tempting to go even further, or perhaps just go through and apply grey tones to the entire thing, but for a page that might end up being rendered in colour, I think this is about as far as you'd want to take it.

Analysing the planes
In the final image, then, we've established three distinct planes. The foreground is made up of lots of solid black and a little bit of screentone, suggesting that it's all pretty much in shadow. Visual interest is created in the middle ground, with strong contrast between spot blacks and large areas of white, while the background features no blacks to speak of, in accordance with the principles of atmospheric perspective. All of this is achieved mainly through the spotting of blacks, although I think it never hurts to throw in some cute extinct animals while you're at it!

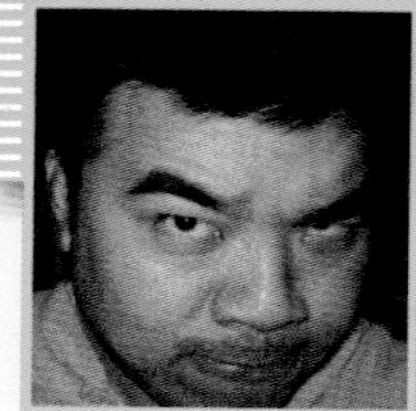

What the experts say

A veteran inker in the comics industry, **Walden Wong** has worked with all of the major studios, and on many high-profile projects. Of the generation of inkers to enter the industry in the wake of the Image Comics formation, Walden is one of the few top inkers who does not owe his development to time spent at a studio. Located in the San Francisco Bay Area, Walden has worked with DC Comics, Marvel Comics, Dark Horse Comics, Top Cow Comics, Disney Adventures, Image Comics and more.

Here, Walden Wong uses an experiment from ***Batgirl #11***, when he was developing an inking style for Lee Garbett's pencils, to try out six completely different inking styles.

The project

A while back, when I started working on ***Batgirl***, I did some sample inking. Lee sent me a high-resolution file of Barbara Gordon.

I Photoshoped the pencilled piece and placed six copies next to each other on an 28 x 43-cm (11 x 17-inch) page to be printed out in blue line for inking, giving it an Andy Warhol feel, which made it an exciting task to complete. I slapped ink over the images and numbered each one.

1: Inked with a brush in heavy thick to thins around the holding line. Interior lines were inked with a brush going thin.

2: Inked with a brush, only this time given a lighter, softer touch throughout.

3: The holding lines were inked with a brush, giving an angular edge. Interiors were inked with a quill, which gave a crisp, and once again an angular, feel.

4: The holding lines were inked with a brush, giving a thick, bold, flat outline. Interior lines were also inked using brushwork.

5: Inked with a quill, giving the whole image an angular feel, not to mention broken lines and lots of dots that allow the imagination to complete the image. The quill was flicked often, from thick to thin and back.

6: Completely inked with Micron pens with different tip sizes.

FINISHED ARTICLE

As a result of the 'bunch of Barbaras' exercise, we chose option 2. When it came time to ink over the original pencils, here's the result.

End result

For as long as I have been inking, I have used various combinations of brush, quill, Microns or any of the tools individually, and made them look exactly like each of the Barbaras left. After a while of working with the tools you have, you learn that each brush, quill or pen can ink something with a certain look quickly and more efficiently. Give me a black ballpoint pen and I can still ink it looking like a comic book page. It'll just take twice or three times as long to complete. Knowing what tools to use just speeds things up.

WHAT THE EXPERTS SAY

Since the early 2000s, **John Heebink** has been teaching about drawing comics, perspective, action figures, clothing, etc., and doing freelance illustration. Comics credits include the graphic novel ***Doll and Creature***, the anthology ***Put the Book on the Shelf*** and the comic book series ***Nick Fury Agent of SHIELD***. John ghosted the Judge Parker comic strip for a month in late 2007 and again in February 2010. John's biggest influences are Jack Kirby, Alex Raymond, Frank Robbins, Wally Wood and Neal Adams.

'TEXTURE AND CONFIDENCE IN INKING' BY JOHN HEEBINK

In inked art the term 'formal qualities' refers to the interaction of black, white, textures and pattern, in service of the overall composition. A fellow art teacher, I think his name was Jeff, told me a few years ago that he always preached 'variety and unity' to his students.

Jeff was teaching graphic design, but it's a perfect description of the paradoxical-sounding – but totally harmonious – goals of comic book page design. For example, nothing brings deadly monotony to a page quicker than drawing all the objects about the same size. But nothing dispels monotony quicker than a little variety. Varying the sizes and crops of faces and figures on a page, in and of itself, actually ties the total page together, I would contend. Unity through variety, if you will.

Texture as unifying variety

By the same token, texture can add unifying variety to a page. I'll propose a radical and only slightly absurd definition of a comic book page:

'A composition that uses formal qualities to guide the reader's eye through a series of story moments.'

We've all had experience looking at a comic book page and thinking that there wasn't enough on it to hold our interest. A stark, too 'open' art style, a lack of black, texture and line-weight variation, and pretty soon you've got a washed-out-looking page that appears to be less than the sum of its parts.

At the other end of the scale are pages where everything is competing for our attention. No part is played down relative to the others; everything is turned up to ten.

Both extremes represent failure to use the formal qualities of a page to guide the eye to the parts of the image that matter: those that tell the story.

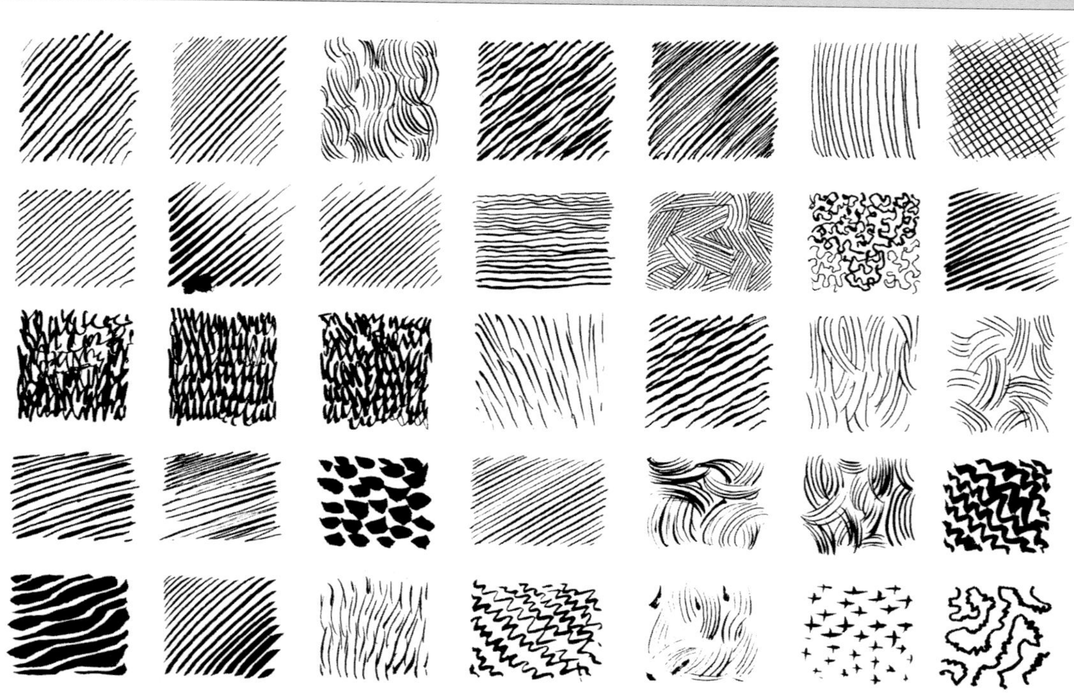

CATALOGUE OF TEXTURES

Before you ink your pencilled art, ink first using warm-ups for practice creating a variety of lines and texture. Experiment and catalogue what textures work best for different types of clothing, buildings, metal, wood, rocks, etc.

Al Williamson

The absolute master of textures and formal qualities was the late Al Williamson, best known for his Star Wars work (***http://en.wikipedia.org/wiki/Al_Williamson***). He had a way, for instance, of doing what we could call 'organic patterning' that I have never seen in another artist. The brush strokes he uses are deft and non-repetitive, full of variety and yet not random. They are given a semi-consistent directionality that hugs and describes the forms in the foreground object. The brush strokes become heavier as the surface rounds away from the light, and that adds a sense of physical solidity.

The coordination of parts in an average Williamson page is positively symphonic. And like a symphony, hierarchical. His pages had to be so, because they were often quite complex, with several textures or patterns in many of the panels. He simply had no rivals in his control of the page's formal qualities in relation to design and storytelling.

Warming up for inking

Never dive into inking a page cold. As much as those sexy lines you pencilled are screaming 'Ink me' at you, you must warm up first. The best way I know is to quickly pencil a series of boxes on scrap Bristol, each an inch or two square, and fill each with a distinctive texture or pattern, whatever comes to mind.

Warming up in the way I'm suggesting is a no-stakes way of putting yourself in touch with what your brush or pen can do. You playfully explore the range of marks you can make. This is a perfect setup for plunging into actual inking with the mixture of gusto, confidence, fearlessness and control that marks a great inker. Plus, if your tools and you aren't in synch on a given day, you don't want to figure that out two hours into your splash page!

Getting to grips with texture

Even if you're not ready to juxtapose patterns and textures and black in a dazzling Williamsonian fashion, that doesn't mean texture is no help to you. Minimal textural indications can add great character and immediacy to a page, even if you're not so terribly analytical about it. Look how just a few classic Marvel 'dit-dits' in an open area turn it from a meaningless void into a physically present thing.

To go beyond this, to develop a range of characteristic marks for different materials – sandstone, glass, fabric, foliage, skin, hair, etc. – is to be on your way to becoming a terrific inker. And filling those little boxes with texture to warm up, can, I promise you, really help.

Pen textures are the easiest to replicate, but, with a little practice copying, you should be able to develop a repertoire of textures that can add variety, unity, character and specificity to your work, with pen and brush.

Other tools and techniques that can add a multimedia effect that makes the page even more interesting to look at include screentones – most available now from manga art suppliers – ink spatter (with a toothbrush), painted-on or spattered white ink, stipple (pen dots), grease pencil, dry brush, electric eraser, razor blade and so on. Keep an eye out for arresting effects to emulate.

BRUSH VS PEN

The brush and the crowquill pen each have subtleties that can make the slightest difference in your work. Both images were inked with both tools, but the image on the right has some additional marks in the background to give it a slightly more kinetic look.

BRIEF HISTORY OF COLOURING

The way comic books are coloured has evolved over the years to keep pace with technology. Now most artists scan their black-and-white line drawings and then add colour using Photoshop. However colour is applied, though, there are some basic rules.

THE YELLOW KID

Richard Felton Outcault was an American comic strip writer-artist. He was the creator of the series **The Yellow Kid** *and considered the inventor of the modern comic strip.*

Before there were comic books and graphic novels, there were comic strips. In 1892, James Swinnerton published the first newspaper comic strip ever, called 'The Little Bears and Tigers', in the ***San Francisco Examiner***. The first successful comic series, though, was Richard Outcault's 'Down in Hogan's Alley', which debuted on July 7, 1895, in Joseph Pulitzer's ***New York World*** as a single picture of life in an urban slum. Its central character was 'The Yellow Kid', a bald, impish tyke with a knowing grin.

Between 1895 and 1905 the comic strip coalesced as a new art form and newspaper feature. The gradual improvement of colour presses throughout the 1890s led publishers, in their frantic circulation wars, to introduce colour supplements to their Sunday papers. Only the doggedly serious ***New York Journal*** refrained from adding comics. In order to meet the demand from readers, most papers reprinted art from humorous magazines such as ***Puck*** and ***Life***. Some political cartoonists began to draw weekly

features, but most of the strip artists came to the new form directly.

Up until the late 1980s, most comic book colouring was produced the way it began since the turn of the century; the artist illustrated the comic in pen and ink before turning the pages over to the printer and supplying them with a colour guide to follow for printing. These colour guides were comprised of simple colour comps, sketches, hand-coloured photostats or photocopies of the black-and-white line art. The printer would then, in turn, produce engraving plates comprised of four colours: magenta, cyan, yellow and black. The combination of the plates and screens would produce a limited colour palette, but have numerous variations of overlapping screens to produce new colours and effects, such as the density of the dots.

Colouring methods changed with the introduction of Adobe Photoshop in the early 1990s. Technology developed new desktop publishing methods for colourists to use and is considered the industry standard today. The finished line art is scanned into a computer and saved as a digital file ready for the colourist.

KEY COLOURS

Comics were known for their newsprint paper quality; light, tan-coloured paper with flat colours, finely printed dots that made up the limited colour palette. Paper quality improved by the mid-1980s when a brighter white paper was being used by the publishers.

XENOZOIC TALES

Mark Schultz's creator-owned comic book series, **Xenozoic Tales,** *is about a post-apocalyptic world where dinosaurs and other prehistoric creatures coexist with humans. Schultz's artwork evokes the style of illustrators and comics artists of an earlier age. Colouring by Jim and Ruth Keegan.*

PRINT BASICS: CYMK

All the colours that you see on the printed comic book page are comprised of three primary colours - red, yellow and blue - or in printers' terms: magenta, yellow and cyan. In the four-colour process (often referred to as CMYK), full-colour artwork is electronically separated into an image composed of cyan (C), magenta (M), yellow (Y) and black (K, for 'key black') dots. Using this method, millions of hues become available using only four inks.

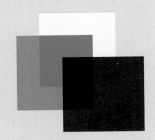

Combining cyan, magenta and yellow gives black

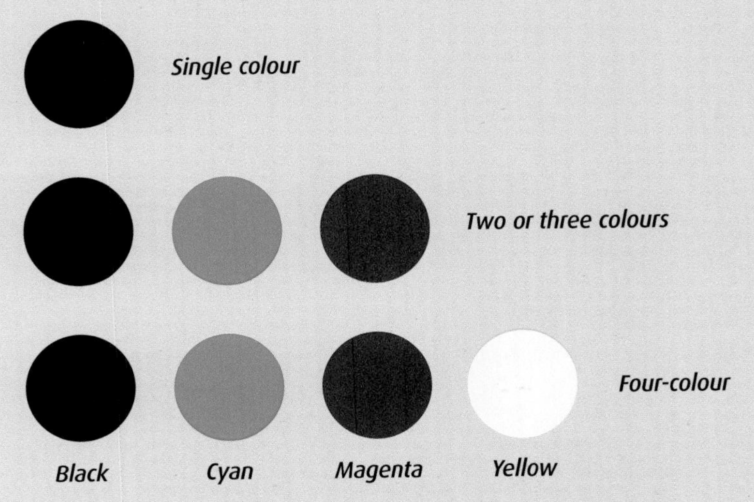

PRINCIPLES OF COLOUR

Colouring comic books is not about being a computer technician, it's about understanding the ideals and principles of being an artist and using the computer as a tool with which to apply this knowledge.

To be a good colourist of your own work or someone else's, you need to understand the foundations of colour and the principles of lighting. Colouring comics is storytelling; learning how to apply colour as a narrative will help you to undestand colour theory and the colour wheel. Familiarise yourself with these concepts before applying the techniques.

Lighting is an important key to good colouring. Plan first where your light source originates from (whether it's natural or artificial light) in the scene you're colouring to help establish mood, a focal point or a central character in action.

Choosing the colour temperature in a scene can adversely affect how storytelling interprets your story. A little restraint goes a long way when applying colour to comics and graphic novels. Colouring comics should complement the work drawn by you or another artist and not conflict or distract a reader from the narrative flow of the story.

COLOUR AND NARRATIVE

Storytelling is your first priority as a colourist. The colouring needs to add impact to the story, support the narrative and keep the reader focused on what's important from panel to panel.

COLOUR THEORY AND THE COLOUR WHEEL

The colour wheel is a vital tool for any colourist in order to understand colour combinations that work well and tell a story.

Primary colours: Red, blue and yellow; all colours originate from these three for colouring comics.

Secondary colours: Green, orange and violet result from mixing pairs of primary colours.
Blue + Yellow = Green
Red + Yellow = Orange
Red + Blue = Violet

Complementary colours: These are pairs of contrasting colours that sit opposite each other on the colour wheel.

Analogous colours: Colours that are adjacent to each other on the colour wheel.

Saturated colours: 'Saturation' refers to the dominance of the hue in the colour. The colours towards the centre of the wheel, where black has been added, are called shades and are considered dull.

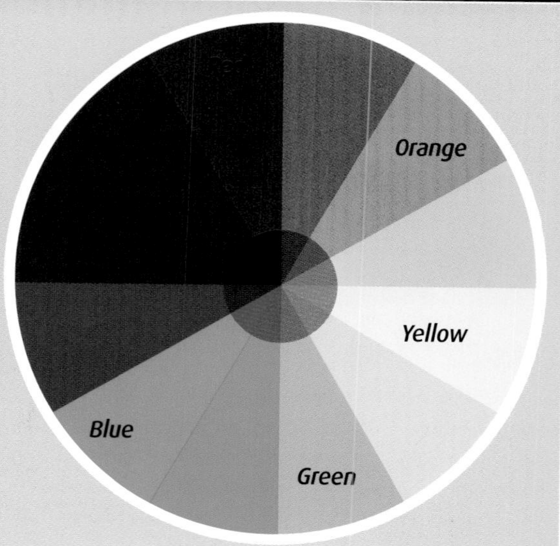

LIGHTING: THE DEPTH OF ILLUSION

Local colour is the actual colour of an object. The grass is green, a banana is yellow and your villain loves to wear red. If you're changing the values of your object, consider using their local colours first. Use local colour when your subject or object is in average light. Use warm colours to highlight the light hitting off your subject, cool colours for shading. Keep in mind where your light source is in each scene, and render light and shadows accordingly.

LIGHTING AND WARMTH

Here, very subtle warm colours are used where light hits an object (the woman on the phone). The colours can be very restrained as so much of the image is taken up by shade, shown in cool colours.

SELECTING COLOURS

Choosing the most effective colours hinges on how they'll add to or impact the story you're telling. Keep in mind that warm colours (like red and orange) advance to the foreground, while cool colours (like blues and greens) recede to the background when placed against a warmer colour.

Advance *Advance*

Recede *Recede*

COLOUR TEMPERATURE

How you choose warm or cool colours depends on the type of emotional reaction you're looking for from the reader.

COOL COLOURS

Cool colours (blues, violets and greens) create a more subdued, quieter and moodier scene. The conversation between these two people (right) needs only cool colours since the action of their exchange is low key.

WARM COLOURS

Reds, yellows and oranges create excitement during a dramatic scene involving tension, action or conflict, like the scene of the woman's fury using an uzi during a gun battle (left).

DIGITAL COLOURING

whether you're colouring comics traditionally by hand or using a computer to digitally colour comics, the most important aspect of colouring is storytelling.

Before you begin colouring, you should read the entire story first. Plot out the scenes thematically using colour as they change throughout the story. For example, when the script calls for a cold and rainy afternoon, you'll know not to use warm colours for this particular scene.

Preparation is key for laying the groundwork of the story before using all the tools Photoshop (what the Pros use) or Corel Painter have to offer. Colour with restraint; just because you have all these cool filters, special effects, gradients and other visual tricks doesn't mean you have to use them all. Read the story, get a feel for what's going on with the characters, the action and the overall mood when you're colouring.

1 CREATING A NEW LAYER

Using the 'Layers' palette in Photoshop, duplicate the background layer by dragging it to the 'Create a new layer' icon. Rename the new layer line art and delete the original background layer.

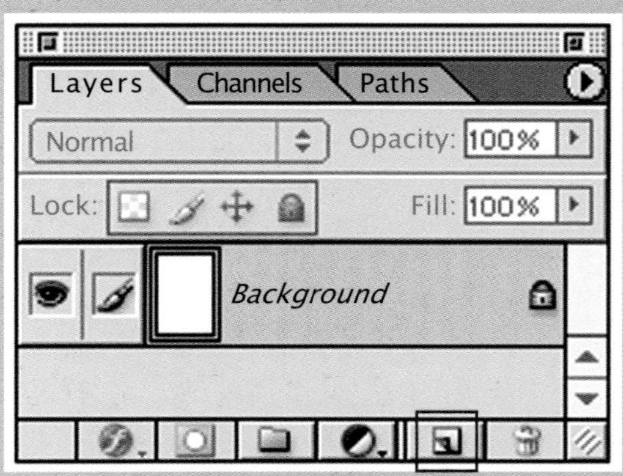

» Comics are printed in CMYK colour (cyan, magenta, yellow, black), so it makes sense to work digitally in CMYK. However, some Photoshop filters, like 'Lens flare' and 'Ocean ripple', are only available in RGB mode (red, green, blue), so you could work in RGB and then convert to CMYK at the end. Be aware that the colours will change subtly when you convert, though.

2 CREATING A TRANSPARENT BACKGROUND

Switch to the 'Channels' tab and click on the 'Load channel as selection' icon. This selects the white background. Press the 'Delete' key so that all the white disappears, leaving a transparent background.

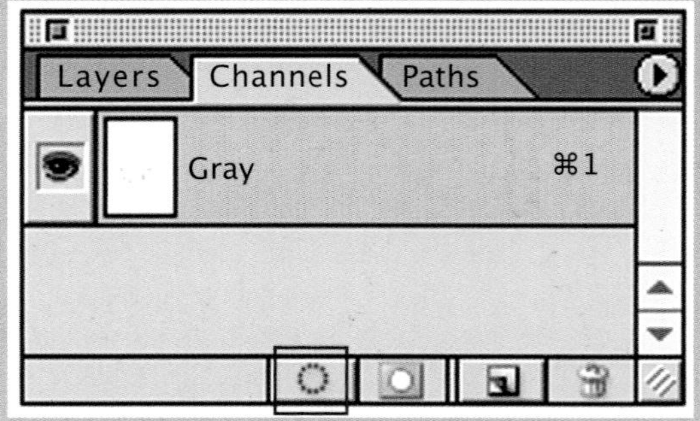

LAYERS AND SELECTIONS

Most drawing, painting and photo-editing programs allow you to select particular areas of an image and experiment with different effects by using layers.

Layers: Layers can be visualised as pieces of transparent film stacked on top of one another. When you make a drawing or scan in an artwork, it appears as a background layer called the canvas. If you create a new layer on top of this, you can work on it without altering the underlying image because layers are independent of each other; similarly, you can work on the canvas without affecting any images on other layers. By organising the linework and different colours onto separate layers, you can make amendments more easily later on.

Selections: To colour a particular area of your artwork, you first need to select it. There are a number of tools for selecting various parts of the image, all of which are found in the toolbar. The 'Marquee' tool is useful for simple geometric shapes, the 'Lasso' tool for drawing around chosen areas and the 'Magic wand' for selecting areas where the colour or tone is distinct.

3 REINFORCING THE LINE ART

Switch back to the 'Layers' tab and then choose 'Inverse' from the 'Select' menu. Make sure the foreground colour is set to black, then choose 'Fill' from the 'Edit' menu. This reinforces the black linework with solid black. Choose 'Mode' from the 'Image' menu and select CYMK to convert the image from grayscale.

4 LOCKING THE LAYER

Now click on the 'Padlock' icon in the 'Layers' palette to lock the line art so that no more changes can be made to it. Then create a new layer beneath the line art layer called white background and fill it with white. This is so that you can see the colours as you put them down.

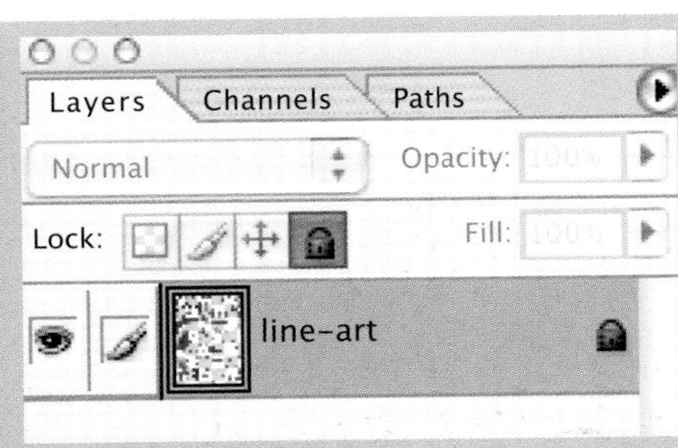

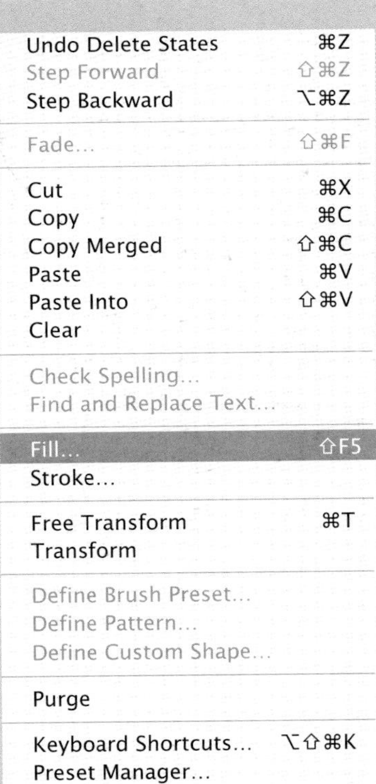

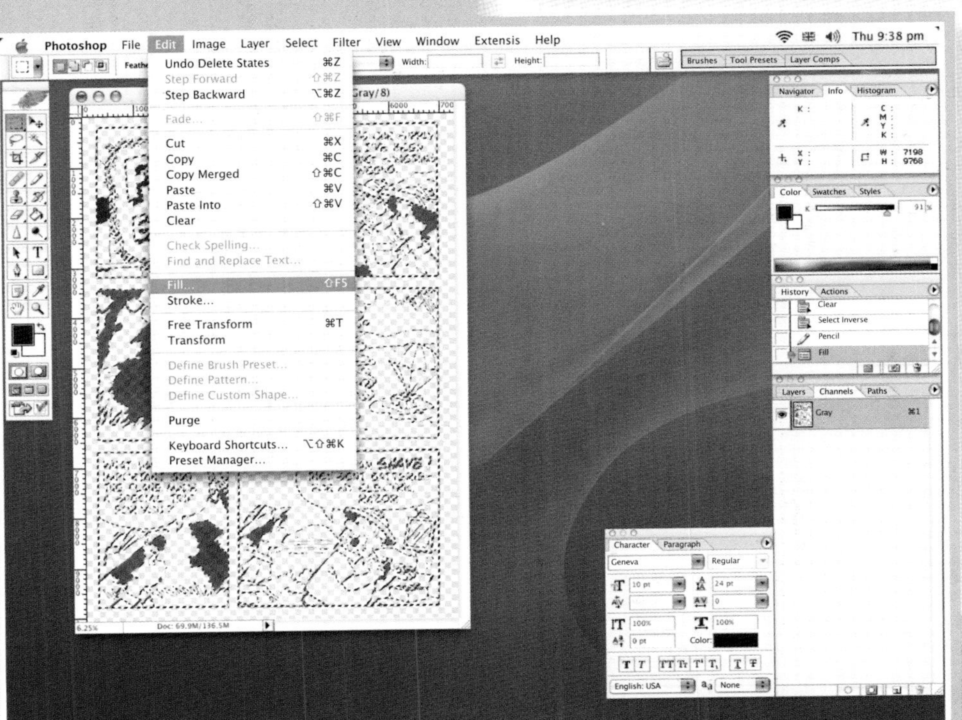

CONTINUES OVER THE PAGE »

Laying down colour

Now that your line art is ready to receive colour, you should start by laying down flat colours and grouping each colour or each type of item together on separate layers. This will help when it comes to touching in bits of colour you have missed at the end of the process.

LAYING DOWN SKIN TONES

Let's start by laying down the basic skin tones. Create a new layer in the 'Layer' palette and name it skin (skin colour is C1 M11 Y25 K0, but you might prefer a slightly different tone). The quickest way is to select the line art layer, then use the 'Magic wand' tool to select an area you want to flood with the base colour.

EXPANDING THE SELECTED AREA

Now choose 'Modify' from the 'Select' menu and go to 'Expand' in the side menu. In the dialogue box set the 'Expand By' value to 4 pixels and click 'OK'. This expands the flooded area so that the edges are slightly under the black linework. If necessary, redo with a slightly larger 'Expand By' value. If you still have pale fringing between the black line and the colour, you might need to clean up the edges of the black line with the 'Eraser' tool.

Select Filter View Window Extensis

All ⌘A
Deselect ⌘D
Reselect ⇧⌘D
Inverse ⇧⌘I
Color Range...
Feather... ⌥⌘D
Modify ▶ Border... Smooth... Expand... Contract...
Grow
Similar
Transform Selection
Load Selection...
Save Selection...

'S OUR SUPPL
. I'VE BEEN

Expand Selection

Expand By: 12 pixels

OK

Cancel

USING THE PAINT BUCKET

Now click on the skin layer and use the 'Paint bucket' tool to flood the area with skin colour. Then just repeat the process with the various areas of the artwork until you have the whole page blocked out with basic colour fills.

SELECTING COLOURS

You can either select colours from a palette or create new 'custom' colours in Photoshop. There are three ways to do this: selecting from a standard or personalised grid of colour swatches; mixing colours using sliders or by specifying the CMYK values (that is, percentages of cyan, magenta, yellow and black); or picking from a rainbow colour bar. It is also very easy to match a colour in your work by clicking on the 'Picker' tool, and then clicking on the colour you wish to match.

Finishing touches

When you have added flat colour to all the areas, you need to double-check your work and then add a few finishing touches.

Retouching

Click off the line art layer to see if you have missed any areas or little spots. If you need to touch up any areas you have missed, make sure you do the retouching on the right layer.

Highlights and shadows

The next thing to do is to add highlights and shadows to give the finished art more of a 3D feel. The best way to do this is to create a new layer above the layer you are planning to place highlights on. So, to add highlights and shadows to the skin layer, create a new layer positioned above the skin layer. Call it skin tones. With the new layer selected, use the 'Airbrush' tool to add highlights and shadows as needed.

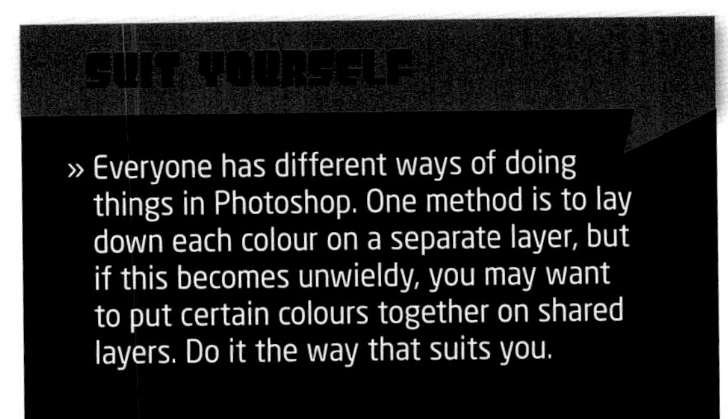

SUIT YOURSELF

» Everyone has different ways of doing things in Photoshop. One method is to lay down each colour on a separate layer, but if this becomes unwieldy, you may want to put certain colours together on shared layers. Do it the way that suits you.

FINAL COLOURED ARTWORK

Once the flat colour work is complete, make any finishing touches you require and ensure that the line art layer is on top of the colour layers.

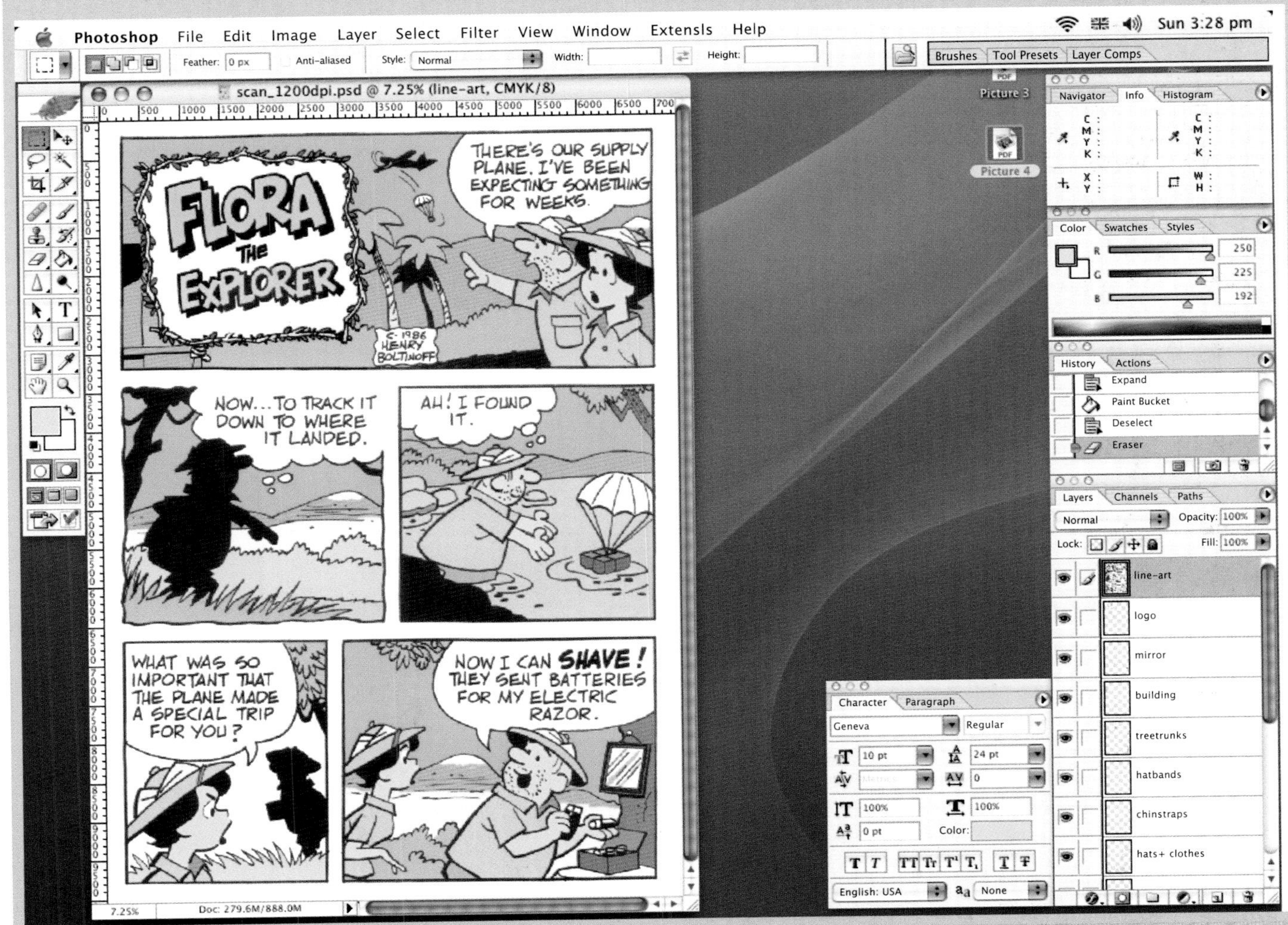

GETTING STARTED WITH HAND LETTERING

Once you've pencilled and inked your story (and, for some of you, coloured it as well), then comes the task of lettering your work.

Before the use of computers spread in the early 1990s, all lettering for comic books, newspaper strips and graphic novels was done by hand. By the early 1990s, lettering was being created on the computer, printed out and pasted onto the comic artwork. As colouring comic books on the computer became the standard, so did lettering comics. Photoshop and Illustrator replaced physically pasting up printed lettering with a more streamlined approach, using digital art files to add lettering.

In this section, you're going to find out how comic books were lettered using the hands-on approach, before moving onto digital lettering. Many of the principles are exactly the same.

TOOLS AND MATERIALS

Some of the most important tools you'll need for lettering by hand are the Ames lettering guide, pencil (standard and mechanical), ellipse/circle templates, an eraser (putty or plastic), pens and ink. You should use a variety of pens for lettering: technical drawing pens and dip (nib) pens. Make sure you have room for a T-square, paper, jars of water (for cleaning your pen nib) and drafting tape around your work area.

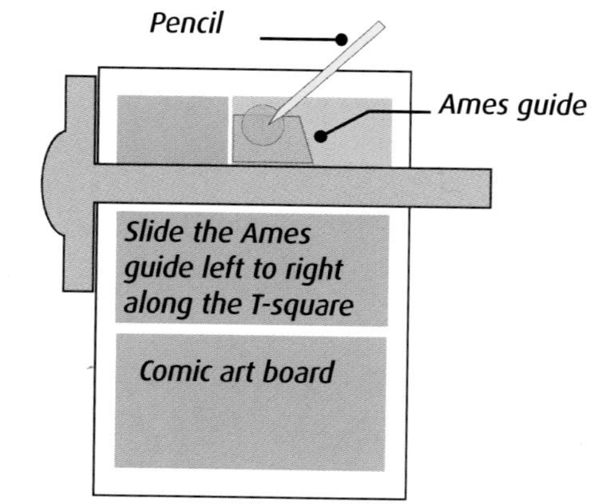

AMES LETTERING GUIDE

The Ames lettering guide is the lettering guide tool for comic book lettering. Set your Ames guide to between 3 and 4, the standard size for lettering comics.

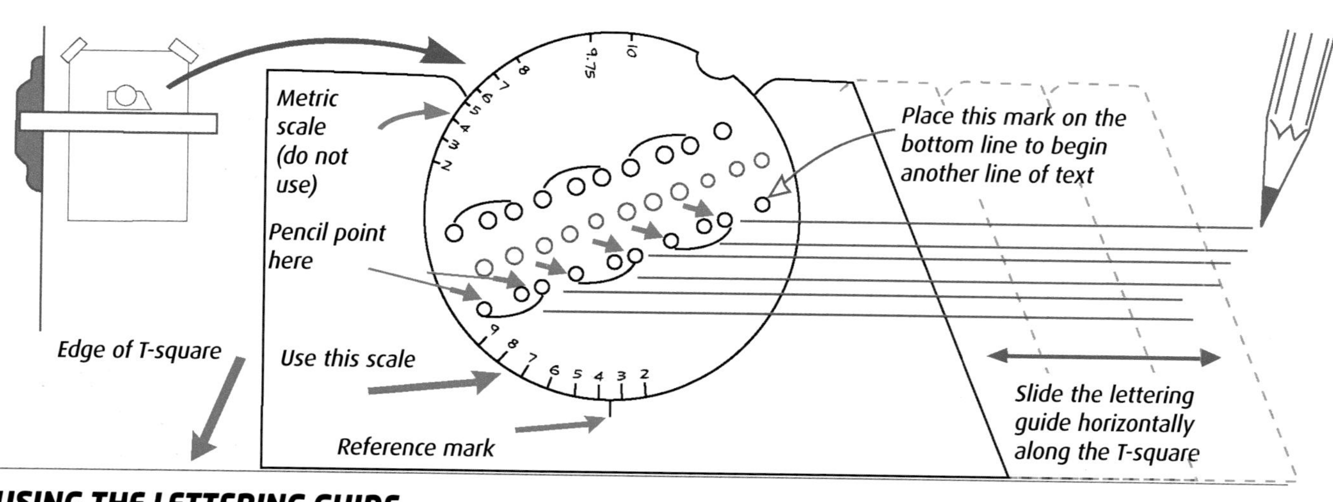

USING THE LETTERING GUIDE

Set up your artboard, T-square and lettering guide as shown above. Set the wheel between 3 and 4; this is the standard size for comic book lettering. Place your pencil point in one of the holes marked and hold the T-square with one hand while you slide the lettering guide across the artboard with your pencil point with the other hand. Repeat with each hole and you will have the guidelines for three rows of letters. If you need additional lines of text, simply place the hole as seen above on the last guideline. Start with the first hole of the set and move across. It's that easy! Wash, rinse and repeat.

T-SQUARE
An 45-cm (18-inch) T-square is perfect for comics. It is a necessity not only for lettering comics, but for perspective as well.

TECHNICAL PEN
The technical pen will require more maintenance than any other tool you'll use for inking or lettering comics, and can be expensive.

ERASER
There is a variety of erasers to choose from for lettering comics; start with a putty eraser or a plastic eraser.

INK
Any brand of ink will do – Higgins, Pelican, Speedball Superblack – what it comes down to is: what works best for you?

PIGMA MARKERS
The Sakura Pigma Micron marker can be used for thicker line widths such as size 08. Fine details may be inked using the pens with 05, 03 and 02 line widths for lettering. These markers are waterproof, disposable and offer an alternative to nib and technical pens for lettering.

TECHNICAL PENCIL
A 0.3-mm or 0.5-mm technical pencil will work best for drawing the guidelines using the Ames lettering guide.

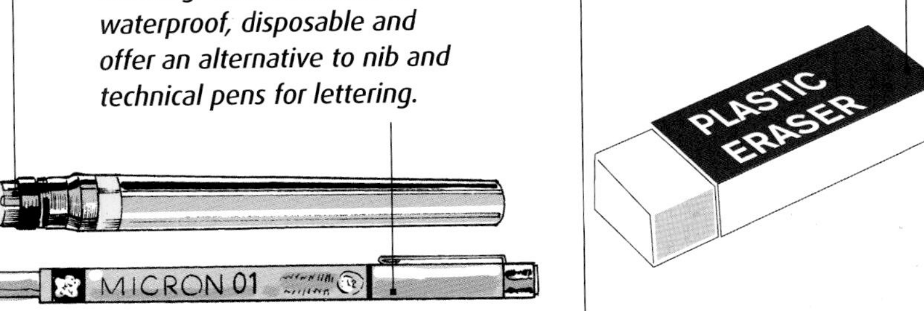

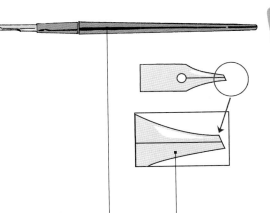

DIP PEN POINTS
For regular lettering try a SPEEDBALL C-6 wedge-shaped point, and a B-6 round point for bold letters. You might prefer the HUNT #107 wedge-shaped point, which requires a smaller pen holder for lettering.

SANDPAPER
If you study comic books before 1990, you'll notice that the letters have different line thicknesses in their vertical and horizontal strokes. You can achieve this classic style of lettering using fine grit sandpaper to file down the tips of your pen nibs. File at an angle as shown in the illustration.

CIRCLE/ELLIPSE TEMPLATES
Use circle or ellipse templates for drawing word balloons.

FRENCH CURVES
Use French curves for drawing balloon tails.

CONTINUES OVER THE PAGE »

Hand-lettering text and balloons

1 SETTING UP
Make sure you have a good drafting table to work on. Take your T-square and line it up on the left or right (whichever works for you), then place your Ames guide along the T-square and use your technical pencil to draw up your guides.Then sketch out the balloon shape. On your comic book art board, your pencil lines should look like this.

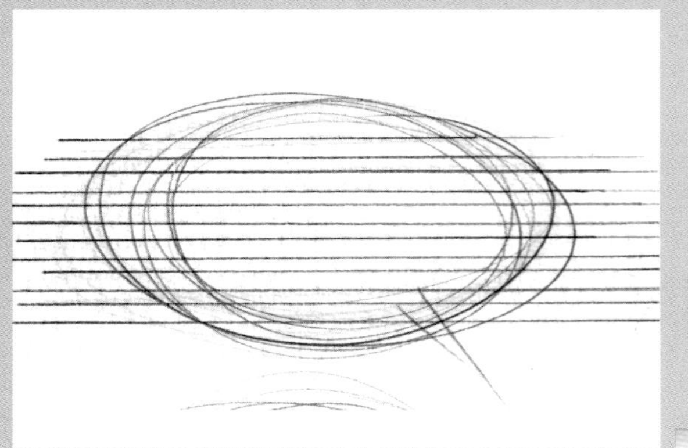

2 LAYING OUT THE DIALOGUE
Use your pencil to lightly lay out the dialogue. It's wise to do this and fix any mistakes before inking your work. Use your elliptical template to refine the sketched word balloon and the French curves for the balloon tail.

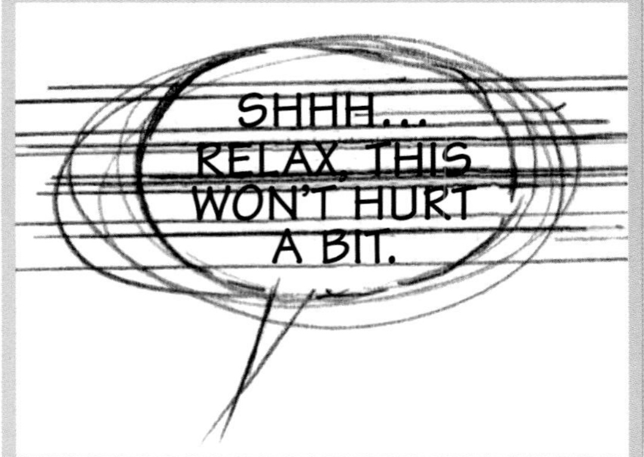

LETTERING CONVENTIONS

Legibility is the prime consideration when hand lettering, and there are some simple guidelines you can follow to ensure that you get it right.

ROUND TOPS

Letters with round tops – C, G, O, Q and S, for example – should hang on the upper guideline.

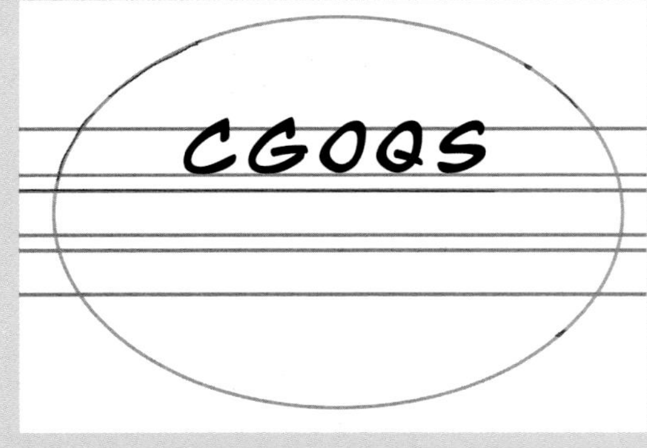

HORIZONTAL STROKES

Letters that contain horizontal strokes – A, E, F, G, H, L, T and Z – are drawn so that the horizontal strokes rise from left to right.

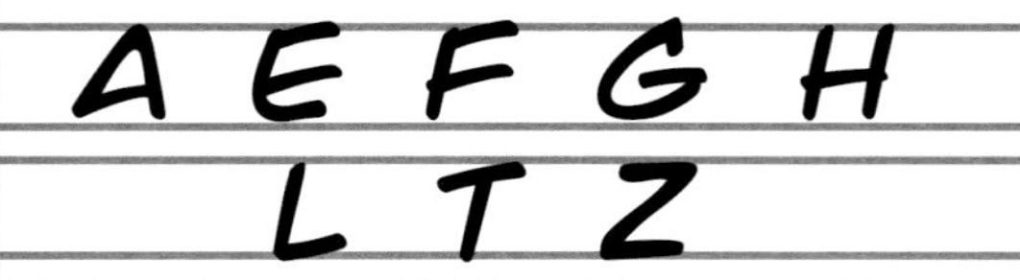

PECULIARITIES

The remaining letters in the alphabet likewise have their little peculiarities when hand-lettered.

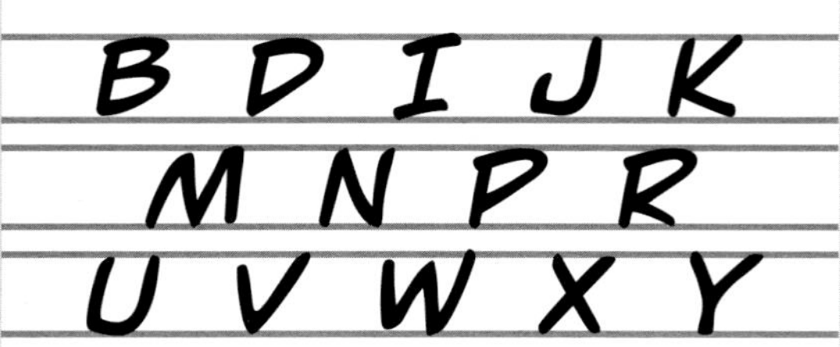

The ascenders and descenders of lowercase letters can interfere with one another.

3 INKING THE BALLOON

Use your technical pen to ink your balloon and tail using the same templates that you used with the pencil. Use different pens for regular and italic dialogue, and for bold lettering.

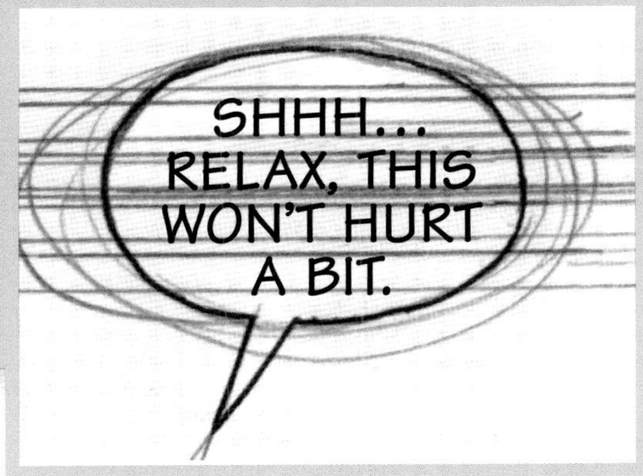

4 THE FINISHED BALLOON

Your finished word balloon should look something like this. Once you've finished the inking, take your eraser and clean up all the pencil lines before scanning your work. All it takes is practice to refine these steps and you'll discover your own style for lettering comic books by hand. The finished result is never perfect, but it gives that 'personal touch' that you can't recreate on a computer.

LOWERCASE

In general, lowercase letters are avoided because the descenders – the tails of the g, j, p, q and y – tend to clash with the ascenders of the b, d, f, h, l and t.

gypja
dfhdbhlt

The letter 'd' has an ascender above the main body of the letter, while a 'g' has a descender below the main body of the letter. An 'a' has neither ascender nor descender.

Roman — *Roman type is the most common type style used.*

Italic — *Italic type adds emphasis or is used for narrative boxes.*

Bold — *Bold type is even more emphatic and is used for shouted dialogue.*

ROMAN VERSUS ITALIC VERSUS BOLD

Roman is the term used to describe 'upright' letters. Roman lettering is used for most speech balloon lettering. This is the easiest of all type styles to read. Italic is the name given to lettering that slopes to the right. Italic lettering is used in speech balloons to add emphasis, or in caption boxes to distinguish them from spoken dialogue. Bold is the name given to text drawn with heavier lines than either roman or italic. Bold is also used to add emphasis to speech balloons or to denote that dialogue is being shouted.

COMPUTER LETTERING

In this section, you'll be introduced to computer lettering using Adobe Illustrator. This is the industry standard software for lettering comic books and graphic novels. Artists now also create their own fonts using programs such as FontLab and Fontographer.

PAGE TWO
Panel One: Medium shot of blonde in the hat sitting in lounge chair gesturing with her right hand that she's had enough champagne, while the captain (leaning over the blonde) puts his right hand around her and attempts to pour more champagne.
CAPTAIN: Please, call me Panos.
BLONDE: Well, Panos…

Panel Two: Medium shot of blonde pushing the bottle away as the captain continues to impose on the woman.
BLONDE: Ease up on the bubbly… for now.
CAPTAIN: But I insist!

Panel Three: Close-up, low angle on the woman looking up at something catching her eye. She is holding her glass of champagne in the panel.
BLONDE: I'm sure you – why rush, when we've…
BLONDE: … got… all… what's he doing?

Panel Four: Pull back to reveal, in the foreground, the Captain's chef preparing the fish for the grill. The fish are on ice along with the cutting tools with the blonde now sitting up looking in the chef's direction. The Captain backs off a bit.
CAPTAIN: My chef?
BLONDE: Wait!

Panel Five: Same shot, only the blonde is now walking towards the chef with the captain following. The chef has his hands on one of the fish and is looking down at it.

Two important programs for digital lettering are Microsoft Word and Adobe Illustrator. Some professionals may use Photoshop over Illustrator, and that's okay, but most use Illustrator (including me) for lettering their comics. The three tools most commonly used in Illustrator for lettering are the ellipse, pen and text tool. Each tool has a specific task to help you create the word balloon, the speaking tail and dialogue for your comic or graphic novel.

1 USING THE SCRIPT
Writers will compose their scripts using a word processing program such as Microsoft Word. The example here was written in Word and then copied and pasted next to the page to be lettered in Adobe Illustrator.

VALENTINE

The artwork being used here is from the assassin series **Valentine***, written and illustrated by Daniel Cooney with colouring by Steve Buccellato.*

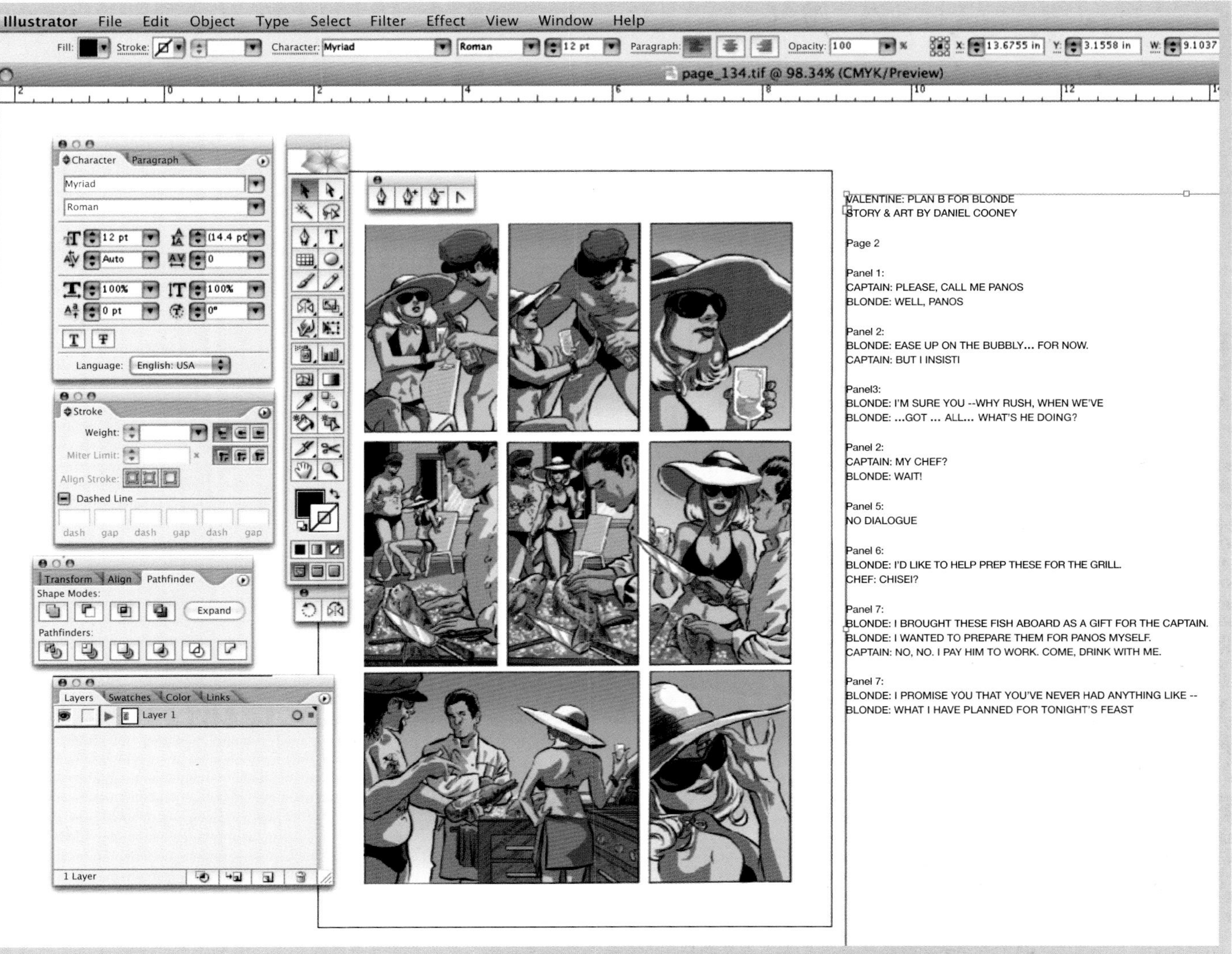

2 SETTING UP THE PAGE

As you can see, this is the setup for lettering a comic book page in Illustrator. The script has been copied into a text box and placed on the right of the image. Notice that the art direction for each panel has been removed, leaving only the dialogue to be copied and pasted into the word balloons.

CONTINUES OVER THE PAGE »

3 STARTING THE BALLOON

Create a new layer and call it 'Balloons'. Next, click on the Ellipse tool in your palette and create a word balloon. Fill the balloon with white and give it a stroke weight of 0.75-1 point. If you want to resize the balloon, use the Selection tool and drag it over the balloon. A box will appear with anchor points that allow you to make the balloon taller, wider and customise it to the shape you want.

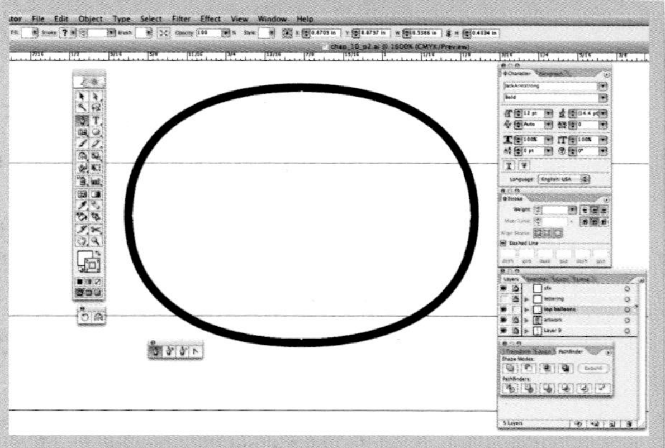

4 CREATING THE TAIL

Choose the Pen tool to create the balloon tail. Click once inside the balloon and drag the Pen tool slightly (this creates an anchor point for manipulation). Click it again for the point and back inside the balloon to complete the tail. You'll need to 'group' the balloon and tail so that it is one object. To do this, choose the Pathfinder tool. If you do not see the Pathfinder tool, go to Window > Pathfinder to reveal the palette. Select 'Add To Shape Area' to create one object. Next, choose the Selection tool and click and drag over both the balloon and the tail. This will reveal a selection box. The colour of the box is linked to the layer.

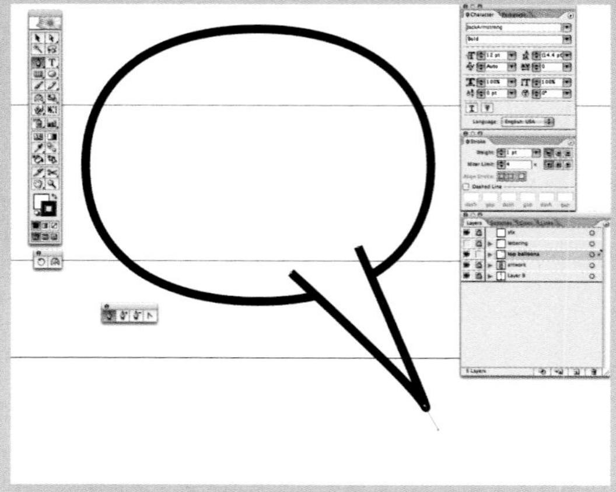

5 PLACING THE BALLOON

Move the balloon to the desired location in your comic art panel. To save time when creating additional balloons, select the balloon, then Copy > Paste. You can use the Direct Selection tool to alter the balloon tail by clicking on its anchor points. Repeat Step 2 to modify the balloon itself.

6 ADDING THE LETTERING

Create a new layer and name it 'Lettering'. Place it above the Balloons layer. Create a text box by selecting the Type tool. Choose a comic book font from your font palette. The recommended font size is 6.5-7 point. Copy the selected text from your script to the right of the artwork and paste into the text box. Once you've positioned it, choose the Paragraph tab in the Character palette to centre justify the type.

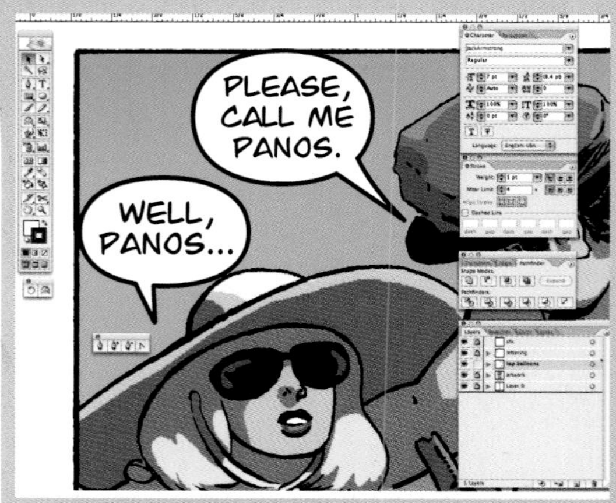

USING LAYERS

The image shown here had all the balloons created in one layer before the lettering step began. The lettering was then added to another layer to keep the process of lettering easier when selecting the balloon or the type for adjustment. The method used in this exercise is just one of many approaches to lettering comics. You may find through practice that another method is more suitable for your needs.

SOFTWARE TOOLS FOR CREATING BALLOONS AND LETTERING

These Illustrator tools are essential for creating word balloons, sound effects, title fonts and dialogue for your comic book or graphic novel. Learn to use them and you'll find how beneficial they are for a professional-looking lettering job.

Pen tool
Using the pen tool allows you to create the tails that attach to the word balloons.

Ellipse tool
The ellipse tool creates circles and ovals that can be manipulated in size and shape to complement the dialogue in word balloons.

The Direct Selection tool
The Direct Selection tool lets you select individual anchor points or path segments by clicking on them, or select an entire path or group by selecting any other spot on the item. You can also select one or more objects in a group of objects.

Type tool
The Type tool creates individual type and type containers and lets you enter and edit type.

Stroke palette
Use the Stroke palette to control whether a line is solid or dashed, the dash sequence if it is dashed, the stroke weight, the miter limit and the styles of line joins and line caps. To display this palette, choose Window > Stroke.

Pathfinder palette
Use the Pathfinder palette to combine objects into new shapes. To display the Pathfinder palette, choose Window > Pathfinder.
The top row of buttons in the palette, called Shape Modes, let you control the interaction between components of a compound shape. You can choose from the following shape modes:

- » Add To Shape Area adds the area of the component to the underlying geometry.
- » Subtract From Shape Area cuts out the area of the component from the underlying geometry.

Swatches palette
Swatches are named colours, tints, gradients and patterns.

ALL ABOUT BALLOONS

Once you've familiarised yourself with Illustrator, you'll begin to create all different types of balloons appropriate to your characters and the storyline. The examples shown here are just a few ideas to get you started.

TYPICAL BALLOON STYLES

Word balloons are recognisable by their oval shape with a tail pointing in the direction of the speaker. There are variations that reflect the qualities of a character to distinguish one from another when necessary.

Stacking word balloons works well when two people are having a conversation in the same panel. You can stack the balloons depending on your panel – portrait or landscape.

I STARTED TALKING FIRST, DO YOU MIND NOT INTERRUPTING?

NO, YOU DIDN'T. I WAS SPEAKING FIRST, YOU'RE JUST NOT LISTENING TO ME.

FINE. GO AHEAD AND FINISHED WHAT YOU STARTED

A WOBBLY BALLOON CAN BE USED FOR SOMEONE TOO WEAK TO SPEAK, DYING, OR FOR THE SUPERNATURAL.

A DOUBLE BALLOON WITH THICK LINES CAN BE USED FOR LOUD SPEECH.

The design of the word balloon has many facets in communicating characters' thoughts, speech or reactions; noises they create using a prop for sound effects; or shouting at the top of their lungs. You can design a word balloon into a sound effect, a narrative caption or someone whispering to another character. The possibilities are numerous as you can see from the examples in this section.

TOP TIPS FOR BALLOONS

Attaching balloons is a great way of giving space to your speech without overcrowding your word balloons. Consider the following when deciding how to break up your sentences:

- Giving your text space to 'breathe' in the balloon.
- Emphasising certain parts of speech.
- Giving pause, building suspense or slowing the pace down.
- Avoid having too many words in a balloon, or a balloon taking up too much space in the panel.

EVERY TIME... EVERY DAMN TIME I TRY TO REMEMBER, THE MIGRAINES...
...LIKE KNIVES... STABBING ME IN THE HEAD.

WHAT YOU GOT SHERIFF?
BANK of ALASKA
IT'S THE DAMNEDEST THING ATTICUS; MAN WALKS IN HERE IN BROAD DAYLIGHT, PULLS A GUN, SHOOTS THE GUARD, TAKES THE MONEY AND THEN JUST VANISHES INTO THE CROWD.
ON UNIT
ATION UNIT

CAPTIONS

Captions are rectangular boxes used for narration, internal thinking and a shift in time and/or place. Captions can be written as the writer's vehicle for omniscient viewpoints from first person to third person, past or present tense, and can be placed anywhere in the panel.

WORD BALLOONS

Word balloons are bordered shapes containing dialogue, usually with a tail that points to the speaker. Word balloons carry the dialogue. Their shape is oval or an ellipse drawn with a template. Word balloon shapes can vary, as can the length of their tails.

SILENT PANELS

Silent panels have no copy in them, but they can be just as powerful, if not more, than words in your story. A silent panel is indicated on a script with the words 'NO COPY' following the visual descriptions.

The outline of this balloon is broken into small dashes that indicate the character is whispering. Another way to indicate a whisper or a character speaking in a low voice is to reduce the size of the lettering or font.

THOUGHT BALLOONS

These uneven cloudlike shapes with bubble tails contain a character's unspoken thoughts.

SOUND EFFECTS

Stylised lettering is used to mimic the sounds of a POW!, SLAM!, KABOOM!, KRAK!, etc. Often, sound effects are overused in graphic novels, so use them sparingly and for more significant moments in storytelling.

ELECTRONIC TRANSMISSION

Word balloons from mobile phones, radios, televisions, computers or anything else along those lines, have a tail shaped like a lightning bolt. The balloon can be rectangular with jagged edges, or the font may have an electronic style for emphasis.

The standard comic book font is block capitals. Bold lettering is generally used to indicate speech rhythms (words that are emphasised in speech or narration). Italic lettering is used similarly to italics in prose writing, where words or phrases in foreign languages are usually lettered in italics. Oversized lettering is used if a character is shouting and you really want to emphasise it. If for any reason you want the lettering to be larger, be consistent in your story for the times you increase the font size.

CONTINUES OVER THE PAGE »

Balloon pointers

As a general rule, make sure the tail pointing to the speaker is generally aimed towards their mouth or head. Make sure you don't put the balloon tail too close to the speaker's mouth; this is just bad design.

Balloon placement

Whether you're lettering for a big publisher like Marvel or DC Comics, or for your own book, there are some general guidelines to follow for balloon placement on a page.

Keep in mind we read across from left to right, move down and back across to left and right again. This occurs inside each word or thought balloon, caption box, within the panel, and the entire page itself. The goal here is for the words and pictures to work together for clarity in storytelling.

Placement guidelines

- Keep in mind that large display lettering or sound effects may conflict with word balloons before your reader has had a chance to follow the sequence correctly. The emphasis should be on storytelling first, and entertaining the reader with splashy sound effects and visuals second.
- Make photocopies of the art pages and draw word balloons, captions and sound effects before lettering digitally. This will help with your word count per panel so that your images do not become overwhelmed with too many words.
- Balloons and captions shouldn't cover up your subject(s) or important aspects of the artwork.
- Don't cover hands and feet with word balloons.
- Never cover faces with word balloons. Sometimes you'll have to cover parts of the characters' heads or hair, and that's okay.
- Word balloons look best when they're spaced away from the speaker.
- Cramming balloons into a confined space with your subject is not a good idea. It confuses the reader and looks too busy.
- Don't squeeze balloons between two characters.
- Be consistent when placing balloons from one panel to the next. Keeping a visual rhythm adds a steady aesthetic for the reader following the sequence of events in your story.
- It's always best if a character on the left speaks first, if at all possible. Otherwise, you're forced to have your word balloon take up more space than necessary, resulting in covering up important elements of the panel.
- Good balloon placement only helps tell the story; bad balloon placement makes the story look unprofessional.

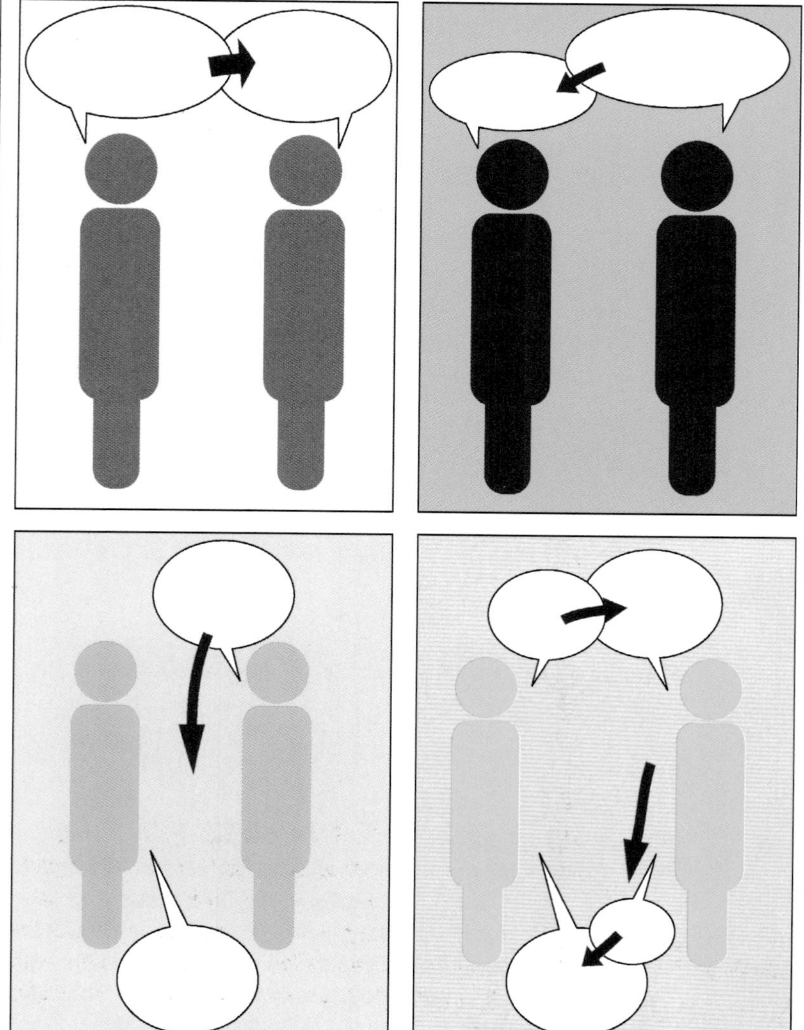

SPEAKING ORDER

The top two panels are examples of speaking order for balloon placement. The green panel (top right) depicts a reverse in reading order from right to left. This order works by having the balloon on the right higher and overlapping the left balloon that is lower, helping the reader in what to read first. The grey panel (bottom right) depicts two characters in a two-way conversation.

NARRATIVE FLOW: THE THEORY

This illustration shows a clear narrative flow helping the reader's eye to follow the balloons from one panel to the next. Word balloons should be read from left to right, then diagonally down to the left, across to the right and back to the left again.

NARRATIVE FLOW: THE PRACTICE

The finished page with the lettering now completed in the word balloons. Notice how some words are emphasised using italics and bold type. An electronic transmission word balloon is used to help the reader distinguish who's speaking on the phone throughout the page.

WHAT THE EXPERTS SAY

Nate Piekos graduated with a BA in Design from Rhode Island College. Since founding Blambot Comic Fonts & Lettering in 1999, he has lettered comics for Marvel, DC, Oni Press and Dark Horse, has become type designer to Harvey Award Winner Mike 'Madman' Allred, and has had his designs licensed by such companies as Microsoft, Six Flags Amusement Parks, ***New Yorker*** Magazine, The Gap and many more. His work has not only been utilised in comics, but on television and in feature films as well. He's been drawing fantasy heroes, giant monsters and buxom women since adolescence and now that he works in the comics industry full time, he can be less embarrassed about continuing the hobby as an adult. Nate lives in rural Rhode Island with his lovely wife.

It may be the last thing you think of, but the logo for your comic book is an important element of its identity.

This is true in all branding, of course, but in comic shops, where books can be stacked in overlapping bins, your comic's logo is often the first thing that a potential new reader sees – and it can't hurt to make it as striking as you possibly can. After all, nobody buys a comic without picking it up and flipping through it first. The goal of your logo (and the entirety of your cover) is to make sure they pick it up!

What it's not

First, let's talk about what a logo isn't. It's my opinion that there is a difference between a logo and a word or phrase typed out in an interesting font, however subtle that difference may be. A logo may start out as a word or phrase typed out in a font, but a good designer never lets it end there. Your logo should convey mood, and there are a million interesting and creative ways to make those letters unique. You are limited only by your imagination and your design ability.

Checklist

In college, I focused on corporate identity design. When I began working professionally in comics, I devised a checklist of requirements for successful logo design. The list was based on some of the lessons I'd learned in class and some of my personal experience. Here goes:

Is this design readable?
If you cannot convey in an instant what the logo says, it's poorly designed. One of my first corporate ID professors taught me to print out the logo at 15 cm (6 inches) wide, tape it to the wall and step back. If you can't read it from more than a few feet away, it's not a legible design.

Does it work in colour/black and white/grayscale?
Make sure you devise a black-and-white and a grayscale version as well as your colour version.

ATLAND
The ATLAND logo was designed with pencil and paper – no fonts were used. Once the design was roughed out, I scanned it into Illustrator and recreated the sketch as smooth, clean vector artwork.

ROBOT HEAD
Uses an icon as the main design element.

HUMAN
Designed to work in black and white.

Take your print needs into consideration. A good logo should work on a 6-m (20-foot) sign in glorious neon, and on a 13-mm (½-inch) phonebook ad in grayscale.

Will this design work on varied backgrounds?
Logos need to be readable on flat coloured backgrounds and busy cover background art. Try it on both, especially if you have action-packed covers. You never know if 10 or 20 issues from now you'll have some insanely detailed panorama that your logo must still be clearly seen on top of.

Will this work in print and on the web?
Print is fairly easy. Inkjet and laser printers have come a long way. You can simply print it out yourself and see. If you have some web space, make different-sized JPEGs, GIFs or PNGs and put them on a dummy index page to view in a few different browsers and on different monitors. This is especially important if you're working on a webcomic.

What colour considerations are there?
The best rule of thumb is this: CMYK is best for print, while RGB is best for the web. You'll want to have both versions. This goes hand in hand with the print test above. No two output devices will give you the same exact results. The best you can hope for is a close match to what you originally intended.

What's the hook?
As I said above, typing out two words with a font does not a logo make. It is text. It lacks a conceptual touch specific to your comic. A logo should have a cohesive, binding, unified sense of purpose to convey a message beyond what the text element tells you. It should convey a 'feeling' that reflects the comic's subject matter.

Is the hook successful?
Sure you know what the image is supposed to convey, but will others? Show other people. If they don't immediately seize on the hook ('Oh yeah, it looks like a pirate flag!'), then try again. This is the point where you need to divest yourself emotionally from the design. I know, you've been working hard on it, but when you show other people, you have to take their criticisms seriously. Furthermore, you have to know which suggestions are helpful and which are not. Only experience can teach you that.

ATOMIC PULP
A logo should work on dark backgrounds as well as light backgrounds.

Should the logo include an icon?
Logos can include icons. Think of the many publishers' marks you see in the top left corner of comic books. Many of them have some sort of recognisable symbol incorporated. Most of the time, I tend to say no to the question of icons in context of a book's logo – it's a slippery slope to go from recognisable icon to totally cheesy. If you do design a purely graphical element to the logo, ask yourself: Can the icon stand alone? Icons are meant to be instantly recognisable and maybe eventually come to be just as understood as their text component.

What materials should I use to design my logo?
We all love to talk shop about paper, ink and computers. But the truth of the matter is that, as you grow as an artist, you come to realise that materials are not the Holy Grail. I have no doubt that Jimi Hendrix could have picked up a $5 guitar at a yard sale and still dazzled an audience with it. The success of your design relies more on your skill, rather than what version of Adobe Illustrator you're using. For the record, I almost always start out doodling ideas on sketch paper. When I've got something I'm happy with, I scan it in and develop the idea to fruition in Adobe Illustrator or CorelDRAW using a Wacom Cintiq. I also use Photoshop and Fontlab quite a bit.

How can I get better at logo design?
It's the answer you don't want to hear: practice. Logos are all around you. You probably see hundreds in a day if not more. Train yourself to notice them. Mentally dissect the logos you see. What makes the good ones work? And I'm not talking about just comic books – comics are usually the last place I look for inspiration for comic logos. I have a huge library in my studio of logo design portfolios, design theory, calligraphy, graffiti, historical art, classic album covers, movie posters and wine labels. And if you're a little short on cash, your local library can come to your rescue.

RECOMMENDED READS

***How to Make Webcomics* by Scott Kurtz, Kris Straub, Dave Kellett and Brad Guigar**

This book covers the basics of what you have to know to get a webcomic up and running.

***How To Create Comics, from Script to Print* by Danny Fingeroth and Mike Manley**

Danny and Mike show step-by-step how to create a new comic from scratch: developing a new character, then going from script and roughs to pencils, inks, colours and even lettering. There's also a section that guides you through the process of getting your comic printed and distributed, and the finished eight-page full-colour comic is included, so you can see the final product.

***The DC Comics Guide to Digitally Drawing Comics* by Freddie E. Williams II**

Gain incredible superpowers... with the help of your computer! ***The DC Comics Guide to Digitally Drawing Comics*** shows how to give up pencil, pen and paper and start drawing dynamic, exciting comics art entirely on the computer. Author Freddie E. Williams II is a leader in digital pencilling and inking - and here, in clear, step-by-step directions, he guides readers through every part of the digital process, from turning on the computer to finishing a digital file of fully inked comic art, ready for print. Creating a template, sketching on the computer, pencilling, and finally inking digitally are all covered in depth, along with bold, timesaving shortcuts created by Williams, tested by years of trial and error.

***Panel One: Comic Book Scripts* by Top Writers**

For future writers and artists, or those who just want to see how it's done, here's a collection of comic book scripts from some of comicdom's top talents. See how Neil Gaiman writes a superhero story, how Marv Wolfman provides a plot for his artist to work from and how Jeff Smith draws a script for ***Rose***.

BREAKING IN

'If you want to break into comics it's easy. Do one, print it, and there you go. If you want a career in comics, do that 20 more times...'

Chris Eliopoulos, artist/writer/letterer ('Lockjaw and the Pet Avengers',

Pitching to a publisher

A good pitch and synopsis are the necessary tools for getting your comic book noticed by a publisher. So, where do you start?

What is a pitch?

A pitch is up front and urgent. If a synopsis is the story boiled down, a pitch is just an idea you're trying to sell. Watch the Robert Altman movie ***The Player*** to get a better idea of the concept of a pitch.

A graphic novel pitch has to be punchy. Not as long or as detailed as a synopsis, the pitch is intended to get the editor interested. It's the idea you're promoting, with a couple of scenes tossed in as examples. You don't need to include a complete story line or list of characters (just the main ones). Chances are, if an editor is keen, he or she will want you to make changes anyway.

The pitch obviously comes first. If you can interest an editor in your idea, then follow with the synopsis and sample script, including sample artwork if there's an artist on board already. The editor will want to read the synopsis for a fuller idea of the story, as well as look at the writing and artwork to get an idea of how the book will look and sound.

(a) This rushes straight in. The first question that leaps into your mind is 'Who's Maldoon?'

(b) The mention of the frozen bodies is out of place - it seems irrelevant.

(c) The whole pitch feels rushed and childish, with relevant plot points poorly explained.

(a) Government agents are keeping Maldoon prisoner.
(b) There are bodies frozen in suspended animation on the site. Maldoon believes he is a member of a group of superheroes, but the agents don't believe him. They claim he is delusional.
(c) Maldoon recounts his adventures for the doctor, but everything the doctor tells them is dismissed and explained away. The frozen bodies look like the characters in Maldoon's stories.

(a) This story is set in the world of black operations. It will be atmospheric (think X-Files), but with a harsh, cynical edge (like 100 Bullets).
(b) A young man named Maldoon is kept prisoner in a government-run facility. He claims to be part of a group of heroic adventurers, but his story is inconsistent.
(c) Yet, though a doctor constantly dismisses his claims, there are bodies – frozen in suspended animation – stored in the same facility.
(d) Bodies, in fact, that closely resemble the members of the group he describes in deliberately comic book-style flashbacks.
(e) It comes down to a simple question: Who is everyone? Nothing is as it seems. Everyone, in some form or another, is lying. Why?

(a) Opening with description of atmosphere.

(b) The main character is introduced quickly.

(c) The next major plot detail is introduced right away.

(d) This tells the editor the story is told in flashback.

(e) Don't explain the whole plot - just supply a taste. Intrigue the editor.

What is a synopsis?

A synopsis is the plot and story line of your graphic novel, usually boiled down to around no more than 1,000 words. In the synopsis you will introduce your characters, outline their motivations and describe how these characters interact. You will also need to give the ending, explaining how everything works out.

The good thing about a synopsis is that no one expects you to stick rigidly to it once the story's been accepted and commissioned. If you feel that it works better by changing a few elements, then fine. But don't depart too far from the original concept.

Remember that the synopsis is there to tell the editor exactly what the book is about. Rambling on – cutting back and forth as though something's just occurred to you – or sounding bored will mean the editor soon loses interest. Writing a synopsis can be harder than writing the real thing, mainly because you have to include all the key elements and explain the story in such a short space, not making it sound like it's been written by someone with a vocabulary of 50 words who still can't manage coherent writing. Take your time, and put in as much effort as you would over the script – no sense rushing everything at this stage.

SAMPLE SYNOPSIS

Here is a typical synopsis for the story we have been trying to pitch. The best way to present it is double-spaced on one side of the paper, with an adequate margin all around. Make sure the title and your name are clearly marked at the top. Most synopses will be more than one page - so have page numbers, name and title in the top right-hand corner on all sheets.

This story is set in the world of black operations. It will be atmospheric (think X-Files), but with a harsh, cynical edge (like 100 Bullets).

Mentioning that the doctor occasionally glances at the two-way mirror helps convey mood and atmosphere, which you want even for a synopsis.

The occasional piece of quoted speech can help speed up the synopsis, as well as show the commissioning editor how well you handle dialogue.

1 VIRTUALLY UNBREAKABLE: MIKE CHINN

SYNOPSIS: VIRTUALLY UNBREAKABLE
MIKE CHINN

A dark office; a scene reminiscent of many a psychiatrist's consulting room. It is almost black and white: deep shadows thrown by stark desk lighting; the doctor/interrogator in a black suit and tie, white shirt, the other in dark coveralls. The 'patient' is always in partial shadow, so his face is never clear (except at the end, when he turns out to be in his sixties, not the young character of the flashbacks at all). There's a long mirror across one wall – typical of the two-way style we're used to seeing in movies and on TV. The 'doctor' often glances at it surreptitiously.

The 'patient' calls himself Maldoon – a young agent with a Black Ops group. The doctor/interrogator is scathing, cynical. The atmosphere of the whole story is a cross between the TV series The Prisoner and The X-Files: the overall paranoia of the first, with the darkness and ambivalence of the second.

Using flashbacks to examples of Maldoon's 'adventures' (which are in gaudy prime colours – almost surreal), the interviewer gradually grinds away at his delusion. How is the interviewer expected to believe that four men can walk away from a plane crash, unhurt in any way – even down to a wristwatch? Why does Maldoon persist in claiming his fellow agents have such ludicrous names (Rex 'Red' Strong, Ace Merrill, Tiff Clayburn – or is that Clayburne?). Why can't he even be consistent in the obligatory female character: is she blonde or black-haired; is her name June Salieri or June Saunders?

And why – since Maldoon wasn't even in the crash to start with – is he suddenly a member when his 'brother' goes missing.

'Isn't it all a typical grandiose delusion?' the interviewer insists. 'First you're Jon Maldoon, the successful pop singer. But that isn't enough. You have to become second in command of a group of super agents. How come, since you're so famous, I've never heard of you? Or my kids? How can you insist – in the 21st century – that you're a major rock star when all you can perform is the kind of bland crap no one's heard since The Monkees!' Maldoon cannot answer any of these questions, and becomes increasingly agitated.

And all the while, there are frequent cuts to several people who seem to be looking through the mirror (later it turns out they are in Plexiglas 'coffins', and are simply gazing blindly through). All look identical to Jon Maldoon's friends – with two women, one blonde, one black-haired – but all are many years older than the ones from the 'adventures...'

CONTINUES OVER THE PAGE »

Dealing with rejection and next steps

Let's not try to be too unrealistic. The chances are that, first time, you'll get an outright rejection. That's not certain, of course. If you hit the market with an idea whose time has come, you'll make it overnight. But most overnight successes take years; you don't think Neil Gaiman's ***Sandman*** sprang fully formed into the world, do you? Neil worked his apprenticeship just like anyone else, writing short fiction, getting to know people, polishing his craft. In fact, Neil is quite an unusual genre writer in that he's conquered both the graphic and conventional novel fields.

If your life follows a less exalted path, you'll probably end up hawking your story to many publishers before one picks it up. If you're lucky, some may tell you why it is being rejected. However, don't ever ask for a detailed criticism of your work if it is rejected. Editors don't have that kind of time.

If the pitch sparks interest, you'll be asked for a synopsis and sample pages. If you've got artwork, submit copies that illustrate the sample script pages for comparison. The editor will want to see how well both artist and writer perform (how well the writer writes and how the artist interprets the words).

DOS AND DON'TS

The next consideration is how to submit the work...

» **DON'T** just turn up at a publisher's office and expect to be let in. Editors are busy and see no one without an appointment.

» **DO** double-space the lines, with a margin of at least 2.5 cm (1 inch) around the sides, top and bottom.

» **DON'T** write back and tell whoever rejected your manuscript that he or she is wrong.

» **DO** put your name and the work's title (in abbreviated form if it's a little on the long side) in the top right-hand corner, along with the page number.

» **DON'T** staple the pages. Editors don't get paid much and they live off the resale of paperclips - and they also quite like to separate pages.

» **DON'T** send original artwork. Not only is it expensive to mail art board, but you don't want to risk losing anything.

» **DON'T** email either script or artwork without checking first. Many editors are happy to receive emailed submissions - but check with them in advance to make sure it's okay.

» **DON'T** worry if you hear nothing for some time.

Artist's portfolios

Portfolios are what artists thrust under commissioning editors' noses and say 'This is what I do'. A portfolio is a catalogue of a body of work that editors can look at to see what the artist has done, is capable of and how his or her style has changed and matured over the years.

Writers have a harder job, since all they can do is hand over a bibliography or a few copies of comics they've scripted. If they're lucky, the editor will be familiar with the issues in question. Otherwise, the editor has to read through the copies and, in today's busy world, might not have the time.

Start your portfolio with your first sale, including copies of the original artwork and the finished comic book. If you want to keep copies of the books on your vanity shelf too, that's okay, but any copies you carry around are going to get worn. Stuff on the vanity shelf should be pristine - it's for gloating over, not reading.

Include material you haven't sold, too - as long as it's good stuff. Your portfolio is there to create an impression, so make sure it's a good one. You could also include studies that you've done, such as landscapes, to show editors you've got range.

Organising and presenting your artwork

A portfolio of your work as it grows and improves is essential. You can organise it by subject matter or chronologically (to show how you've improved). It's up to you. The main point is that you can show examples of your work in a tidy and professional manner. If you use a ring-binder portfolio, samples can be removed for passing around at meetings.

- Don't use too large a folder. Remember, you have to carry it, and editors don't want something the size of a table dropped on their desks.
- If the originals are large, get good-quality copies made: photocopies or scanned-in prints.
- Use separate, detachable wallets for each piece of work. These can be handed around easily, while being protected.
- Only show material you're happy with. If you include work that you're not sure about, the editor will pick up on it. You're there to sell yourself.
- Do present each page on a separate board or strong paper that you've mounted on board (but only at the corners).
- Don't leave too much white space at the edges. Excess white will simply be trimmed off

during reproduction. Because boards are expensive, not using as much as you can is wasteful.

• Do cover each board or sheet with clear layout or visualising paper. This not only protects both art and paper, but provides space for any special proofing requirements or sizing notes (either yours or your publisher's) to be written.

• Don't use different-sized boards – a carefully packed, uniform-sized package stands the best chance of surviving both the mail and publishers.

• Do write the title of the book and publisher on each board – in case the protection sheet gets lost. Also, add the page number (book page, not manuscript) and your name.

Contracts and Agents

When negotiating a contract, it pays to be careful. In other areas of art and writing the creators hire themselves an agent and let him or her do all the work. But in the comics' field, this method of working is rare. That's not to say there aren't agents for the field.

The alternative is to source a book that details an author's and artist's rights. ***Artist's Market*** or ***Writer's Market***, for example, include sections on rights, copyright and intellectual property – as well as lists of publishers and societies throughout the world. Or, if you want more detail, seek out a specialist title, such as ***The Rights of Authors, Artists, and Other Creative People*** (Norwick and Chasen) or ***The Internet and Authors' Rights*** (Pollaud-Dalian, ed.).

And, finally, there are artists' collectives, whose aim is to look out for the rights of comic book creators. They can be found on the web.

Copyright

Now we're approaching the sticky stuff – copyright. Who owns what, and for how long.

Copyright is something with which you're going to have to get acquainted. All published work is copyrighted – the very act of publishing is recognised as registering copyright for that particular work. The purpose of copyright is to prevent plagiarism – the theft of your work by someone who presents it as his or her own. Full-time writers and artists don't want to spend months over something just to have it stolen from under their noses. Sadly, all the copyright laws in existence still don't prevent it from happening.

Copyright exists on a work for the duration of the creator's life plus a specified term after death. In the United States and the European Union that presently stands at life plus 70 years.

You'll often see the term 'intellectual property' – this is the law covering copyright as well as patents and trademarks. To all intents and purposes 'intellectual property' can be considered your book or script and the Intellectual Property Law stands as Copyright Law.

When you make a sale, the ideal situation is to just sell first U.S. publication rights, or first foreign publication rights. This means that the company buys, from you, the right to publish – just once – your book. Your contract will determine how long the publisher retains the rights to your work (it could be for life, or it could be when the book goes out of print). It also covers whether you will receive a flat fee or advance against future royalties – royalties are an agreed percentage that you will receive from the book's sales, but the book has to earn back your advance first.

However, often you will find that publishers buy all rights. And this is just what it sounds like. Once you've signed on the dotted line, the book belongs to the publisher. The story and all characters contained within are now the intellectual property of the publisher. You get no royalties, and any movie sales go to the publisher. You may get the chance to write further adventures of your hero, except he won't be your hero any longer. Also, the publishers might want to develop him in ways you hate.

MAKE YOURSELF MEMORABLE

There are several ways that artists can present themselves and be remembered by commissioning editors.

» Try postcards with an example of your work on one side and your contact details on the other.
» Use your own personal logo on letters, business cards, invoices, compliments slips, postcards and fliers.
» Produce fliers or one-page ads.
» A website or blog can contain a gallery of your work, reproduced perfectly and almost cost-free.

SELF-PUBLISHING

Your story is done, or nearly completed, right? It's time to share it with the world, but those publishers just aren't buying it. Let's look at the alternatives of getting your story published.

ENTERING THE DIRECT MARKET

The direct market are the stores, primarily comic book shops, that buy comic books and graphic novels on a non-returnable basis. That means that once the store buys the book, the author gets to keep the money, even if the shop never sells it.

First, ask yourself which avenue for self-publishing your work is best for you.

DEALING WITH RETAILERS

Some retailers prefer only to order through Diamond Comic Distributors, the world's largest comic book distributor, while others will support their local creators and order directly from them. Generally, the breakdown is 50/50 and it's negotiable, but don't get greedy!

The upside of being your own boss is eliminating the middleman and getting more money in your pocket. The downside is more responsibility for making sure your books are well packaged and delivered on time. This is where you manage your time in making one trip to the post office for all of your orders to retailers rather than running to the post office every time you make a deal with a retailer.

The other downside is reducing the orders through Diamond. If you take enough business away from them, they may have second thoughts about continuing to solicit your books. Remember, comic book publishing is a business and companies want to make money.

Be consistent with your deals to retailers and treat the transaction agreement equally. You don't want to be playing favourites if word gets around, and it does!

There are a lot of advantages to dealing directly with local and regional retailers. You can have in-store signings to promote your new book, special limited edition work exclusive to the retailer and some stores give sizeable discount to friendly creators.

USE THE INTERNET

The are many advantages to using the internet these days for publishing your book, and the ever-growing social media on the web is one of them. Promoting your work on the web is an inexpensive

MAINSTREAM DISTRIBUTION

Diamond Comic Distributors is the world's largest comic book distributor. If you're looking to have your comic book or graphic novel in shops throughout the country, then Diamond might be your solution.

Every month Diamond sends out a catalogue to retailers called *Previews*, which contains mostly comic books, trade paperbacks and graphic novels, collectibles, apparel and more.

The retailers decide what books they want to carry and then they'll place their order. Customers have access to *Previews* as well and can inform the retailer that they would like to order books from the catalogue.

The first step in getting Diamond to carry your book is to send them a copy. You don't have to have the book actually printed yet. A photocopy of the completed work to Diamond's purchasing department is all you need to send. Go to vendor.diamondcomics.com/public/ for contact information in dealing with Diamond.

Let's do a rundown of what Diamond wants to know about your book:

- A photocopy of your completed book.
- Length and format – explain how many pages and if it's hard or softcover.
- Cover price of the book – price of book on cover and what shops will sell it for.
- Terms of sale – how much of a portion you want to be paid from the cover price.

The terms of the sale of your book work like this: you get 40% of the cover price. If your book cost £10, that means you get £4 per book. Suddenly you see why it's not easy to make a living publishing your own books. Yes, that is the industry standard; Diamond will charge the retailer who orders your book 55% of your cover price for the book and keep 15% in return for distribution services. The retailer in turn charges cover price to the buyer, keeping the 45% profit to pay for rent, employees and all the other books they didn't sell.

If you charge more than 40%, Diamond's going to feel there isn't enough profit for the stores carrying the book. The less you charge, the more savings Diamond passes on to the retailers.

way of having your work accessible to anyone, anywhere.

Educate yourself about the tools that are just one click away from a search engine. Make sure you have the basics: a website, a Facebook page, LinkedIn, Twitter, YouTube, a blog. If you don't use the tools to promote and sell your book on the web, you're missing an opportunity that many of your competitors are already doing.

Print-on-demand

If you really want a hard copy of your own work, then what avenue do you take? One option that has been growing in popularity in recent years over normal printers with high cost volumes is print-on-demand (or POD). Print-on-demand uses a high-tech process that can print small quantities of a book relatively affordably. The individual books aren't nearly as cheap per copy as if you printed several thousand copies the normal way, but print-on-demand has a much lower startup cost.

Ashcans, minibooks and zines

These are all known as photocopy comic books. This method uses cheap copy paper and a decent cardstock. It's cheap, and that's how you start, by keeping your overheads low. If you're publishing your own story, why not go to your local copy place and make some books on a small budget. See how they sell at a convention or your local comic book shop before spending a thousand pounds on your first comic book.

Advantages:

- Affordable.
- Print any amount you want with no minimum.
- If you have typos and other errors, you can fix them at little to no cost.
- Digest size, photo album size, just about any format a copier will allow you to use.

The tough part of putting together a minibook is making the original fit into a smaller format. You need to photocopy your originals down to a size to scan, digitally letter and print. These are usually copied onto A4 paper (letter size) folded in half like pamphlets. You can send your file via email, FTP or on a CD to your local copy centre, and have them output directly onto the paper.

Book yourself into a gig

Most comic book distributors won't solicit handmade or photocopy booklets. In order to get your work to readers, you're going to have to try some direct selling methods.

The best way is to register for a table at your local comic book convention. Some conventions are for the mainstream superhero crowd, and you're not likely to do well there. Some shows specialise in small press and alternative works where your chances will be greater. These shows typically give cheaper table rental space than the large mainstream shows.

For a list of comic book conventions around the country and abroad check out www.conventionscene.com.

Local comic shops may be willing to carry your photocopied books. Most will take a handful on a consignment basis, which means they'll put them on the shelves and pay you for any copies that sell. A fair deal is a 50–50 split: if they sell your book for £2, you get £1. Make sure you get a receipt for the copies that you deliver them so you can keep track of the books they've sold.

Whichever way you decide to take your graphic novel, good luck!

Digital distribution

Another option would be to open your own internet store, have it attached to your website or blog, where readers can click on a link and either download copies of your comic book or purchase physical copies to be shipped to them.

Webcomics

Webcomics are another publishing option that doesn't have the huge expense of publishing your book through a traditional printer and can potentially reach a wider audience. They're becoming increasingly popular for independent creators for publishing work. Advantages are as follows:

- The web gives millions of people easy access to your work.
- Work in full colour without spending a penny on printing.
- Design your web-based comics specifically for the web.
- It's virtually cost-free.
- Link to other artists' and writers' blogs and websites.
- Set up a PayPal account and earn money back on your work (though it may be very little at first).

Webcomics are broken down into three categories:

Serialised strips

Also known as cartoon strips – which consist of a landscape orientation comprised of three to four panels that tell a joke, a fragment of conversation or can feature 'episodes' in an ongoing series.

Graphic novel

These usually are more complex in terms of story and artwork, which can feature a full-length page.

Single-panel comic

This format is usually comprised of a single panel, often found in editorial comics, and has comedic and social commentary content.

WHAT THE EXPERTS SAY

Eric Trautmann writes for videogames and comic books, including ***DC's ACTION COMICS, ADVENTURE COMICS, THE SHIELD*** and others, as well as the webcomic 'Wide Awake' (co-authored with Brandon Jerwa). He can be found online at ***www.eric-trautmann.com***.

At the time of this writing, the comic publishing 'marketplace' is fairly conservative; obviously, there are exceptions to this, but mainstream comics houses seem locked in the superhero arms race, and smaller publishers – weathering both the primacy of the capes-and-cowls choking the comics racks and a not-insignificant economic downturn – have tended towards concentration on their own, homegrown 'house' properties or TV and movie licenses.

So, if you've got a good idea, and a story to tell, the options are self-publishing in print or publishing via the web.

The primary advantage of the webcomic, then, is a lower cost; you're not putting ink on paper, so you're also not paying for warehousing, shipping, order fulfilment and all the other expenses of traditional dead-tree publishing.

Instead, your costs are simply the creation of the artwork and story, and simple web hosting and site design; for our webcomic, 'Wide Awake', we opted for an online What-You-See-Is-What-You-Get website creation service, which is inexpensive and robust enough for our needs. There are several such providers, and researching which is the most affordable, easiest to use and best suits you is not terribly difficult.

The disadvantage of the webcomic is a perceived lack of legitimacy, though with more and more mainstream creators moving into this space (notably Warren Ellis's wonderful ***Freakangels*** series) the 'legitimacy' problem is diminishing.

When my co-creator (Brandon Jerwa) and I decided to bite the bullet and attempt a webcomic, I did a fair amount of preparatory research – looking at successful webcomics, and determining what, if anything, they had in common. We determined that some of the ingredients to success for a webcomic are a) quality of material; b) originality of concept; c) frequency and reliability of updates; d) ease of use.

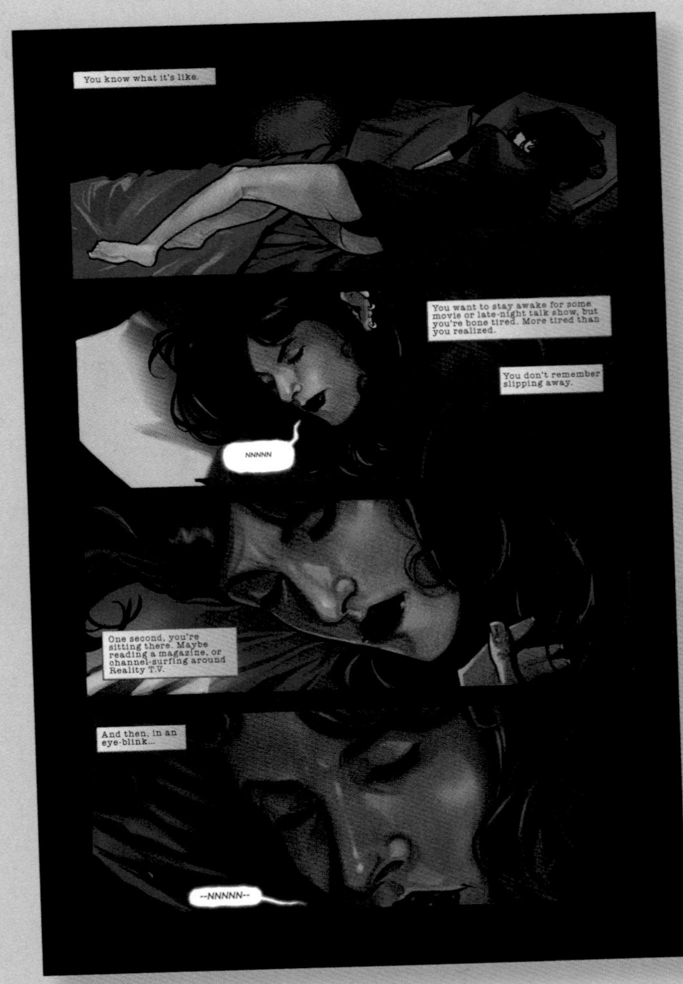

AMANDA IN DREAMLAND

Comic book artist Brandon Jerwa illustrates this sequence of Amanda sleeping, while the caption boxes give the reader insight into what she's thinking about. This works well for establishing a setting and moving the story forward, as each panel progresses closer to Amanda as she goes into dreamland.

Quality of material

The only real wild card in the bunch. The most successful webcomics tend to feature high-quality, attractive visuals and/or outstanding wordsmithing. ***Penny Arcade, PvP, Diesel Sweeties, Freakangels*** – these all excel in these areas, to varying degrees.

Originality of concept

Web-based audiences of webcomics seem to be fiercely tribal, and often have moved their reading to the internet precisely to avoid the more conservative, familiar material found in mainstream comics. In many cases, the focus of the material is aimed at a specific, core 'niche'. ***Penny Arcade*** has amassed a tremendous following by providing content to an audience with a narrow focus: videogame enthusiasts. Often, to the uninitiated, the comics and accompanying news posts read like an undeciphered code, but the end product is undeniably successful.

For your webcomic, have a good, strong logline; if you can't describe it in one sentence, it's time to refine the idea substantially.

Frequency and reliability of updates

Most successful webcomics have a regular update schedule, and they meet it. Nothing will stall the momentum of a webcomic faster than failing to provide new material to a waiting audience hungry for content. ***Penny Arcade*** manages three new 'strips' each week (plus news posts); ***Freakangels*** delivers six story pages every Friday; and so on.

In addition to building anticipation in your audience, providing them with reliable content will make it more likely that they, in turn, will share links to your work with their friends, readers of their blogs and so on. Word of mouth builds or breaks most webcomics, and this is a simple way to encourage reader loyalty.

Ease of use

Webcomics should be easy to use. Images should fit on the screen and type should be of readable size; multiple clicks to get through pay gates or past ads are all barriers between you and your reader.

More importantly, complex panel layouts (found in most mainstream comics) can be difficult to read on the screen, and will turn away non-comics readers.

Again, a look at successful web series shows some similarities. ***Penny Arcade*** (for the most part) is a traditional three-panel strip, similar to a newspaper comics section cartoon. ***PvP*** follows a newspaper strip model as well.

This is likely not accidental; as the comics market shrinks, there's a considerably larger potential readership that isn't acclimatised to double-page spreads, complicated panel flow and so on.

The newspaper strip model is one approach; ***Freakangels*** is built on a matrix of four vertical panels (see right), but panels can be combined for varying pacing effects or a full-page splash.

For our own series, we opted to build the pages on a four-panel layout as well, though we determined that horizontal panels (see left) made more sense given modern laptop screen dimensions. Panel flow is ALWAYS left to right, and there's an iron-clad rule to avoid vertical panels that break this flow.

Experiment with your own panel layouts, but remember that what might work well on the printed page will have a different effect on the computer screen - create for the medium you're working in.

CHANGE OF PACE

The pace quickly changes as Amanda is speaking out loud through word balloons as she defends herself from the creature. The use of various camera shots, angles, tilts and sound effects are well designed for a dynamic action sequence on the comic page.

GLOSSARY

Action: Visual movement of the subject within the panel.

Angle shot: Composition within the panel from a different point of view, or a different angle of the action from the previous panel.

Antagonist: Principal character in opposition to the protagonist or hero of a narrative.

Background: General scene or surface against which characters, objects or action are represented in a panel.

Bird's-eye view: Point of view elevated above an object, with a perspective as though the reader were a bird looking down at the action of the panel.

Bleed: The art is allowed to run to the edge of each page, rather than having a white border around it. Bleeds are sometimes used on internal panels to create the illusion of space or to emphasise action.

Burst: Speech balloon with jagged edges to indicate volume/stress or broadcast/electronic transmission, such as a mobile phone or radio.

Camera angle: Angle of the point of view from the reader's perspective to a subject or scene, the camera angle can greatly influence the reader's interpretation of what is happening on the comic book page.

Captions: Comic book captions are a narrative device, often used to convey information that cannot be communicated by the art or speech. Captions can be used in place of thought bubbles, can be in the first-, second- or third-person, and can either be assigned to an independent narrator or one of the characters.

Close-Up (CU): Concentrates on a relatively small object, human face or action. It puts an emphasis on emotion to create tension.

Composition: The arrangement of the physical elements (or the subject matter) within a comic book panel. A successful composition draws in the reader and directs their eye across the panel so that everything is taken in.

Crop marks: Registration marks placed at the corners of an image or a page to indicate to the printer where to trim it for final print size for publication.

Dialogue: Conversation between characters in a narrative.

Double-page spread: Two comic book pages designed as one large page layout.

Double truck: Refers to a pair of facing pages (pages both seen visibly), found in newspapers, magazines and comic books with content that stretches over both pages.

Dots Per Inch (DPI): Measure of printing resolution. The higher dpi you scan your artwork, the larger the file size and sharper the image for printing. The industry standard is 400 dpi.

Establishing shot: Sets up the context for a scene by showing the relationship between its important figures and objects.

Exterior (EXT): A scene that takes place outside any architectural structure.

Extreme Close-Up (ECU): Subject or action in a panel is so up close that it fills the entire panel.

Extreme Long Shot (ELS): Typically shows the entire object or human figure in some relation to its surroundings.

Eye movement: Arrangement of words and pictures in the panel, directing the narrative eye of the reader throughout the page layout.

File Transfer Protocol (FTP): Facility on the internet that allows you to copy files from one computer to another. The address (or URL) is usually something like ftp://ftp.somewhere.com.

Flashback: An interjected scene comprising of panels that takes the narrative back in time from the current point the story. Often used to recount events that happened before the story's primary sequence of events or to fill in crucial backstory. Character-origin flashbacks specifically refers to flashbacks dealing with key events early in a character's development.

Focal point: Emphasis of action, subject or any element in a panel on a page.

Foreground (FG): Objects, characters or action closest to the reader in a panel.

Full Shot (FS): Composition that illustrates the entire subject comprised of one individual, a group or the centre of the action in one panel.

Graphic novel: Narrative work in which the story is conveyed to the reader using sequential art in either an experimental design or in a traditional comics format. The term is employed in a broad manner, encompassing non-fiction works and thematically linked short stories as well as fictional stories across a number of genres.

Grid: Series of panels organised on a page, often found to be consistent in size and shape for visual storytelling. The artwork is traditionally composed within each panel separated by the equal spacing of gutters.

Hook: Inciting incident at the beginning of the story to immediately engage the reader.

Inker: The inker (also sometimes credited as the finisher or the embellisher) is one of the two line artists in a traditional comic book or graphic novel. After a pencilled drawing is given to the inker, the inker uses black ink (usually India ink) to produce refined outlines over the pencil lines.

Inset panel: Panel within a larger panel, often used as a close up on the action to invoke emotion or to drive the narrative.

Interior (INT): Setting that takes place inside a structure such as a house, office building, space ship or inside a cave.

Lettering: The art of lettering is penned from the comic book creator responsible for drawing the comic book's text. The letterer crafts the comic's 'display lettering': the story title lettering and other special captions and credits that usually appear on a story's first page. The letterer also writes the letters in the word balloons and draws in sound effects. The letterer's use of typefaces, calligraphy, letter size and layout all contribute to the impact of the comic.

Line quality: Variance in the thickness and design of the line drawn with a pencil, inked with a brush, or penned with a crowquill/pen nib.

Long Shot (LS): Typically shows the entire object or human figure and is intended to place it in some relation to its surroundings.

Medium Shot (MS): Subject and background share equal dominance in the panel. A medium shot of a character(s) will take in the body from the knees or waist up, with incidental background decided upon by the discretion of the writer/artist.

Mini-series: Tells a story in a planned limited number of comics or graphic novels.

Montage: Combination of illustrated images used for flashbacks, accelerated pacing of a story, transition between scenes and emotional devices to engage the reader.

Narrator: The person who tells the story to the audience. When the narrator is also a character within the story, he or she is sometimes known as the viewpoint character.

Pacing: Time it takes for the plot to unfold throughout the story.

Page: Art board your original work is created on, consisting of one or more panels on the page.

Panel: Individual frame in the multiple-panel sequence of a comic strip or comic book. Consists of a single drawing depicting a frozen moment.

Panel transition: Method a creator takes the reader through using a series of static images. Clearly transitions the contents of the action of one panel to the next panel.

Penciller: Artist who works in the creation of comic books, graphic novels and similar visual art forms. The penciller is the first step in rendering the story in visual form and may require several steps of feedback from the writer. These artists are concerned with layout (positions and vantages on scenes) to showcase steps in the plot.

Plot: Literary term for the events a story comprises, particularly as they relate to one another in a pattern, a sequence, through cause and effect or by coincidence.

Point of View (POV): Camera angle positioned for a key character, allowing the reader to view the action as a character within the panel can view it.

Roughs: Conceptual sketches or thumbnails of layouts that help plan the story visually.

Scene: Setting in a narrative sequence throughout several panels that can run for a page or more in a story involving key characters.

Script: Document describing the narrative and dialogue of a comic book. Comic book equivalent of a television program teleplay or a film screenplay. In comics, a script may be preceded by a plot outline, and is almost always followed by page sketches, drawn by an artist and inked, succeeded by the colouring and lettering stages.

Sequence: Series of panels/pages involving character, situation and place in a visual narrative.

Setting: Time, location and everything in which a story takes place, and initiates the main backdrop and mood for a story.

Sound Effects (SFX): Lettering style designed to visually duplicate the sound of a character, object or action within a panel or page.

Speed lines: Often in action sequences, the background will possess an overlay of neatly ruled lines to portray direction of movements. Speed lines can also be applied to characters as a way to emphasize the motion of their bodies.

Splash page: Full-page drawing in a comic book, often used as the first page of a story. Includes the title and credits. Sometimes referred to simply as a 'splash'.

Spotting blacks: Process of deciding what areas in a comic panel should be solid black. Gives the illustration depth, mass, contrast and a focal point on the character or action of the panel.

Stat panel: Artwork within the panel copied, and then repeated in subsequent panels from the original.

Story: Common term for a description of a sequence of events involving a narrative arc from beginning to end.

Story arc: Extended or continuing storyline in episodic storytelling media such as television, comic books, comic strips, board games, video games and, in some cases, films.

Story line: Plot or subplot of a story.

Tangent: When two objects within a panel, or in separate panels close in proximity, confuse the eye and create unusual forms thereby disrupting the visual narrative. Often, it's the panel border, or similar linear composition in a nearby panel, that creates unwanted tangents.

Thought balloon: Large, cloud-like bubble containing the text of a thought.

Tier: Row of panels horizontally from left to right. Traditionally, comic page layouts were designed with three tiers of panels.

Tilt: Cinematic tactic used to portray psychological uneasiness in the subject or compounding action within a panel.

Whisper balloon: Word balloon broken up by small dashes throughout its border to indicate a character is whispering.

Word balloon: Oval shape with rounded corner used to communicate dialogue or speech.

Worm's-eye view: Low angle shot from the ground looking up at the focus of the composition. Used to make the subject more imposing and larger than it appears to be.

Zoom: Proximity of the camera, that moves towards or away from the central character or focal point of a composition in a panel.

INDEX

Figures in italics refer to illustrations.

CREDITS

Publisher's acknowledgments:
Quarto would like to thank and acknowledge the artists listed below who kindly allowed us to reproduce examples of their illustrations and photographs.

Joko Budiono p.76, 77t, 77c, 80, 81t, 81c, 82b, 83
Chad Hardin p.58, 59
John Heebink p.68, 69, 70, 71t, 72, 122, 123
Eda Kaban p.77b, 78t, 81b
Chris Marrinan p.15, 16, 147
Pete McDonnell p.5t, 10tl, 10br, 11bl, 12tl, 12b, 64tr, 64br, 65
Diane Pascual p.8b
Nate Piekos p.104, 144, 145
Jeremy Saliba p.19, 28, 29, 37t
Mark Schultz p.36
Mark Simmons p.102, 103, 118, 119
Chad Weatherford p.63

1001 Arabian Nights: The Adventures of Sinbad #8 by Dan Wickline, art by Eduardo Ferigato p.54, 55
Batgirl #11 by Lee Garbett, art by Walden Wong p.120–121
Brandon Pike Batman © DC Comics. All rights reserved. p.106, 112, 113
Flash Gordon, Alex Raymond © King Features Syndicate p.34br
Friends of a Friend by Brian Schirmer, art by Mark Simmons p.42, 43
Green Lantern © DC Comics. All rights reserved. p.2, 5b, 6, 9, 10tr, 10bl, 11br, 12t, 12tr, 12bl, 12br, 13, 17, 18, 20, 21, 23, 24, 25, 26, 32, 35b, 41, 46, 48, 49, 50, 51, 53, 60, 64bl, 71b, 74, 75, 78b, 79, 82t, 85, 86t, 86b, 87b, 90, 91, 93, 95, 96, 97, 98, 99, 108, 109, 110, 111; Daniel Cooney 114b, 115b, 116b, 117t, 117c, 126t, 127b, 132, 133, 134, 135, 136, 137, 138, 139, 140, 141t, 141c, 142, 143
"Heads, Hands, and Emotion" art by Mark Simmons, colors by Adam Wallenta p.73
Homeless Channel by Matt Silady p.56, 57
Life is Funny by Christopher Beckett. Writer, Jason Copland; artist, Osmarco Valladão p.127t
The Martian Confederacy: From Mars With Love by Jason McNamara, art by Paige Braddock p.46, 47
Mary Perkins On Stage, Leonard Starr © Tribune Media Services p.35t
Monkey In A Man Suit by Jason McNamara, art by Rahsan Ekedal p.38, 39, 44, 45
Novella © Carolina Cooney, art by Daniel Cooney, colors by D.J. Welch p.18
No U-Turn © Tim Andrick 2010. Used with permission. By Tim Andrick, art by Jeff Himes p.89, 100, 101
The Rocketeer © Dave Stevens p.47, 141b
Valentine and cast of characters © Daniel Cooney. Pencils, Bill Reinhold; Inks, Linda Reinhold p.21
Valentine: Russian Roulette story and art by Daniel Cooney, colors by D.J. Welch p.99t, p99c
Wide Awake by Eric Trautman, art by Brandon Jerwa p.154–155
The Yellow Kid by Richard Felton Outcault p.124
Xenozoic Tales © Mark Schultz p.33, 34tl, 125bl

RKO / THE KOBAL COLLECTION p.37b
Photographer: Annie McKelvey; model: Natalie Brooke Edwards p.84, 86t

Author's acknowledgments:
For Carolina and Dashiell

My gratitude goes out to the wonderful and talented people who helped make this book an exciting, fun, and unforgettable experience! They are:
Kate Kirby and Chloe Todd Fordham, my editors at Quarto Publishing. A special thank you to Chloe for your insight and patience in helping me produce this book. Caroline Guest, the art director, for assembling together a great-looking book. Penny Dawes, the jacket designer, for composing such dynamic front and back covers. Sarah Bell, the picture researcher, who tirelessly kept track of all the copyright ownership forms.

Special thanks to all the professional artists and writers who donated their work (this book wouldn't have been what it is without you): Mark Schultz, John Heebink, Jason McNamara, Brian Schirmer, Joko Budiono, Nate Piekos, Peter Palmiotti, Bill Reinhold, Dan Wickline, Matt Silady, Walden Wong, Eric Trautman, Brandon Jerwa, Jason Copland, Paige Braddock, Chad Hardin, Adam Wallenta, Pete McDonnell, Chris Marrinan, Jeremy Saliba, Mark Simmons, Jeffrey Himes and Chad Weatherford – thank you for taking the time out of your professional commitments to contribute articles and artwork for this book.

The numerous art students from The Academy of Art University, who provided their student work and time for teaching points and examples for this book.

I want to personally thank the people who taught me just about everything I know about comics and graphic novels while I was a student at The School of Visual Arts: Klaus Janson, Walt Simonson, Gene Colan, Sal Amendola, Joe Orlando and Jack Harris, as well as artists and writers past, present and future that continue to inspire me. I have had the opportunity to teach others willing to learn about writing and drawing comics for several years now. As an educator and practitioner of sequential art, the learning never stops. I feel that because I do both as a career, I am fortunate to experience the rewards that each profession brings to me.